Immanuel Kant

Key Concepts

Key Concepts

Immanuel Kant

Key Concepts

Edited by Will Dudley and Kristina Engelhard

ACUMEN

First published in 2011 by Acumen

Acumen Publishing Limited
4 Saddler Street
Durham
DH1 3NP
www.acumenpublishing.co.uk

ISBN: 978-1-84465-238-9 (hardcover)
ISBN: 978-1-84465-239-6 (paperback)

British Library Cataloguing-in-Publication Data
A catalogue record for this book is available
from the British Library.

Designed and typeset in Classical Garamond and Myriad.
Printed by Ashford Colour Press Ltd, UK.

Contents

Contributors

Emily Carson is Associate Professor of Philosophy at McGill University.

Will Dudley is Professor of Philosophy at Williams College.

Kristina Engelhard is Assistant Professor of Philosophy at the University of Cologne.

Katrin Flikschuh is Reader in Modern Political Theory at the London School of Economics.

Patrick Frierson is Associate Professor of Philosophy at Whitman College.

Michelle Grier is Professor of Philosophy at the University of San Diego.

Paul Guyer is Professor of Philosophy at the University of Pennsylvania.

Dietmar Heidemann is Professor of Philosophy at the University of Luxembourg.

Stephen Houlgate is Professor of Philosophy at the University of Warwick.

Georg Mohr is Professor of Philosophy at the University of Bremen.

Kirk Pillow is Interim President of Corcoran College of Art and Design.

Ulli F. H. Rühl is Professor of Legal Studies at the University of Bremen.

Kenneth R. Westphal is Professor of Philosophy at the University of Kent.

John Zammito is Professor of History at Rice University.

Günter Zöller is Professor of Philosophy at the University of Munich.

Abbreviations

PM   *Physical Monadology* (1756)
PP   *Towards Perpetual Peace* (1795)
PracR *Critique of Practical Reason* (1788)
RBR   *Religion within the Boundaries of Mere Reason* (1793)
TP   *On the Use of Teleological Principles in Philosophy* (1788)
UH   *Idea for a Universal History with a Cosmopolitan Aim* (1784)

Unless stated otherwise, the translations used by the authors are from *The Cambridge Edition of the Works of Immanuel Kant in Translation* (20 vols), Paul Guyer & Allen W. Wood (eds) (Cambridge: Cambridge University Press). See Bibliography.

Introduction

Will Dudley and Kristina Engelhard

Immanuel Kant revolutionized philosophy. He spent the first half of his career as a prominent rationalist in the tradition of Gottfried Leibniz, before his mid-life encounter with the empiricism of David Hume spurred him to reconsider his most basic beliefs. Kant subsequently undertook a thorough "critique" of reason, in order to specify its capacities and limitations. The result was a truly novel philosophical position, transcendental idealism, with which Kant claimed to save the possibility of knowledge from Hume's scepticism, and to establish the reality of human freedom and moral agency.

Kant's achievements transformed philosophy immediately and irrevocably. The initial consequence was the German idealism of Fichte, Schelling and Hegel. Subsequent movements indebted to Kant (if sometimes primarily as an inspiration for criticism) included Romanticism, naturalism and existentialism. Anglo-American philosophy, which early in the twentieth century defined itself in sharp distinction from the German tradition, has more recently incorporated Kantian insights in every domain. A thorough understanding of Kant is thus indispensable to contemporary philosophers of every stripe.

The significance of Kant's thought is matched by its complexity. Kant's revolutionary ideas are systematically interconnected and presented in a forbidding technical vocabulary, which makes his main works especially difficult for the uninitiated. The systematic and technical character of Kant's philosophy also offers, however, a means by which to understand it. A careful and patient investigation of the key concepts that structure Kant's philosophical project gradually leads to comprehension of the whole.

This book aims to provide an accessible introduction to Kant by explaining the key concepts of his philosophy. The book is organized into three parts, which correspond to the main areas of Kant's transcendental idealism: I. Theoretical Philosophy; II. Practical Philosophy; III. Aesthetics, Teleology, Religion. The individual chapters, written by highly regarded Kant scholars, are each devoted to the explication of a single key concept. Each chapter is readable on its own by those seeking to understand a particular topic, while the whole provides a clear and comprehensive account of Kant's philosophical system.

Historical background

The primary feature of the philosophical landscape in Kant's time was the conflict between rationalism and empiricism. The basic rationalist thesis is that all knowledge is gained purely by rational insight, and thus can be justified *a priori*, independently of experience. Rationalism regards knowledge claims based upon experience as unreliable and inferior to those based upon intellectual intuition and deductive inference. Empiricism asserts, to the contrary, that all knowledge is dependent upon experience, and all justification must therefore be *a posteriori*.

In eighteenth-century Germany, the species of rationalism developed by Gottfried Wilhelm Leibniz was the dominant philosophical doctrine. Leibnizian rationalism made the strong claim that all truths, even those pertaining to facts about the world that would seem to be accessible only by experience, are ultimately grounded in conceptual relations that can be deduced by reason alone. Leibniz held that intellectual intuition reveals the truth of a small number of fundamental principles, which serve as the basis of all other truths. From these fundamental principles Leibniz derived a distinctive metaphysics. Its basic entities are simple substances called monads, which Leibniz understood to be indivisible, immaterial substances that constitute everything in existence.

Before 1770, in what has come to be known as his pre-critical period, Kant was a well-known and productive member of the Leibnizian rationalist tradition. He shared Leibniz's assumption that simple substances make up the basic level of reality, and that they constitute space without themselves being spatially extended.

During this period Kant focused primarily on theoretical philosophy, and in particular on the philosophy of nature. He was concerned that philosophy and the natural sciences were drifting apart, a situation he regarded as intolerable for reason. Kant, unlike most Leibnizians, thus expended considerable effort attempting to reconcile the metaphysical claims of rationalism with the empirical science of his time. He aimed to demonstrate that although philosophy and empirical science employ different methods in their shared quest to know the truth, their results are nonetheless compatible.

Kant was especially concerned that rationalism seems to imply a commitment to metaphysical idealism, whereas the natural sciences are committed to realism. Metaphysical idealism is the view that the ultimate nature of reality is constituted by minds or ideas. Realism holds, on the contrary, that the nature of reality is mind-independent. In his *Physical Monadology*, published in 1756, Kant developed a theory of monads that he intended to be consistent with a realist theory of space and extended objects. His theory maintained the Leibnizian view that simple, non-extended substances are the fundamental elements of space and extended bodies, and thus that the most basic level of reality is immaterial. But Kant also held that space and extended objects are themselves real, in virtue of the fact that the substantial forces of monads provide their constitution.

Kant refined his version of rationalism for nearly fifteen years after the publication of the *Physical Monadology*. But around 1770, in his mid-forties, Kant began to question the basic premises of his own philosophical views. He abandoned rationalism, which he now disparaged as "dogmatic metaphysics", and spent the next ten years working reclusively on an alternative that he called "critical philosophy". The first fruit of this labour was the *Critique of Pure Reason*, published in 1781. In this book, Kant argued that philosophy must begin with a thoroughly critical examination of the capacities and limitations of reason, and that such a critique yields a new philosophical perspective that resolves the long-standing impasse between rationalism and empiricism. Kant would continue to work out the systematic consequences of his critical philosophy until his death in 1804.

In his *Prolegomena to Any Future Metaphysics* (1783), Kant famously referred to the scepticism of David Hume as "the very thing that ... first interrupted my dogmatic slumber and gave a completely different direction to my researches in the field of speculative philosophy" (*PFM* 4:260). Hume's scepticism was a consequence of his unwavering commitment to the empiricism developed by his great predecessors, John Locke and George Berkeley. The empiricist principle that all ideas come from sensory experience undermined the rationalist confidence, previously shared by Kant himself, that facts about the world can be known through reason alone.

Hume emphasized that knowledge of matters of fact depends upon causal inference. We infer from a sense impression (light outside the window) to a causal explanation (the sun is shining). In doing so, we use our past experience of the world as the basis for an inductive generalization (having observed a regular association between exterior illumination and sunshine, we come to regard the sun as the cause of daytime light).

Hume recognized, however, that no degree of regular association – not even "constant conjunction" – could ever demonstrate a truly necessary connection. The most carefully drawn causal inferences always remain vulnerable to falsification (perhaps my neighbour has recently aimed a spotlight at my window).

Moreover, Hume argued, our reliance upon induction cannot be rationally justified. Inductive reasoning infers that x will be the case in the future because x has been the case in the past. But the only reason we can give for believing that the future will resemble the past is that in the past it has been the case that the future resembles the past. And this is manifestly circular: we justify the practice of inductive inference by means of an inductive inference.

Hume concluded that our knowledge of matters of fact rests ultimately upon faith. Empirical knowledge rests upon causal inference, which rests upon induction. And although induction is an indispensable guide to the formation of beliefs, we cannot give a non-circular explanation of why inductive reasoning should be reliable. We have a powerful faith in the reliability of induction, which sustains our expectation that past experience will serve us well in the future. But such faith is not rational, and thus Hume advocated scepticism concerning the ability of reason to justify our beliefs about the world.

Hume's scepticism also extended to the ability of reason to guide and motivate human action. He pointed out that we have no impression of free will, and argued that our experience gives us no reason to attribute such freedom to ourselves. Human behaviour is no different, Hume contended, from that of animals: living creatures attempt to satisfy their desires as best they can in response to the circumstances in which they find themselves. If desires or circumstances change, so do behavioural responses. Rational creatures, on this account, are those that respond to their environment in ways that maximize the satisfaction of their desires. Reason is a tool that can determine the best means to achieve the ends that desire dictates – it is "a slave of the passions" (Hume 2000: 266) – but it cannot motivate us to adopt alternative goals. Hume concluded that human action is based entirely upon habits formed in reaction to natural forces, rather than upon freely willed responses to rational norms.

Kant's critical philosophy

Kant quickly realized that Hume's rigorous exploration of the consequences of empiricism threatened not only philosophical rationalism, but also the fundamental aspirations of the Enlightenment. The Enlightenment demanded that belief and action be rationally justified, rather than imposed by unquestionable authorities. This call for freedom, which found powerful expression in the American and French revolutions, insists on the right to rational self-determination in morality, politics and religion. Hume's scepticism and determinism, however, deny the very possibility of the free and rational agency that is the *sine qua non* of the Enlightenment project.

Kant understood that he could defend knowledge and freedom only by developing a wholly new philosophical alternative. He therefore undertook a "critique" of reason, with the intention of showing that Hume had failed to demonstrate that reason is incapable of grounding belief or directing action. At stake was nothing less than the possibility of intellectual, moral and political freedom.

Kant thus declared that "the concept of freedom ... constitutes the *keystone* of the whole structure of a system of pure reason" (*PracR* 5:4). He presented this system in three interconnected books: the *Critique of Pure Reason* argues that determinism cannot be known to be true, and thus that freedom is possible; the *Critique of Practical Reason* argues that the reality of human freedom is established by our experience of moral obligation; and the *Critique of the Power of Judgment* argues that it is reasonable to hope that the fulfilment of moral obligation will ultimately accord with happiness.

The *Critique of Pure Reason* is concerned with epistemology and metaphysics, charged with answering the general question: "What can I know?" It also attempts to determine what we *cannot* know, in order to identify and resist dogmatic claims that overstep the bounds of reason. Finally, it gives an account of why we are perpetually prone to the temptation to ignore these bounds and lapse back into dogmatism.

Kant's epistemological investigation begins with the revolutionary insight that all objects of knowledge must have whichever features are required to enable them to be experienced by knowing subjects. Because these features apply necessarily and universally to the objects of experience, knowledge of them would qualify as "metaphysical" in the only meaningful sense of the word. It is therefore possible to establish metaphysics as a legitimate discipline, but only if it is preceded (and constrained) by an account of the mental capacities by means of which subjects encounter and represent the world. Kant identified three such capacities – sensibility, understanding and reason – and his investigation of them generated a number of principles that he claimed must be true of all objects that could ever appear in human experience.

Kant emphasized, however, that nothing whatsoever can be known about that which transcends human experience, and on this basis he rejected not only Leibnizian metaphysics (which aspired to know the truth about the soul, the universe and God) but also Hume's determinism. Kant agreed with Hume that we do not experience freedom. Indeed, Kant claimed that we *cannot* experience freedom, because it is a condition of the possibility of experience that every event necessarily appears to be the effect of prior causes. But from this it does not follow, Kant insisted, that determinism is true. Although we can know with certainty that things as we experience them, or appearances, are causally determined, we can know nothing of what things are like in themselves, or independently of being experienced by us. The only intellectually respectable position on determinism is thus agnosticism: to assert or deny the truth of free will is to engage in dogmatic metaphysics.

The negative conclusion that we cannot know whether or not determinism is true is one of the most important results of the *Critique of Pure Reason*. Kant described it as "limiting knowledge to make way for faith" (*CpR* B xxx). By showing that we can never demonstrate the truth or falsity of determinism, critical philosophy shows that it is permissible to have faith in freedom.

The possibility of freedom provides the starting point of the *Critique of Practical Reason*, in which Kant endeavoured to show that reason is indeed capable of setting ends and motivating us to pursue them. Without freedom, reason could not be "practical" in this sense, and Hume would be right that our ends and motivations are thoroughly determined by natural desires. The modern aspiration to rational self-determination can thus be legitimated only if the reality of freedom can be established.

The *Critique of Practical Reason* proceeds towards this goal by pointing out that moral obligation and responsibility – being absolutely required to adopt a particular intention and being held accountable for doing so – make sense only on the supposition of freedom. If we are not free, then the intentions upon which we act are beyond our control. And we cannot be obligated to adopt an intention if we are literally incapable of doing so (as Kant famously put the point, "ought implies can"). Only if we have the freedom *not* to act upon the ends that desire would dictate, as well as the freedom to adopt the intentions that reason prescribes, can we be responsible for fulfilling moral obligations.

Kant further contended that we are in fact immediately aware of the absolute necessity of abiding by moral principles, and that this awareness reveals to us the reality of freedom and the practicality of reason. Every rational agent, he claimed, is conscious of being obligated and able to sacrifice the satisfaction of desire – even to the point of being able to sacrifice his or her own life – when moral principles are at stake. But to be capable of meeting absolute obligations we must be able to recognize them and give them priority over the ends urged upon us by desire. And this we can do only if reason is capable of setting ends and motivating us to pursue them independently of the influence of natural inclination. The experience of absolute obligation thus makes us aware of the reality of the freedom that theoretical reason cannot demonstrate.

Once I am aware of my freedom, it becomes meaningful and urgent to ask: What should I do? Creatures lacking freedom do not confront such a question, for they cannot choose between alternative courses of action. Because as human beings, we do have choices, we must decide how we will act.

Kant's moral philosophy responds to this question by attempting to determine the criteria by means of which we can know that we have a duty to adopt, or to refrain from adopting, a particular intention. These criteria are then applied to specify not only our moral duties, but also our rights, the legitimate demands we can place upon fellow rational agents, either to pursue, or to refrain from pursuing, certain aims.

Kant's political philosophy is a natural extension of his account of morality. We are obligated, he argued, to establish and sustain communities that are conducive to our moral striving. And these political entities are obligated to interact in ways that do not corrode the moral agency of their citizens. In particular, Kant contended, it is a duty to strive towards international peace, since the conditions of war are especially detrimental to morality.

The *Critique of the Power of Judgment* responds to a problem left unresolved by the first two critiques. The *Critique of Pure Reason* argues that freedom can never be observed in the natural world. But the *Critique of Practical Reason* argues that we must attribute freedom to ourselves in order to regard ourselves as moral agents. Consequently, there seems to be an unbridgeable gap between our theoretical, scientific perspective on the natural world and our practical, moral perspective on our own agency. The third critique aims to reconcile these two perspectives by showing that we are in a position to judge (although not to know) that freedom is operative in the natural world.

Kant's goal is to demonstrate that we are justified in regarding nature as a system that contains not only efficient causes but also purposive beings. His strategy, as in the first two critiques, is to construct a transcendental argument that begins with a given fact and deduces the necessary conditions of its possibility. The third critique moves from the fact that we make aesthetic and teleological judgements to the conclusion that such judgements are possible only if we regard nature as a unified whole, purposefully organized so as to be conducive to the operation of freedom. Kant classifies aesthetic and teleological judgements as two species of "reflective" judgement, each of which implicitly attributes a distinctive sort of purposiveness to nature.

The first part of the third critique is devoted to aesthetic judgements, which we make when we perceive either a natural object or a work of art to be beautiful. Kant claims that encountering a beautiful object activates two mental capacities – understanding and imagination – simultaneously. Understanding tries to conceptualize the object as a particular kind of thing, while imagination associates the object with a wide variety of pre-conceptual intuitions. This triggers an ongoing interaction, with understanding applying concepts to the intuitions generated by imagination, and imagination inspired by these concepts to produce still more associations. The harmonious engagement of these two mental capacities in response to the beautiful object provides the perceiver with a distinctively aesthetic pleasure. This is neither the practical pleasure that comes from using an object to satisfy our desires, nor the theoretical pleasure that comes from the successful classification and comprehension of an object. Aesthetic pleasure stems from the awareness that the form of an object is suited to stimulate our mental capacities, and that these capacities are suited to complement each other. We experience nature as beautiful when it appears to serve the purpose of pleasing subjects like ourselves by initiating and sustaining the play of our minds. Judging natural objects to be beautiful thus involves regarding nature as "subjectively purposive".

Judging nature to be "objectively purposive" involves attributing purposes to nature itself, either to the natural world as a whole, or to particular beings within it. We do this implicitly, according to Kant, when we make teleological judgements, to which the second part of the third critique is devoted.

We make a teleological judgement when we deem a natural entity to be a biological organism. To experience something as an organic unity is to regard the existence and function of its parts as being determined by the roles they play in serving the needs of the living whole. To take Aristotle's famous example, a hand is only a hand in virtue of its relationship to the rest of the body. Severed from that organic relationship, the hand is no longer a hand, but merely a decaying lump of flesh. Kant argues that we cannot account for the existence of organisms by mechanistic processes, and must regard these living beings as having been purposefully arranged. Teleological judgements thus presuppose that nature is "objectively purposive".

Kant further believes we must postulate, although we cannot know, that God exists and has arranged the natural world in such a way that happiness will ultimately be proportionate to moral worth. This postulation of divine providence completes the project of critical philosophy by bridging the gap between nature and morality.

Kant's legacy

The significance of Kant's achievements, not only for philosophy but also for many other disciplines, cannot be overstated. His work had a direct and powerful impact on his contemporaries, and continues to exert a profound influence across the humanities and social sciences.

The first and most dramatic consequence of critical philosophy was the collapse of rationalism. The *Critique of Pure Reason* persuaded many of Kant's philosophical peers that human cognition does not have epistemic access to things in themselves, the soul, the universe or God. This conclusion brought to an abrupt end the metaphysical project that defined the rationalist tradition.

The philosophers who followed Kant had no choice but to rethink the aspirations, problems and methods of their own discipline. A number of his immediate successors sought to complete the project of critical philosophy by rectifying various omissions and inconsistencies that they claimed to discover in Kant's own work. These efforts gave rise to the philosophical movement known as German idealism, which spanned the careers of Fichte, Schelling and Hegel. Other thinkers who rejected this new tradition – including Schopenhauer, Nietzsche, Frege and Russell – nonetheless developed their own views by critically evaluating Kantian theses and arguments. In the second half of the nineteenth century, the neo-Kantian movement emerged as a negative reaction to philosophy's increasing drift from the fundamental principles of transcendental idealism, advancing its programme under the slogan: "Back to Kant!"

One of Kant's most enduring philosophical legacies is the structure of transcendental argumentation, which stipulates a given fact and then seeks to establish the necessary conditions of its possibility. Such arguments continue to be employed in both theoretical and practical philosophy. One especially prominent application is found in the discourse ethics of Jürgen Habermas, which seeks to justify certain ethical norms by demonstrating that they are necessary presuppositions of human communication.

Kant's own moral philosophy continues to serve as the prototype for contemporary species of deontological ethics, which take the concept of obligation to be fundamental. Influential advocates of this important approach to moral theory include Onora O'Neill and Christine Korsgaard. In political philosophy, the social contract theory of John Rawls represents a deontological position explicitly indebted to Kant's concept of the person as a free and rational agent. Moreover, Kant's argument in favour of the creation of a league of nations motivated political action in the early twentieth century and remains an important basis for the configuration of the United Nations.

Ongoing debates in theoretical philosophy also take inspiration from Kant, even when they call his views into question. Important examples include Donald Davidson's challenge to the idea of a conceptual scheme and Saul Kripke's argument that analytic truth can be decoupled from *a priori* justification. Kant is also an influential precursor to current work in the philosophy of mathematics, philosophy of physics and philosophy of science.

Finally, Kant has left an especially deep mark on aesthetics and the philosophy of religion. His formalist account of beauty and his conception of the sublime have been seminal for both aesthetic theory and art criticism. And his distinctive account of rational faith – of the role that a religion stripped of metaphysical superstition can play in moral life – has opened entirely new perspectives in the philosophy of religion and theology.

Kant's transcendental idealism is among the most significant intellectual developments of the past two centuries. It has shaped the evolution of the methods, problems, arguments and positions in every area of philosophy, as well as in legal, social, political, aesthetic and religious theory. A full appreciation of the present state of those fields depends upon an adequate understanding of the key concepts that structure Kant's critical philosophy. It is with the intention of furthering such understanding that the essays in this volume have been written.

PART I

Theoretical philosophy

ONE

Critique: knowledge, metaphysics

Günter Zöller

This chapter draws on Kant's key term, "critique", and its relation to Kant's central concern with the possibility of knowledge and the status of metaphysics in order to present the basic character, the overall orientation and the general strategy of Kant's mature work in theoretical philosophy. In line with the introductory intent of the chapter, Kant's train of thoughts is not presented in its intricate details and technical terminology but in the form of a broadly conceived argumentative reconstruction of Kant's project that seeks to avoid partisan interpretations and is intentionally kept free of scholarly discussions, interpretive controversies and exegetical minutiae.

The primary texts underlying the portrayal of Kant's critical stand on knowledge and metaphysics are the prefaces and introductions of the first and second editions of the *Critique of Pure Reason* (*CpR* A vii–xxii and 1–16; *CpR* B vii–xliv and 1–30) along with §14 of the first *Critique* (contained in both editions of the work but so numbered only in the second one; *CpR* A 92–4; *CpR* B 124–9) and the introduction along with §§57–60, entitled "On the Determination of the Boundary of Pure Reason", of the *Prolegomena to Any Future Metaphysics* (4:350–65), a popularly cast companion piece that Kant published between the first and the second edition of the *Critique of Pure Reason*. For the *Prolegomena*, refer to Kant (2004a).

Critique and reason

The term "critique" can serve to designate and characterize Kant's entire mature philosophy, which was propagated by him and his followers as "critical philosophy" after it had initially been presented by Kant in three works bearing the term "critique" in their very title: *Critique of Pure Reason* (1781; second, in part revised, edition 1787), *Critique of Practical Reason* (1788) and *Critique of the Power of Judgment* (1790). Yet Kant did not set out to write a set of three critiques. Neither did he plan the second *Critique* when writing the first one, nor the third *Critique* when writing the second one. Rather, the critical trilogy grew out of the initial critical project, as contained in the *Critique of Pure Reason*, by extending the primary enquiry into the theoretical–cognitive potential of reason first into the investigation of reason's practical–volitional potential and finally into the survey of the potential of the power of judgement to reflect on the purposive organization of things in nature and culture. Hence "critique" in Kant refers to addressing and solving philosophical problems in a manner that was first methodically developed and carried out in the *Critique of Pure Reason* and subsequently taken over into further fields of philosophical investigation.

In the preface to the first edition of the *Critique of Pure Reason* Kant refers to the broader contemporary context for his critical project by calling his own times "the age proper of critique" (*CpR* A xi n), referring to the Enlightenment project of questioning traditional authority and replacing justification and validation by appeal to established and cherished beliefs with achieving insights through the use of one's own powers of reasoning. In Kant's adaptation of the term "critique" to his own work in philosophy the word retains the general meaning of a detection of prejudice and error in received views but also assumes the more specific sense of a principled assessment of the extent to which claims in general, or claims of a specific kind, may be justified or justifiable. Most importantly, Kant throughout ties the term "critique" to the revisionary assessment of the claims of reason or of the claims made by or on behalf of reason, as opposed to claims based on experience or other claimed sources of insight.

In Kant's usage, "reason" designates at the most general level the higher mental powers in their entirety, as opposed to the lower mental powers based on the senses. To critically assess reason therefore means to enquire into reason's ability to provide insights that are not based on the senses, or at least not only based on the senses, but that rely specifically, if not exclusively, on the resources of reason or on the powers of thinking and conceiving, as opposed to those of sensing and perceiving.

The particularly close connection between "critique" and "reason" in Kant, manifest chiefly in phrases such as "critique of reason", "critique of pure reason" or "critique of pure speculative reason", typically takes the grammatical form of a genitive construction in which reason is at once the object that is being criticized and the subject that is undertaking the critique. With no other, external, authority suited to judging and adjudicating the claims of reason, which exceed, in principle, the scope of experience and thus are open only to non-empirical, strictly argumentative forms of validation, reason itself must undertake the business of critique. Hence the critique of reason is, in essence, the self-critique of reason. To be sure, reason cannot be the subject and agent of its own critique in the literal sense of carrying it out, as it were, in person. After all, reason, on Kant's understanding, is not some magical supra-human mind or spirit but the sum total of the principles regulating thinking in beings like us, finite rational beings, that possess the ability or, in Kant's preferred term, the "faculty" [*Vermögen*] to think. For Kant to undertake the self-critique of reason means to engage in an examination of reason by means of reason in order to assess, in a principled manner, what reason is capable of – and what not.

Critique and knowledge

On Kant's view, reason is not easily capable of a radical self-examination of the extent of its potential. For the most part, reason, or rather the human being in his or her use of reason, misjudges its abilities and lets itself be misled into illusions about the extent of its powers. That reason is entrusted with its self-critique reflects not its past or present actual performance but its future, possible accomplishment in Kant's assessment. Moreover, for Kant the critique of reason is not only a possible enterprise to be undertaken at one's discretion but a requirement in order to settle, once and for all, the factual dispute about the claims of reason.

The claims of reason under critical scrutiny in Kant are, in the first instance, reason's cognitive claims or claims to cognition to be achieved by means of reason. Kant uses the term "cognition" [*Erkenntnis*] to cover knowledge claims of all kinds and any possible extent, regardless of whether they turn out, upon closer inspection, to be justified or unjustified. Typically, though, the cognitive claims of reason are maintained in the stronger sense of asserting the cognition in question to be justified and true. Kant designates the cognitions claimed and proven to possess justification and truth as "knowledge" [*Wissen*], a term closely connected in German with the word for scientific knowledge or science [*Wissenschaft*].

In light of the epistemological distinction between asserted or claimed cognition, that is, mere cognition, and validated or warranted cognition, that is, knowledge, the task of a critique of reason can be described as the sorting of the cognitive claims of reason according to whether or not they pass the test for warranted assertibility as well as truth and can be considered knowledge. Kant himself highlights the justificatory dimension of the critique of reason by drawing extensively on the imagery and conceptuality of jurisdiction and casting the critique of reason as a contested case before a court of law.

Kant distinguishes several kinds of cognitions or cognitive claims. In the *Critique of Pure Reason* and its associated works, especially the *Prolegomena to Any Future Metaphysics* (1783), the focus is on cognitions regarding what is, or is purported to be, the case. Cognitions of this kind, as well as the corresponding knowledge in case of possible or actual epistemic justification, are termed "theoretical". By contrast, the *Critique of Practical Reason* and the associated work in foundational moral philosophy, the *Groundwork of the Metaphysics of Morals* (1785), focus on cognitions regarding what ought to be the case, or is so claimed. Interestingly, Kant avoids applying the term "knowledge" [*Wissen*] to sufficiently justified practical cognitions, effectively limiting the use of the term "knowledge" to the sphere of theoretical cognition and its critical examination in theoretical philosophy. To be sure, this terminological practice in Kant does not imply a lack of possible justification for certain claims to practical cognition, in particular those practical claims regarding the very principle of morality (the categorical imperative) and its various formulations and variant specifications.

A main reason behind Kant's asymmetrical treatment of the distinction between cognition and knowledge with respect to the spheres of the theoretical and the practical may be the close association of the concept of knowledge with the cognitive orientation towards objects, either particular objects (individuals) or classes of such objects (kinds). While theoretical cognitions and the corresponding knowledge serve to determine the *object* by ascertaining the latter's existence and properties, practical cognitions function by determining the *will*, with an eye towards realizing something that is not yet the case. On Kant's understanding, theoretical cognition as well as (theoretical) knowledge, as opposed to practical cognition, involve a determining reference to an object or to objects, or, in short, *objective reference*.

In the *Critique of Pure Reason* Kant's chief concern is with assessing the objective reference of cognitions and specifically with accounting for certain cognitions with claims to objective reference being justified and true and hence instances of knowledge. Given the philosophical nature of Kant's interest in the objective reference of cognitions, his investigation does not target the contingent circumstances under which such objectively valid cognition, or knowledge, might be given, but the conditions that are in principle necessary for such cognition, or for knowledge, to obtain. In Kant's parlance, his enquiry concerns the "conditions of the possibility" of objectively valid cognition or of knowledge. On Kant's understanding, the necessary conditions of knowledge do not involve contingent psychological features pertaining to the mental make-up of beings like us, who are capable of theoretical cognition. Rather they involve the necessary structural conditions for the objective validity of cognitive claims, which alone are the conditions that allow us to distinguish between beliefs about objects that we may happen to hold, for whatever reason (including adherence to authority, prejudice and illusion), and warranted cognitive claims about objects that are justifiably true.

Knowledge and metaphysics

Considering the normative intent of Kant's assessment of cognitive claims in the *Critique of Pure Reason*, the critical project might be considered a work in the theory of knowledge or epistemology, even though the latter term, or rather its German equivalent [*Erkenntnistheorie*], is not to be found in Kant himself but rather has been coined and used under the influence of Kant's critical philosophy beginning in the nineteenth century in order to distinguish the psychology of cognition from the epistemic logic of knowledge. Yet the *Critique of Pure Reason* is not an epistemology in the more recent sense of a general theory of knowledge, as opposed to, say, a theory of scientific knowledge investigated in the philosophy of science. Kant's critical epistemology is primarily targeted at knowledge of a special kind, or rather at a special kind of cognitive claims that are to be examined with regard to their possible qualification as knowledge. Only secondarily and as a by-product of that primary investigation does the *Critique of Pure Reason* address other or more general cognitive claims.

The special kind of cognition (and possible knowledge) that the *Critique of Pure Reason* has in view is knowledge regarding supersensory objects, or objects that, by definition, elude verification or falsification by appeal to objects given by the senses. Kant has strong reasons for choosing the special focus of the *Critique of Pure Reason* on the epistemology of metaphysical knowledge. Historically, and well into Kant's own time, metaphysics was considered the core area of philosophical study or, in the words of Aristotle, "first philosophy" (Greek, *prote philosophia*; Latin, *prima philosophia*). In medieval times Aristotelian metaphysics had been incorporated into Christian theological thinking, resulting in a doctrinal system of school philosophy or scholasticism (from the Latin word for "school", *schola*).

Even the early modern period, marked by the triple renewal of humanism in literature, renaissance in the arts and reformation in religion and theology, to a large extent retained the ambition of academic philosophy as a system of doctrinal metaphysics in which the nature of God, the world and the human beings in it was to be ascertained and proven by means of reason alone. In the German lands (there was no politically unified Germany at the time, Kant himself being a citizen of the fairly recently established kingdom of Prussia) the reigning school of philosophy had been built on the foundations of the metaphysical system of Gottfried Wilhelm Leibniz (1646–1716) by Christian Wolff (1679–1754) and his students, chiefly among them Alexander Gottlieb Baumgarten (1714–62). The Wolffians had divided metaphysics into general metaphysics (*metaphysica generalis*), which they identified with the study of being as such or the investigation of the general kinds and features of being (*ontologia*), and special metaphysics (*metaphysica specialis*) or the study of three special object domains of being, namely, God, the human soul and the world in its entirety, to be investigated in philosophical theology (*theologia*), philosophical psychology (*psychologia*) and philosophical cosmology (*cosmologia*), respectively.

Through his academic upbringing Kant inherited the project of the German school of philosophy of establishing the system of metaphysics and specifically of establishing such a system on the basis of rational inference alone, unaided as well as unhindered by empirical evidence. Yet from early on Kant combined his adherence to the traditional metaphysical programme with a keen awareness of the methodological requirements and epistemological difficulties involved in basing cognitive claims about being in general, God, the soul and the world on reason alone. In particular, Kant shared the principal doubts raised by the British empiricists – John Locke (1632–1704), George Berkeley (1685–1753) and David Hume (1711–76) – who each in their own way had questioned the very possibility of purely rational knowledge and insisted on the deliverances of the senses as the ultimate basis of all knowledge.

A particular influence on Kant's increasing scepticism about the very possibility of metaphysics in the traditional, rationalist vein was David

Hume's paradigmatic critique of causal cognition. Hume denied the possibility of any insight into the inner nature of things that might make intelligible the connection of one distinct entity's change of state ("cause") with that of another one ("effect"), instead basing causal claims on the behavioural criterion of the constant conjunction of distinct events and the psychological mechanism of experience-induced future expectations. While Kant did not share Hume's sceptical solution to the problem of causal knowledge and its concomitant substitution of probable belief for certain cognition, he took over Hume's critical analysis of causal claims, generalizing it into a query into the possibility of metaphysical cognitions of all kinds.

In order to widen Hume's specific problem regarding causal cognition into the general problem of metaphysical knowledge, Kant applied a twofold classification of cognitive claims. With respect to their origin, cognitions are either based on experience and therefore hold *a posteriori* (Latin for "from afterwards", literally meaning "after empirical evidence has come in"), or they are not based on experience and hence hold *a priori* (Latin for "from before", literally meaning "before any empirical evidence has come in"). In line with Kant's general epistemological approach to the critique of knowledge, the difference between cognitions *a posteriori* and cognitions *a priori* is not intended as a distinction with regard to the acquisition of cognitions but in view of their validity status, that is, whether the cognitions in questions are valid on empirical grounds or valid on other, non-empirical grounds that are yet to be specified. In logical terms, cognitions *a posteriori* are contingent and particular (or hold contingently and particularly), while cognitions *a priori* are necessary and universal (or hold necessarily and universally).

The second epistemological distinction developed by Kant to pose the general problem of metaphysical knowledge concerns not the mode of origin but the content of cognitions. Reconstructing cognitions as judgements involving a subject term and a predicate term linked by the copula "is" or "are", Kant distinguishes between cognitions in which the predicate term unfolds only what is already contained in the subject term, or *analytic* judgements, and cognitions in which the predicate adds a determination that is not yet contained in the subject term, or *synthetic* judgements. Again Kant's point is not a psychological distinction between what a given person believes or assumes to be contained or not contained in a given subject term, but the logico-epistemological distinction between what is and what is not definitionally included in a given subject term. Kant's paradigmatic examples are the analytic judgements that gold is yellow (given gold's definition as a yellow metal) and that a triangle has three angles, on the one hand, and the synthetic judgements that gold is heavy and that the sum of the interior angles of a triangle equals 180 degrees, on the other hand.

Based on the mutually independent distinctions between judgements *a posteriori* and judgements *a priori* and between analytic and synthetic judgements, Kant generates a typology of three possible forms of judgements designed to address the array of possible epistemological claims. All analytic judgements are valid – and can be known to be valid – *a priori*, due to the complete inclusion of the predicate in the subject and the former's partial identity with the latter. By contrast, synthetic judgements are either *a posteriori* and valid – as well as known to be valid – on the basis of experience, or else they are *a priori* and valid – as well as known to be valid – independently of experience.

In terms of Kant's basic concern with the objective reference of cognitions in general and that of metaphysical cognitions in particular, the types of judgement so differentiated allow us to distinguish between cognitions involving an *a posteriori* reference to objects that is based on experience and cognitions involving an *a priori* reference to objects that is not based on experience. Accordingly, metaphysical cognitions can be described as claims to objective reference that find their logical expression in synthetic judgements *a priori* or judgements that claim to enlarge the cognition of objects independently of experience. Restating the problem about metaphysical cognition as a problem about synthetic judgements *a priori* allows Kant to change the focus of his enquiry from the alleged *objects* of metaphysics (being, God, soul and world) to the *mode of cognition* that can be termed metaphysical, namely, a kind of cognition that does not involve resorting to experience for purposes of confirmation or disconfirmation of its claims.

The logico-epistemological restatement of cognitive claims about metaphysical objects in terms of synthetic judgements *a priori* does not yield a unique and exclusive description of metaphysics. On Kant's account, two established sciences share this type of judgement with metaphysics, while surpassing metaphysics in their proven success as sciences containing extensive bodies of objectively valid cognition or knowledge. Those actual sciences are mathematics, in particular pure mathematics as the science pertaining to the pure geometrical and arithmetical forms subject to instantiation in nature, and natural science, in particular pure physics as the science concerned with the formal laws governing objects in nature. While the actual success of these two sciences serves to establish that synthetic judgements *a priori* indeed are possible, this does not yet guarantee the possibility, much less the actuality, of specifically metaphysical synthetic judgements *a priori*. On the contrary, the reference of both mathematics and physics to natural objects, of which those two sciences exhibit the *a priori* forms and laws, is apt to raise doubts about the possibility of metaphysics as a science given that the latter's objects (being, God, soul, world) by definition cannot be encountered by the senses.

The possibility of metaphysical knowledge

In order to ascertain whether or not metaphysics, that is, metaphysical knowledge, is possible, Kant proposes to study the methodological approach of the established, proven sciences, pure mathematics and pure natural science, with an eye towards the possible exploitation of the secret of their success for the problem case of metaphysics. Kant's point is not the rigid transposition of the procedures and methods proven in one discipline to another one. On the contrary, Kant is keenly aware of the errors committed by previous philosophical attempts, especially in rationalist metaphysics, in applying specifically mathematical methods of enquiry and techniques of proof to the specifically different object domain of metaphysics. Rather, Kant is enquiring into the basic mode of investigation that the paradigm examples of a successful science – mathematics and natural science – can be seen to share.

On Kant's account, both classical, Euclidean geometry and modern physics from Galileo to Newton owe their scientific success to a change in approach that can be called a "revolution" in the word's modern political meaning of a radical reversal. In both cases, the dramatic methodical change concerns the mode of the relation between the scientific investigator and the object of investigation. Rather than seeking instruction from their objects of investigation and reducing the investigator to the role of a passive recipient of cognitive data, the classical geometer and the modern physicist subject their objects to a purposively designed investigation, thereby determining the conditions under which the objects are observed and measured and so actively provoking the relevant data output of the objects. The point of this procedure is the manipulation of the objects under investigation into a position that informs the investigator according to previously fixed terms of cognitive engagement. Rather than falsifying or distorting the scientific results through foreign interference, the intervention of the investigator serves to bring forth what otherwise, under conditions of passive data gathering, would have gone unnoticed and is revealed only under the artificial constraints of a methodically designed investigation.

The lesson Kant extracts from his interpretation of the epistemic conditions for scientific success is the need for scientifically ambitioned cognition to complement the passive gathering of data with the active seeking of such data. Again the point is not to manipulate the cognitive data themselves but to artificially shape the conditions under which the data present themselves so that they turn out to be informative with regard to the investigator's cognitive interests. On Kant's analogy the scientist is to approach nature not as an obedient pupil receiving instruction but as an independent judicial examiner who forces nature to answer to pre-formulated questions (*CpR* B xiii).

When considering transposing the investigative strategy of knowledge acquisition from the paradigm cases of mathematics and natural science to the problem case of metaphysics, Kant radicalizes the methodological reflections about the "revision of the manner of thinking" [*Umänderung der Denkart*] (*CpR* B xxii n) to be found in particular sciences to a general reversal in assessing the requirements for knowledge. In epistemically pre-revolutionary times cognition was supposed to orient itself towards the object. The correspondence (Latin, *adaequatio*) entailed by justified true cognition or knowledge was thought to consist in the representation taking its measure from the object. Based on the revolutionary epistemic practice of mathematics and natural science, Kant proposes the radical reversal of the cognitive relation between representation and object by having it be the object that is to accord with the representation and that is to take its measure from the representation.

On the face of it, this might seem an absurd move that replaces the traditional normative concern of cognition with objectivity and truth through the fabrication of the epistemic object by the representational activity of the subject. But Kant is not about to give up on the normative intent of cognition to achieve the status of knowledge. Nor is he set on replacing all previous object-bound, reproductive cognition with subject-bound, productive cognition. Rather, Kant considers a division of labour between the subject and the object standing in a cognitive relation such that the object contributes the matter and the subject contributes the form of the object to be cognized. Moreover, on Kant's proposal it is not the subject in its individuality and through its particular constitution that contributes the form factor to cognition but the subject in general, regardless of its individuality and considered only in its generic identity as the subject of cognition and (possible) knowledge. Accordingly, the form contributed by the subject in general is not some contingent particular form but the basic form of the object in general. Strictly speaking, then, the subject provides only the *a priori* form or forms of the object of cognition, while the latter contributes the particulars to the cognitive relation between representation and object.

Kant himself likens the envisioned revolutionary change in the epistemic relation between the subject and the object of *a priori* knowledge to the reversed roles of the earth and the stars in the explanation of the motion of the celestial bodies undertaken by Copernicus (1473–1543), according to whom the appearance of celestial motions is due to the motion of the earth (*CpR* B xvi) and not that of the celestial bodies themselves, which are at rest. However, the phrase "Copernican revolution", often attributed to Kant and more often yet used to describe Kant's major epistemological accomplishment, is not used by Kant himself, neither with respect to Copernicus's innovation nor to his own. Moreover, when Copernicus employs the term "revolution", as in the title of his main work, *De revolutionibus orbium coelestium*, it refers to the periodic movements ("revolutions") of the celestial spheres and not to the reversal in their astronomical explanation.

The primary intent of Kant's revolutionary account of the epistemic relation between representation and object is a re-evaluation of that relation in the specific case of metaphysical cognition. Previous, pre-Kantian metaphysics has the representations involved in metaphysical cognitions conform to their objects. Yet by definition the objects of metaphysics lie beyond the reach of the senses and hence are unavailable for the passive, essentially receptive gathering of cognitive data. Short of limiting the purview of metaphysical cognition to the mere conceptual elucidation of independently given concepts or independently established claims in analytic judgements, there seems to be no way to account for the possibility of metaphysical knowledge. But if one adopts Kant's revolutionary epistemological proposal, it becomes at least conceivable that there is metaphysical knowledge understood as the cognition of the *a priori* forms that objects possess independently of their material particulars and which yet pertain to those objects in their particular material determinations.

To be sure, the features attributable to objects through metaphysical knowledge under Kant's revolutionary reinterpretation of *a priori* cognitive reference do not originate in the objects themselves but reflect the prior and principal formative influence of *a priori* cognitive forms originating in the subject as an integral part of the latter's representational activity and being brought to bear on the representation of objects. The major challenge to Kant's novel epistemology is how to reconcile the subjectivity of *a priori* cognitive forms it entails with the claim of cognitions, including metaphysical ones, to objectivity and truth.

The bounds of metaphysical knowledge

Kant's basic solution to the threatening lack of objectivity on the part of cognitions like those, typical of metaphysics, that claim to refer to objects without deriving from them is a re-evaluation of the very conception of objectivity. On Kant's novel account of the possible objects of cognition, objectivity consists not only and not even primarily in the cognitive representation being informed by the object. Rather, to a significant extent the object of cognition – more precisely, every object to be cognized – is shaped by *a priori* subjective form. Moreover, on Kant's novel account, the very status of the object as an object of possible or actual cognition is dependent on the presence of such forms originating in the subject but pertaining to the object. The basic strategy employed by Kant to ensure the objectivity of *a priori* cognitions, including possible metaphysical knowledge, is to have those very cognitions represent the necessary conditions for the very objectivity of cognition. Those *a priori* cognitive forms without which no cognition of objects is possible can legitimately be considered *a priori* forms of the very objects of such cognitions.

Kant's crucial move is to turn metaphysical knowledge from alleged cognitions of the content of special metaphysical objects into the *a priori* knowledge of the formal conditions for there to be any cognition of objects at all, and by extension for any objects of such cognitions. Metaphysical knowledge is not some super-cognition of super-objects but the meta-cognition of the conditions for any cognition of objects and for the objects so cognized. Kant reserves the term "transcendental", which had been employed in traditional metaphysics for the most general features shared by every being as such, for the essential formal features that any object must possess in order to be an object of cognition (*CpR* A 11ff./B 25). Given the universality and necessity of those formal conditions of the possible cognition of objects and the possible objects of cognition, transcendental cognitions and the logical form in which they present themselves can be described as a body of cognitions *a priori* to be expressed in synthetic judgements *a priori*. Kant calls the system of such meta-cognitions regarding the *a priori* forms of possible objects of cognition "transcendental philosophy" (*ibid.*).

Transcendental philosophy is not just a redescription and an alternative form of justification for the traditional metaphysics and its claims to substantial cognition of being in general, the existence of God, the immortality of the soul and the overall structure of the world. In tying metaphysical knowledge to the formal conditions rendering possible any and all cognition of objects, Kant changes the object domain of metaphysics from that of alleged non-empirical entities to that of the objects of possible cognition, more specifically to the very possibility of those cognitions. Moreover, the subjective origin of the *a priori* forms of the objects of cognition introduces an essential formal dependence of the object of cognition on the subject of cognition, or of the known on the knower. Accordingly, the objects so cognized are not cognized as they are in and of themselves ("things in themselves") but only as they present themselves or, in Kant's favoured phrase, "appear" under the subject's cognitive conditions ("appearances").

In particular, Kant distinguishes two sets of *a priori* subjective conditions of the possible cognition of objects and therefore also of the possible objects of cognition, space and time as the *a priori* forms for the cognition of particulars through immediate representations (intuitions) and the twelve categories (among them causality) as the *a priori* forms for the cognition of universal features through discursively mediated representations (concepts). The combined result of the intuitive and the conceptual cognitive conditioning of objects of cognitions is the cognition of objects that are located in space and time and structured by the categories, that is, empirical objects. Kant's term for the sum total of the domain of possible cognition so constituted is "experience" [*Erfahrung*]. Hence metaphysical cognition, to the extent that it can be justified and rightly regarded as knowledge, is restricted to synthetic *a priori* judgements about the intuitional and conceptual conditions of the possibility of experience and of the objects of experience.

Yet while metaphysics-turned-transcendental-philosophy has its cognitive claims severely restricted and strictly limited to objects located in space and time and standing under categorial concepts, the transcendental claims themselves are not based on experience or empirical in nature. Rather, the claims of metaphysics-as-transcendental-philosophy involve non-empirical cognitions about empirical objects. They address only that and all that which makes experience and its objects possible, and in that very capacity they may be considered metaphysical knowledge. As a body of knowledge, metaphysics in Kant consists in the system of non-empirical concepts and principles that provide the necessary metaphysical foundation for the possibility of the experience of objects and for the objects of such experience.

The peculiar type of cognition to which Kant reduces metaphysical claims turns on the intrinsic linkage between their exclusively *a priori* origin and their exclusively *empirical application*. Only by restricting the object domain of metaphysics from its previously alleged extension beyond the limits of experience to the very confines of experience can metaphysical cognition lay claim to objective reference, namely, one that concerns the metaphysical underpinnings of experience. The secret of metaphysics is the metaphysical secret of experience: that experience itself, along with its objects, possesses non-empirical, metaphysical foundations.

Kant's radical reinterpretation of metaphysical knowledge as transcendental knowledge about the non-empirical conditions of experience and its objects has far-reaching consequences for the overall conception of philosophy. With all cognitive claims of metaphysics that exceed the domain of possible experience critically rejected and refuted, metaphysics as a system of genuine knowledge, as opposed to ultimately unwarranted cognitions, is reduced to the metaphysics of empirical objects and their sum total, namely, nature. But restricting metaphysical knowledge to the transcendental conditions of experience is not only a *negative* move that denies the applicability and validity of metaphysical cognitions outside of possible experience. It is also, on Kant's considered view, a *restrictive* statement that limits metaphysical knowledge to the domain of possible experience, thereby opening up a conceptual space for the things as they are in themselves and independently of the *a priori* cognitive conditions and delimiting an object domain for claims to be made on other than theoretical or cognitive grounds.

By limiting metaphysical knowledge to the empirical domain, the non-empirical domain, once the very province of alleged metaphysical cognitions, becomes available for alternative claims that resemble the claims of metaphysical knowledge in one regard but that also differ from them in another important respect. The alternative claims regarding the non-empirical domain are *a priori* and synthetic, like the transcendentally revised metaphysical claims regarding the empirical domain. But unlike the transcendental claims of the critically revised and restricted metaphysics, which aim at theoretical cognition or the cognitive determination of objects, the alternative claims regarding the non-empirical domain aim at practical cognition and at the orientation and motivation of the will. On Kant's overall scheme of philosophy, the place vacated by the critical curtailment of the unjustifiable metaphysical ambitions of theoretical philosophy is to be occupied by the justifiable metaphysical claims of practical philosophy, effectively substituting the discredited theoretical metaphysics with a practical metaphysics or metaphysics of morals [*Metaphysik der Sitten*] based on the practically established reality of freedom.

While the foundation and erection of the projected metaphysics of morals falls outside the sphere of theoretical philosophy, the preparation of its conceptual space lies entirely within the sphere of theoretical philosophy and forms an integral part of the self-critique of reason. Furthermore, on Kant's view, making possible the metaphysics of morals, and more generally a non-empirical understanding of matters of morality, is even the ultimate gain if not the purpose of the critical self-limitation of the metaphysical part of theoretical philosophy to the domain of empirical objects. In restricting theoretical metaphysics to the empirical domain, the *Critique of Pure Reason* prepares the non-empirical domain for its subsequent occupation through practical philosophy and specifically through a metaphysics of morals.

TWO

Sensibility: space and time, transcendental idealism

Emily Carson

Kant's characteristic distinction between sensibility and understanding is generally taken to mark the shift from his pre-critical period to the mature critical period. It is at the heart both of his explanation of the possibility of synthetic *a priori* cognition and of his critique of speculative metaphysics. As we shall see, for Kant, sensibility both extends our cognition, allowing us to go beyond mere concepts to synthetic *a priori* cognition, and constrains our synthetic *a priori* cognition to objects of possible experience.

Sensibility in the pre-critical period

Kant introduced a fundamental distinction between the faculties of sensibility and intellect in his Inaugural Dissertation of 1770, *De mundi sensibilis atque intelligibilis forma et principiis* (*On the Form and Principles of the Sensible and Intelligible World*), in which he makes clear the importance of this distinction for metaphysics. He describes *De mundi* as a specimen of a "propaedeutic science" for metaphysics that "teaches the distinction between sensitive cognition and the cognition which derives from the understanding" (ID 2:395). If we keep straight the sources of our concepts, Kant claims, we can avoid certain longstanding metaphysical disputes. One such dispute that had concerned Kant at least as early as 1755 revolved around an apparent conflict between the metaphysical doctrine of indivisible monads and the infinite divisibility of geometrical space. In his *Physical Monadology*, Kant asked:

How, in this business, can metaphysics be married to geometry, when it seems easier to mate griffins with horses than to unite transcendental philosophy with geometry? For the former peremptorily denies that space is infinitely divisible, while the latter, with its usual certainty, asserts that it is infinitely divisible.

(*PM* 1:475)

The metaphysicians' response to this challenge, which Kant attributes to Wolff (ID 2:395), was to reduce sensible knowledge, including geometry, to confused knowledge of what is known more clearly by the intellect: geometrical concepts like infinite divisibility apply to sensible appearances, but not to the ultimate monadic reality that those appearances confusedly represent. Kant objected to this that instead of appealing to the "reliably established data" of geometry to provide "secure foundations on which to base its reflections", metaphysics turns mathematical concepts "into subtle fictions, which have little truth to them outside the field of mathematics" (2:167–8).[1] I shall describe briefly how the doctrine of sensibility Kant introduces in *De mundi* addresses this apparent conflict between metaphysics and mathematics.

To introduce the distinction between the faculties, Kant appeals to examples that later reappear in the *Critique of Pure Reason* as the Antinomies of Pure Reason. One of them bears directly on the conflict just described: the concept of a simple. By means of the understanding, Kant says, we "arrive without difficulty" at the abstract concept of a simple part, but we cannot always "follow up" this general concept by the sensitive faculty of cognition (2:387). The sensible representation of a simple "in the concrete by a distinct intuition", Kant explains, rests on conditions of time. But in the case of a continuous magnitude like a line, the division into parts has no limit and so cannot be completed in a finite period of time. Thus, "according to the laws of intuitive cognition", we never arrive at – and so cannot represent – a simple part of a continuous magnitude.

This difference with respect to the representation of simple parts reveals a "lack of accord between the sensitive faculty and the faculty of the understanding" (2:389). Instead of taking this to reveal the confused nature of sensibility, as the metaphysicians did, Kant takes it to reflect the fact that sensibility and understanding have different objects. Sensibility is "the receptivity of the subject in virtue of which it is possible for the subject's own representative state to be affected in a definite way by the presence of some object"; intelligence is "the faculty of a subject in virtue of which it has the power to represent things which cannot by their own quality come before the senses of that subject" (2:392). The apparent conflict between geometry and metaphysics dissolves once we recognize that they concern different objects: the objects of sensibility are phenomena, governed by the laws of sensibility and subject to conditions of space and time, while the objects of the understanding are noumena, governed by the laws of the understanding. By getting straight the distinction between sensibility and the understanding and by keeping straight the sources of our concepts, we can protect the claims of geometry from those of metaphysics. Geometry applies to the objects of sensibility, objects given in space and time; metaphysics applies to the objects of the understanding, that is, God and moral perfection (2:396).

On the basis of this characterization of sensibility as receptive, Kant introduces the crucial critical claim that "things which are thought sensitively are representations of things as they appear" (2:392). By contrast, "things which are intellectual are representations of things as they are". He offers two grounds for the claim about sensible cognition. First, because it depends on the subject's affection by the object, it "is dependent upon the special character of the subject insofar as the subject is capable of this or that modification by the presence of objects" (*ibid.*). Second, because "objects do not strike the senses in virtue of their form", we have to distinguish the matter of sensory cognition, sensation, from its form, which must be "an internal principle in the mind" that "coordinates" what is given by the senses "in accordance with stable and innate laws" (2:393). All phenomena, then, are subject to the principles governing the form of the sensible world, but the applicability of those principles is limited to phenomena. Crucially, this does not diminish the epistemic status of sensitive cognition relative to intellectual cognition. Indeed, this is what constitutes Kant's fundamental break with the Leibniz–Wolff treatment of sensibility: "from this, one can see that the sensitive is poorly defined as that which is more confusedly cognised, and that which belongs to the understanding as that of which there is a distinct cognition". While the representations of geometry – "the paradigm of sensitive cognition" – can be very distinct, those of metaphysics – "the organon of everything which belongs to the understanding" – can be very confused (2:394). Thus Kant explicitly rejects the metaphysicians' view that geometry gives us confused cognition of what is known clearly by the understanding: sensibility is a source of genuine cognition in its own right.

In *De mundi*, then, we see how Kant's new characterization of the distinction between the faculties eliminates the apparent conflict between mathematics and metaphysics. The faculties of sensibility and understanding seem to operate more or less autonomously on distinct objects. This allows both for a "science of sensory things" (2:398) – geometry

– and cognition of intellectual things – in ontology and rational psychology – by means of the understanding (2:396). Although by the time of the first *Critique*, Kant's characterization of the faculty of sensibility remains virtually unchanged, the characterization of the understanding and its relation to sensibility is radically revised in such a way as to undermine speculative metaphysics.

Sensibility in the *Critique of Pure Reason*: the Transcendental Aesthetic

All we need to know to begin a critique of pure reason, Kant says in the Introduction to the first *Critique*, is that there are two stems of human cognition, namely sensibility and understanding (*CpR* A 16/B 30). Sensibility is "the capacity (receptivity) to acquire representations through the way in which we are affected by objects" (A 19/B 33). In contrast with the account in *De mundi*, now both sensibility and understanding are essential for any cognition at all: "without sensibility, no object would be given to us, and without understanding none would be thought" (A 51/B 75). Human cognition is essentially discursive. The Transcendental Aesthetic is the science of the *a priori* principles of sensibility: it considers the conditions under which objects are given to us. It will turn out that there are two *a priori* principles of sensibility: space and time.

Corresponding to the faculties of sensibility and understanding are two kinds of representations of objects: intuitions and concepts. Intuitions are the representations by which objects are given to us in sensibility; they relate immediately to objects and are singular (A 320/B 377).[2] Concepts, through which objects are thought, relate mediately to objects by means of characteristic features that several objects may have in common: concepts are thus general. Since sensible intuition is the only way in which objects are given to us, concepts, if they are to have objects, must "ultimately be related to intuitions", and so, for us, to sensibility (A 19/B 33). So sensation is the effect of things on our representative capacity: when we are thus affected through sensation we acquire empirical intuitions; the object of an empirical intuition, what it represents, Kant calls an appearance. Appearances have both matter and form: the matter of an appearance is what is given in sensation, while the form of appearance is what allows the manifold or multiplicity given in sensation to be "ordered in certain relations" (A 20/B 34). This form of appearance is the subject matter of the Transcendental Aesthetic.

As the *a priori* science of sensibility, the Transcendental Aesthetic examines the conditions under which objects are given. To determine what those conditions are, Kant proposes first to "isolate sensibility by separating off everything that the understanding thinks through its concepts", leaving only empirical intuition. From that we remove "everything that belongs to sensation". We shall then be left with "all that sensibility can make available *a priori*": that is, as we shall see, "pure intuition and the mere form of appearances" (A 22/B 36).

The contention that something is left over, that there is over and above empirical intuition a pure intuition "in which nothing is to be encountered that belongs to sensation", rests on the claim that "that within which the sensations can alone be ordered and placed in a certain form cannot itself be in turn sensation" (A 20/B 34), which sounds much like the claim in *De mundi* that objects do not strike the senses in virtue of their form. It follows that "the pure form of sensible intuitions in general is to be encountered in the mind *a priori*, wherein all of the manifold of appearances is intuited in certain relations". Kant substantiates this claim in the Metaphysical Expositions, where he argues that there are two pure forms of intuition: space and time.[3]

The metaphysical exposition of the concept of space

A metaphysical exposition of a concept, Kant tells us, presents the content and *a priori* origin of that concept. Kant's argument begins with the claim that by means of outer sense, "we represent to ourselves objects as outside us, and all as in space" (*CpR* A 22/B 37). Objects in space have determinate shape, magnitude and positions with respect to each other. Similarly, by means of inner sense we represent mental states as in temporal relations. That spatial and temporal relations are such basic features of our experience gives rise to the question: what are space and time? Kant proposes three answers to this question. Space and time might be actual entities, a view Kant associates with Newton, or they might be only relations of things that hold of those things even if they are not intuited, as the Leibnizians would have it. On both these views, things have their spatial and temporal properties independently of our intuiting them. Kant's own proposal, by contrast, is that space and time are relations that "attach to the form of intuition alone, and thus to the subjective constitution of our mind" without which spatial and temporal properties "could not be ascribed to anything at all" (A 23/B 37). Kant will argue in the Metaphysical Exposition that the representation of space is an *a priori* intuition. From this he concludes that the representation of space "has its seat merely in the subject as its formal constitution for being affected by objects", thus is "the form of outer sense in general" (B 41), and finally that space itself "is nothing other than merely the form of all appearances of outer sense" (A 26/B 42).

The first two arguments of the Metaphysical Exposition show that the representation of space is *a priori*, and not *a posteriori*. Kant begins by arguing that the representation of space is not "an empirical concept that has been drawn from outer sense" (A 23/B 38).[4] Recall the basic claim that by means of outer sense we represent objects "as outside us and all as in space". Kant argues that for my sensations to be thus related to "something outside me" and to things that are "outside and next to one another", we must represent them not just as different, but as "in different places". In other words, to represent objects as in spatial relations, as we evidently do, we must represent them as occupying regions of space. This in turn presupposes the representation of the space of which those regions are a part. It follows that "the representation of space can't be obtained from the relations of outer appearance through experience, but rather this outer experience is itself first possible only through this representation" (*ibid.*). The representation of objects as spatially related presupposes the representation of space, and so the representation of space cannot be acquired empirically from experience of objects in spatial relations.[5]

It may seem that the *apriority* of the representation of space does not follow from the fact that outer experience presupposes the representation of space, because the representation of space might also presuppose the representation of outer objects: perhaps the two representations are reciprocally necessary. The second *apriority* argument is meant to show, against this, that the representation of space does not presuppose that of outer objects. It then follows that the representation of space is a necessary representation *a priori* "that is the ground of all outer intuitions".

The argument proceeds from the claim that "one can never represent that there is no space", although "one can very well think that there are no objects to be encountered in it" (A 24/B 38). What does it mean to say that we can never represent that there is no space? We can take this to be a restatement of the previous conclusion: we cannot represent outer objects without representing them as in space. By contrast, we can represent space with no objects. To understand Kant's claim here, it helps to compare it to the parallel argument about the representation of time (A 31/B 46): to say that we can represent space with no objects is to say that we can "take the appearances away from space". This seems to be what Kant described at A 20–21/B 35:

[If we] separate from the representation of a body that which the understanding thinks about it, such as substance, force, divisibility, etc. as well as that which belongs to sensation, such as impenetrability, hardness, colour, etc., something from this empirical intuition is still left for me, namely extension and form.

In other words, if we remove from the representation of a body all its conceptual and sensory content, we are still left with its purely spatial features. To say that we cannot represent that there is no space is to say that we cannot remove the spatial content of appearances. The spatial content that is left over just is a representation of space with "no objects to be encountered in it". Understood this way, we can take the second argument to be telling us more about this *a priori* representation, that, as Parsons has put it, the representation of space is "a fundamental phenomenological given" (Parsons 1992: 69) with content of its own.[6]

At this point, Kant takes himself to have established that the representation of space is *a priori* and is a necessary condition of outer intuition. The next step is to show that it is a sensible representation, that it is an intuition. Again, there are two arguments for this thesis, both of which depend on the different part–whole relations of intuitions and concepts. Kant's strategy is to show that the representation of space is such that it cannot be a concept and – since all cognition "is either an intuition or a concept" (A 320/B 377) – it must therefore be an intuition. More precisely, he argues that the original representation of space, from which all concepts of space are derived, is an intuition.

The key features of our representation of space that Kant appeals to in these arguments are that it is singular and infinite. What Kant means by the singularity of space here is that "if one speaks of many spaces, one understands by that only parts of one and the same unique space" (A 25/B 39). These parts are not components of the single all-encompassing space, but rather are "only thought in it": the parts of space rest "merely on limitations" of the already-given singular space. In a text from 1790 on Kästner's treatises, Kant describes it as "a peculiarity found in no other concept … that all spaces are only possible and thinkable as parts of one single space, so that the representation of parts already presupposes that of the whole" (Ak 20:419). He seems to take this as a datum of experience, appealing to phenomenological claims about the space of experience (cf. Parsons 1992: 72). This comes out more clearly in the parallel passage from *De mundi*, where Kant talks about how one conceives to oneself a part of space:

> The concept of space is a singular representation embracing all things within itself; it is not an abstract common concept containing them under itself. For what you speak of as several places are

only parts of the same boundless space related to one another by a
fixed position. And you can only conceive to yourself a cubic foot
if it be bounded in all directions by the space which surrounds it.

(ID 2:402)

Parts of space are determined by their relation to the all-encompassing
space (a part is delimited "by the space which surrounds it") and different parts of space are distinguished by their respective relations to
that "same boundless space".

Why does it follow from this that space is not a concept? We have
already seen that concepts are inherently general, and intuitions are
singular: the representation "which can only be given through a single
object is an intuition" (*CpR* A 32/B 47). The relation between particular spaces and space is one of parts to whole, not of instances to
concept. Moreover, a conceptual representation of a single object is
"given through" other representations – its characteristic marks – that
are the parts of the concept. By contrast, the representation of space is
not given through other representations that are its parts; rather its parts
presuppose the whole. Space is only "given through a single object"
and is therefore an intuition.

These phenomenological facts also ground Kant's claim to the infinity of space in the second intuition argument. Thus the argument begins
with the claim that "space is represented as an infinite given magnitude"
(A 25/B 39). This is not to say that we perceive space as an infinite
whole. Kant is again more explicit about what he means in the parallel argument for time: "The infinitude of time signifies nothing more
than that every determinate magnitude of time is only possible through
limitations of a single time grounding it. The original representation,
time, must therefore be given as unlimited" (A 32/B 48). The infinitude of space is supported by the phenomenological claim that any
given space, however large, is bounded by more space. Thus in the
A-edition version of this argument, Kant refers to the "boundlessness
in the progress of intuition" (A 25). Moreover, this succession of intuitions can proceed without limit in both directions: "space and time
are *quanta continua* because no part of them can be given except as
enclosed between boundaries (points and instants), thus only in such a
way that this part is again a space or a time. Space therefore consists only
of spaces, time of times" (A 169/B 211). The result of limiting a space
results in another space, which can in turn be limited: space is infinitely
divisible. Thus Kant says that space is thought as containing "an infinite
set of representations within itself" (A 25/B 41); concepts, although
they can contain an infinite set of representations under themselves,

cannot contain an infinite set of representations within themselves. Kant explains this in his lectures on logic (see e.g. Ak 24:911). A concept contains under itself those concepts that are obtained from it by adding differentia to make it more specific. For example, the concept of body contains under itself more specific concepts of particular bodies. Since we can continue adding differentia indefinitely – no matter how many differentia you add, it is always possible for there to be still smaller differences among the things answering to the concept – a concept can contain under itself indefinitely many concepts. The concept contains within itself those concepts that are its characteristic (defining) marks. Any given concept can contain within itself only finitely many concepts because a finite mind could never grasp infinitely many concepts. But the representation of space does contain within itself infinitely many representations, so it is not a concept. The boundlessness in the progression of intuition allows for the representation of space to contain indefinitely many representations. Thus "the original representation of space is an *a priori* intuition, not a concept" (B 40). This is not to say that we do not have concepts of space and of spaces, but Kant takes himself to have shown that all our spatial concepts are grounded in the original intuition of space.

In the Metaphysical Exposition, then, Kant argues on the basis of the way in which we represent objects "as in space" that our representation of space is *a priori*. On the basis of the special way in which the representation of space is given to us, Kant argues that the original representation of space is an *a priori* – or pure – intuition. In the Transcendental Exposition of the Concept of Space, Kant bolsters this conclusion by showing how it provides an explanation of the possibility of geometry as synthetic *a priori* cognition.

The transcendental exposition of the concept of space

A transcendental exposition, Kant says, explains a concept – here, the concept of space – "as a principle from which insight into the possibility of other synthetic *a priori* cognitions" – geometry, in this case – "can be gained" (B 40). It does this by showing that those cognitions "actually flow from the given concept" and that they "are only possible under the presupposition of a given way of explaining this concept" (*ibid.*). So the key question of the Transcendental Exposition is: what must the representation of space be for geometry to be possible? As we have seen, Kant has already argued that the original representation of space is an *a priori*, or pure, intuition. He goes on to show how thus taking the representation of space as a pure intuition makes "comprehensible" the possibility of geometry as "a science that determines the properties of space synthetically and yet *a priori*" (B 41).

Geometrical propositions are all necessary or apodictic. Kant argued in the Introduction to the *Critique* that "necessity and strict universality are secure indications of an *a priori* cognition" (B 4): the necessary proposition that space has only three dimensions could not be an empirical judgement, nor can it be inferred from empirical judgements (B 41). Rather, the *apriority* of the representation of space accounts for the apodictic nature of geometrical propositions.

Kant also asserted in the Introduction that geometrical propositions are synthetic. We cannot arrive by analysis at the geometrical principle that the straight line between two points is the shortest because "my concept of the straight contains nothing of quantity, but only a quality". The concept of the shortest therefore "cannot be extracted out of the concept of straight line by analysis" but is "entirely additional to it". Thus the synthesis of the concepts of shortest and straight line can be effected only with the help of an intuition added to the concept (B 17).[7] We can now see that that intuition is a pure intuition of space. So the fact that the representation of space is an intuition accounts for the syntheticity of geometry.

Kant takes himself to have shown in the Metaphysical Exposition that the original representation of space is an *a priori* intuition, and in the Transcendental Exposition that this *a priori* intuition can explain the synthetic *a priori* status of geometry. But this gives rise to a further puzzle: "how can an outer intuition inhabit the mind that precedes the objects themselves, and in which the concept of the latter can be determined *a priori*?" (A 25/B 41). Kant has given a general argument that there must be an *a priori* intuition of space, but there remains the question of how we are to make sense of the notion of *a priori* intuition.

The problem is set out clearly in the *Prolegomena*, where Kant begins with the question of how pure mathematics is possible.[8] The distinguishing feature of mathematical cognition, he says, is that it "must present its concept beforehand in intuition and indeed *a priori*" (PFM 4:281). So the condition of the possibility of mathematical cognition is that "it must be grounded in some pure intuition or other, in which it can present, or ... construct all of its concepts *in concreto* yet *a priori*". If we could discover this pure intuition and its possibility, Kant continues, we would have our explanation of the possibility of pure mathematics. Now in the Metaphysical Exposition, we have discovered this pure intuition. But, Kant continues in the *Prolegomena*, "with this step the difficulty seems to grow rather than diminish. For now the question runs: How is it possible to intuit something *a priori*?" An intuition is a representation that depends on the presence of an object, but it seems that an *a priori* intuition would have to occur without an object being present: "how can the intuition of an object precede the object itself?" (4:282). What could the object of such an intuition be?

It is to answer this question that Kant first moves from the argument of the Metaphysical Exposition that the representation of space is an *a priori* intuition to the claim that the representation "has its seat merely in the subject" (*CpR* A 25/B 41). Again, the *Prolegomena* is more expansive. The puzzle about *a priori* intuition arises only if we take our intuition to represent things as they are in themselves: on that view, there could be no *a priori* intuition. I can only know what is in the object itself if the object is present and given to me. Even if the thing in itself were thus given to me, and even if its properties could somehow "migrate over" into my power of representation, my cognition would be only empirical. But geometry is *a priori* cognition, so cannot be cognition of properties and relations of things as they are in themselves. So the explanation of geometry as synthetic *a priori* cognition depends on the possibility of *a priori* intuition of geometric objects; that in turn can be explained only if the spatial properties of geometric objects "have their seat" in our subjective constitution for being affected by objects. As Kant puts it in the *Prolegomena*:

> There is therefore only one way possible for my intuition to precede the actuality of the object and occur as an *a priori* cognition, namely if it contains nothing else except the form of sensibility, which in me as subject precedes all actual impressions through which I am affected by objects. (4:282)

The first two arguments of the Metaphysical Exposition showed that the representation of space is the ground of all outer intuitions. The argument of the Transcendental Exposition shows that we can explain our cognition of geometry if we take this ground as a "formal constitution for being affected by objects and thereby acquiring immediate representation, that is, intuition, of them, thus only as the form of outer sense in general" (*CpR* A 25/B 41). Geometry can present its objects *in concreto* and *a priori* because it concerns only the formal properties that objects have by virtue of the subjective conditions of outer intuitions, not objective features of things in themselves.

Transcendental idealism

The final step of the Transcendental Exposition thus turns on the claim that the only way to make sense of an *a priori* intuition of space is to take that intuition to be of the form of sensibility. Accordingly, in "Conclusions from the above concepts" Kant generalizes the argument of the Transcendental Exposition from geometric objects to all objects. Once again, he raises the question of how an intuition can both precede and determine the objects themselves "for neither absolute nor relative determinations can be intuited prior to the existence of the things to which they pertain, thus be intuited *a priori*" (*CpR* A 26/B 42). We represent empirical objects as determined in space; the representation of space has been shown to be an *a priori* intuition. Kant takes it to follow that "space represents no property at all of any things in themselves nor any relation of them to each other" (*ibid.*). The spatial properties and relations of objects are not objective properties and relations of things themselves but rather reflect the subjective conditions of sensibility. The key to the argument for the subjectivity of space is the claim that the only way to explain the possibility of *a priori* intuition (whose actuality was established in the Metaphysical Exposition) is to take it to be the "subjective condition of sensibility under which alone all intuition is possible for us" (*ibid.*).[9]

This way of understanding the argument forestalls the common objection that Kant's argument for transcendental idealism rests fatally on the assumption of the necessity of Euclidean geometry, an assumption that no longer stands. Resting the argument on geometry in this way would conflict with Kant's claim that in the *Critique* he is following the synthetic method, which "takes no foundation as given except reason itself" and "therefore tries to develop cognition out of its original seeds without relying on any fact whatever" (*PFM* 4:274). This method is opposed to the analytic or regressive method of the *Prolegomena*, which must "rely on something already known to be dependable, from which we can go forward with confidence and ascend to the sources, which are not yet known" (4:274–5). Accordingly, in the *Prolegomena*, Kant presents an "argument from geometry"; but this is explicitly opposed to the synthetic methodology of the *Critique*. I have thus tried to present the argument for the subjectivity of space in the *Critique* as independent of any claims about geometry. In the Transcendental Exposition, Kant appeals to geometry to bolster the independent argument of the Metaphysical Exposition and to show how taking space to be subjective makes sense of the notion of *a priori* intuition. But the argument for the subjectivity of space rests on the general question of how to make sense of an *a priori* intuition of space, the existence of which is established in the Metaphysical Exposition, and so is in keeping with Kant's synthetic method.

We have now arrived at the full-blown conclusion of the transcendental ideality of space. Kant takes it to follow from the fact that space "represents no property at all of any things in themselves, nor any relation of them to each other" that space "is nothing other than merely the form of all appearances of outer sense" (*CpR* A 26/B 42).[10] This provides us with Kant's answer to the question set out at the beginning of the Aesthetic with regard to the nature of space (and time). Space and time are neither actual entities, as Newton would have it, nor determinations or relations of things that pertain to them independently of their being intuited, as Leibniz would have it: rather, space and time are "relations that attach to the form of intuition alone, and thus to the subjective constitution of our mind" (A 23/B 37). It follows that we can "speak of space, extended beings, and so on, only from the human standpoint" (A 26/B 42). The representation of space "signifies nothing at all" considered apart from the subjective conditions of sensibility. Space is thus ideal in regard to things considered in themselves, but this does not take away from the reality of space "in regard to everything that can come before us externally as an object" (A 28/B 44). Because it is a necessary condition of the possibility of all outer experience, space is empirically real with respect to all possible outer experience: spatial claims are "universally valid" of "all things that may appear to us externally" (A 27/B 43). But because space is nothing other than the form of all appearances of outer sense, it is transcendentally ideal: "it is nothing as soon as we leave aside the condition of the possibility of all experience, and take it as something that grounds the things in themselves" (A 28/B 44). All and only objects of possible experience are spatially determined.

With this move from the subjectivity of space to the conclusion that space is nothing other than the form of appearances of outer sense, Kant moves from claims about the representation of spatial objects to conclusions about space itself. This move has been the subject of much commentary, centred around possible responses to the problem of the "neglected alternative". The objection, raised in Kant's time, is that Kant does not consider the possibility that space is both a subjective form of sensibility and an objective determination of things "that attaches to objects themselves and would remain even if one were to abstract from all subjective conditions of intuition" (A 26/B 42). Why could it not be, for example, that because of the constraints imposed by the subjective form of sensibility, we can only perceive objects that really are spatial?

Guyer suggests that Kant rules out this possibility on the basis of geometrical considerations. The absolute necessity of geometry requires that whatever is asserted of spatial figures in geometry is necessarily true of those figures; if, however, their conformity to the conditions of our sensibility were merely contingent (we perceive only the objects that happen to conform to those conditions), then geometry would not be absolutely necessary. The only way to ensure that objects necessarily conform to our form of intuition is if "they are reduced to our necessarily spatial representations" (Guyer 1987: 266). On Guyer's view, then, the argument for transcendental idealism depends essentially on an assumption of the necessary truth of geometry.

I earlier suggested reasons why we might not want to take Kant's key arguments in the *Critique* to rest on geometrical considerations.[11] But what underlies this picture and (arguably) gives rise to the problem of the neglected alternative is what has come to be called a "two-worlds" interpretation of transcendental idealism according to which there are two distinct domains of objects: non-spatiotemporal things in themselves and spatiotemporal objects. If we reduce the latter to representations, as Guyer suggests, then it is natural to think of things in themselves as the objects of those representations. This in turn leads quite easily to what Parsons (1992) has called "the Distortion Picture" of the distinction between appearances and things in themselves according to which we represent objects as having properties – including spatial properties – that they do not in fact have. There is no doubt that Kant's language sometimes invites this reading: to take just one example, he says that "the things that we intuit are not in themselves what we intuit them to be, nor are their relations so constituted in themselves as they appear to us" (*CpR* A 42/B 59).

On the other hand, this reading comes uncomfortably close to the Leibniz–Wolff view of sensibility that Kant rejected in the Inaugural Dissertation: recall that the metaphysicians' response to the problem of infinite divisibility was to reduce sensible knowledge to confused representations of what is known clearly by the intellect. Kant objected that this turned mathematical concepts into "subtle fictions", not true of ultimate reality. But taking things in themselves to be non-spatiotemporal objects that we represent to ourselves as spatiotemporal seems to have the same effect: there is a sense in which our geometrical knowledge – indeed our knowledge of sensible objects in general – turns out to be false.[12] It is true that the critical Kant does not claim that we have clear knowledge of ultimate reality through the intellect, as the Leibniz–Wolff tradition would have it; instead, he denies that we have any purely intellectual knowledge at all. But it is not clear why the mere unknowability of things in themselves puts the geometer in a better position than the metaphysicians' view does: it would still be the case that our geometrical concepts are not true of ultimate reality.

Considerations such as these have led some commentators (e.g. Parsons 1992; Allison 2004) to reject the "two-worlds" interpretation of transcendental idealism in favour of a reading that emphasizes texts where Kant speaks instead of a single object "taken in a twofold meaning, namely as appearance or as thing in itself" (B xxvii), or of the critical "distinction between things as objects of experience and the very same things as things in themselves" (B xxvi). The idea is that the distinction is not between two distinct systems of objects, but rather between different ways of conceiving of the same objects. When we conceive of things "from the human standpoint", we conceive of them under the subjective conditions of intuition, and so we consider them as spatiotemporal. But we can also conceive of them from a transcendental standpoint, abstracting from those sensible conditions, and so as things in themselves. This provides a neat solution to the problem of the neglected alternative: if things in themselves just are things considered in abstraction from sensible conditions, then there is no possibility of their being spatiotemporal.[13]

In the end, despite Kant's attempt to "preclude all misinterpretation" of his view of "the fundamental constitution of sensible cognition" (A 42/B 59), the text admits of different interpretations. What is clear by the end of the Aesthetic, however, is how Kant sees his correction of the "falsification of the concept of sensibility" perpetrated by the "Leibnizian–Wolffian philosophy" (A 44/B 61) as contributing to the solution of the "general problem of transcendental philosophy" (B 73). Synthetic *a priori* judgements are possible because the pure *a priori* intuitions of space and time allow us to go beyond a given concept to discover "that which is *a priori* and synthetically connected with it in the intuition that corresponds to it". But because space and time are merely conditions of sensibility, they also "determine their own boundaries" (A 39/B 56): synthetic *a priori* judgement can never "extend beyond the objects of the senses and can hold only for objects of possible experience" (B 73).[14]

Notes

1. For a more detailed treatment of these issues, see Carson (1999).
2. Although human intuition is necessarily sensible, and thus dependent on affection by a given object, Kant allows the possibility of intellectual intuition. A divine understanding would not represent given objects; rather the objects would be given or produced through the representation (B 145).

3. The following discussion focuses on the case of space. Kant offers analogous arguments for time as a pure form of intuition in the Metaphysical Exposition of Time, but I shall not consider those here.

4. Actually, Kant says that "space is not an empirical concept", but here and throughout the Metaphysical Exposition his claims should be construed as claims about the representation of space, and not about space itself.

5. This formulation of the main claim of the first *apriority* argument is given in Parsons (1992: 68) and developed in Warren (1998). Falkenstein (1995) gives a similar reading of the argument.

6. That content, the spatial features of objects – their extension and form – is what is studied in geometry, the science of space. Understood this way, the argument leads naturally into the next argument in the A-edition version of the Transcendental Aesthetic: "the apodictic certainty of all geometrical principles and the possibility of their *a priori* construction are grounded in this *a priori* necessity" (A 24). This argument was removed from the B edition and replaced by the Transcendental Exposition, which will be discussed below.

7. The argument for the syntheticity of geometry in the Introduction is not very strong, as has often been pointed out by commentators. I take it that Kant does not intend to offer a conclusive argument here, but is merely indicating or motivating what he will go on to establish conclusively in the *Critique*. This means, however, that he cannot help himself to the synthetic *a priori* status of geometry in the arguments of the Transcendental Aesthetic. In particular, he cannot be arguing in the Transcendental Exposition from the premise of the synthetic *a priori* status of geometry to the conclusion that our representation of space is an *a priori* intuition. In any case, there is no need for such an argument from geometry, because that conclusion has already been established at this point. For more on the supposed argument from geometry, see Shabel (2004).

8. In the *Prolegomena* Kant adopts the regressive method of arguing from an already-known body of cognition to its unknown sources, as opposed to the synthetic method of the *Critique*. I discuss this further below.

9. Kant is quite explicit about this in several passages in the *Prolegomena*: for example, "There is therefore only one way possible for my intuition to precede the actuality of the object and occur as an *a priori* cognition, namely if it contains nothing else except the form of sensibility, which in me as subject precedes all actual impressions through which I am affected by objects" (4:282); "by the very fact that they are pure intuitions *a priori* they prove that they are mere forms of our sensibility" (4:283). Parsons (1992) contains an extended discussion of the limitations of such an argument.

10. With this, Kant has substantiated the claim made at the beginning of the Aesthetic that we can separate from outer representations that which is contributed by the understanding and that which belongs to sensation to arrive at the *a priori* form of sensible intuition which "lies ready for it in the mind *a priori*" (*CpR* A 20/B 34): once we see that space is the subjective condition of sensibility, "it can be understood how the form of all appearances can be given in the mind prior to all actual perceptions, thus *a priori*" (A 26/B 42).

11. Guyer acknowledges these reasons, but argues that Kant does not observe his methodological prescriptions in the *Critique*. Cf. Guyer (1987: 80; 2006: 48–9).

12. Guyer describes transcendental idealism as "the harshly dogmatic insistence that we can be quite sure that things as they are in themselves cannot be as we represent them to be" (Guyer 1987: 333).

13. This "two-aspect" view also comes at a cost. For a helpful survey of the merits and difficulties associated with these alternatives, see Gardner (1999: 290–98).
14. I am grateful to Lisa Shabel and Janet Folina for comments and discussion.

THREE

Understanding: judgements, categories, schemata, principles

Dietmar Heidemann

Overview

It is one of Kant's central claims that sensibility and understanding are the only sources of knowledge with which the human cognitive faculty is furnished. In the *Critique of Pure Reason*, the major work of his transcendental philosophy that is supposed to answer the key question of theoretical philosophy, "What can I know?" (A 804/B 832), Kant writes: "All that seems necessary for an introduction or preliminary is that there are two stems of cognition … sensibility and understanding" (A 15/B 30). This claim is mainly, though not exclusively, directed against the Leibnizians. The Leibnizians concede that sensibility and understanding are in many respects different; however, they assign both of them to a single cognitive capacity, the faculty of representation: sensibility is the faculty of confused representation whereas the understanding is the faculty of clear and distinct representation. According to this view, sensibility and understanding are not essentially distinct sources of knowledge, but rather indicate nothing more than the difference between confused and distinct representation. Since cognition cannot consist in confused representation, the Leibnizians argue, only the understanding is capable of acquiring genuine knowledge by means of clear and distinct representation.

Kant considers the conception of the difference between sensibility and understanding in terms of a psychological graduation from confused to distinct representation to be fundamentally mistaken. He explains why with the help of the following example:

Without doubt the concept of right that is used by the healthy understanding contains the very same things that the most subtle speculation can evolve out of it, only in common and practical use one is not conscious of these manifold representations in these thoughts. Thus one cannot say that the common concept is sensible and contains a mere appearance, for right cannot appear at all; rather its concept lies in the understanding.   (A 43–4/B 61)

What Kant means is that the confused representation of something does not automatically render it a representation of sensibility. For occasionally even the understanding represents its objects in a confused manner, yet the confused representation of a concept – for example, the concept of right – does not make the concept a sensible appearance like an object of sense perception.

In Kant's view this difficulty signals that the Leibnizian theory is flawed. Thus in the *Critique of Pure Reason* he sets out to demonstrate and explain the independence of sensibility and understanding as two distinct sources of knowledge.[1] Whereas the Transcendental Aesthetic outlines the theory of sensibility, arguing for space and time as forms of intuition, the Transcendental Logic delivers the theory of the understanding, depicting logical functions and categories as the forms of thinking.

Despite the independence of sensibility and understanding, however, according to Kant they must cooperate in order to make cognition possible. This idea is behind the famous quotation from the *Critique of Pure Reason*: "Thoughts without content are empty, intuitions without concepts are blind" since "[w]ithout sensibility no object would be given to us, and without understanding none would be thought" (A 51/B 75). Thus although sensibility and understanding are self-reliant, neither of them provides cognition on its own. Cognition requires the cooperation of sensibility and understanding, or intuitions and concepts.

In the *Critique of Pure Reason*, Kant is not interested in an empirical theory of sensibility or understanding. He aims for a non-empirical, transcendental theory of the sources of knowledge. A transcendental theory is a theory that expounds the *a priori* conditions of the possibility of experience and cognition. Such a theory can determine, independently of experience, Kant maintains, the formal character of all possible objects of human experience or cognition. For example, it can be determined that for the human mind objects of sense perception necessarily appear in space and time.

This chapter outlines the transcendental theory of the understanding.[2] We shall first consider the meaning of "transcendental logic", the doctrine that develops the theory of the pure understanding. Then we shall explore the key concepts of that theory: understanding itself as the faculty of thinking; categories and judgements as the forms of thinking; the transcendental deduction that demonstrates the conditions under which the use of the forms of thinking can be objectively justified, and the role that apperception and imagination, as the main cognitive capacities of the understanding, play in that demonstration; the schemata of the imagination that demonstrate how concrete objects of sensibility can be subsumed under the abstract forms of thinking, which include not only the categories but also the principles of the pure understanding, the most abstract *a priori* laws that govern all possible human experience and cognition.

Transcendental logic

To make the fundamental difference between sensibility and understanding as clear as possible, Kant defines the understanding as "a non-sensible faculty of cognition" (A 67/B 92), a cognitive faculty that by definition does not rely on sensible input. Making sense of this conception of the understanding requires first examining its theoretical domain, the "transcendental logic".

Transcendental logic is a special kind of logic. It is special in that, unlike "general logic", it does not abstract "from all content of cognition" (A 55/B 79). Whereas general logic concerns nothing over and above "the form of thinking", "transcendental logic" explicitly considers the relation of cognition to its objects, and in doing so it takes into account the sources of knowledge (A 56/B 79). Transcendental logic is therefore very different from general logic, although, as we shall see, they are related.

With respect to "general logic", two important things must be noted: first, Kant is the inventor of the now-common term "formal logic" (cf. A 131/B 170); however, second, his use of the term "formal" or "general" logic is somewhat different from its contemporary use. Kant describes general logic as the doctrine that "considers representations" irrespectively of their origin, and "deals only with the form of the understanding" (A 56/B 80). Contemporary logicians would deny that formal or symbolic logic by itself involves representations or operations of the understanding. They would rather restrict the domain of formal logic to purely formal relations that obtain between symbols, terms, propositions and statements, while completely ignoring the understanding as cognitive faculty. Nevertheless, Kant and contemporary logicians agree that formal or symbolic logic essentially considers abstract logical relations or rules within which the variables can mean anything at all. From a formal point of view it simply does not matter what *a*, *b* or *c* mean, since it is always logically true that if *a* implies *b* and *b* implies *c* then *a* also implies *c*.

In transcendental logic, however, the content and source of thought do matter. For Kant, the meaning of the content of thought originates in the sources of knowledge. The transcendental aesthetic shows that space and time are the *a priori* forms of sensibility; as such they are the transcendental conditions of the possibility of sensible intuition. Analogously, the transcendental logic determines the *a priori* forms of thinking objects through the understanding. Such *a priori* forms determine how we must necessarily think of all objects possible for us, not in a concrete but in a purely formal manner. Whereas the transcendental aesthetic informs us *a priori* that objects of sensible intuition are spatiotemporal, the transcendental logic informs us *a priori* how we must formally think of objects in order to be able to conceive of them at all. For example, it demonstrates that we must think of predicates as belonging to subjects. In this sense, Kant says, transcendental logic reveals "concepts that may be related to objects *a priori* ... by means of which we think objects completely *a priori*" (A 57/B 81–2).

Thus whereas general logic does not care about whether its cognitions are pure or empirical, transcendental logic is exclusively concerned with concepts in so far as their relation to objects is established *a priori*. That the concept "table" refers to certain objects in space is something we do not know *a priori* through the understanding, since we derive that concept from sense perception and can therefore establish the empirical fact of its relation to certain objects only *a posteriori*. However, that we must formally think of tables as substances to which certain predicates pertain is something we know *a priori*. For Kant there is a whole set of concepts whose relation to objects can be cognized *a priori*. It is the task of transcendental logic to tell us which concepts they are, and how these concepts refer to objects *a priori* as the necessary conditions of the possibility of cognition. Hence the transcendental logic enables us to determine *a priori* how we must think of all objects of cognition. The first important step towards performing this task is to examine the faculty of the understanding.

Understanding

The understanding, like sensibility, is not only a source of knowledge but also a faculty of cognition. Following the rationalist tradition, Kant employs the term "faculty" to characterize mental capacities. In the Kantian sense, a faculty of cognition can be attributed to a rational being with respect to one or more mental capacities exercised by that being. Accordingly, the human mind is furnished with the understanding as a faculty of cognition that most fundamentally exercises the capacity to think. It does so by means of concepts, which it uses in judgements that establish or apply rules of thinking. Kant describes this in the following way:

> We have explained the understanding in various ways – through a spontaneity of cognition ... through a faculty of thinking, or a faculty of concepts, or also of judgements – which explanations come down to the same thing. Now we can characterize it as the faculty of rules. (A 126)[3]

In contrast to sensibility, the understanding's distinguishing mark is the spontaneity with which it employs concepts in judgements. Sensibility is the only way cognition immediately relates to objects, since in sensibility we intuit things just as they are given to us (A 20/B 33). Intuition is, Kant points out, that "representation ... which can only be given through a single object" (A 32/B 47). Via the affection of our senses we represent only single objects like *this* chair, *this* particular length or *this* shade of colour. By contrast, the faculty of the understanding represents its objects by means of concepts. Concepts, however, refer to objects indirectly, and for that reason they are discursive representations. The discursivity of concepts means that they are general, representing not single objects but collections of marks that have been abstracted from more concrete representations. For instance, the concept "chair" is general in that it does not represent any particular chair but a collection of common marks – seat, leg, back rest – that the understanding abstracts from the representations of particular chairs. There are arm chairs, camp chairs, bar chairs, beach chairs, baby chairs, metal chairs, wooden chairs, plastic chairs and so on. Although these particular chairs are different in many respects, we can employ the concept "chair" in order to refer to all of them. In this sense a concept can be described as the representation of an analytic identity of that which we represent as the same in different objects. This is why concepts are general representations, as opposed to the singular representations of intuition. The fact that they are general representations explains why they cannot be given in sensibility, and why they are products of the spontaneous activity of the understanding. Whereas external objects are given to the senses, concepts are not given to the understanding.

Rather, concepts are built by means of the spontaneous operations of the understanding. In this context "spontaneous" simply means that there are no sensible constraints forcing the understanding to "act"; instead, the understanding causes itself to "act" on the manifold of representations (cf. among other places A 67–8/B 92–3, B 153ff.; A 76–7/B 102–3, B 143). Although Kant refers to the understanding as "acting" cognition, he does not unjustifiably hypostatize it. Rather, he employs traditional vocabulary in order to describe the cognitive processing of the understanding as a spontaneously operating faculty.[4] So, to put it in a nutshell, the understanding is spontaneous and discursive because as the "faculty of thinking" (A 69/B 94) it is the "faculty of concepts" (A 166/B 199).

As has already been emphasized, the fundamental characterization of the understanding as the faculty of thinking by means of concepts is non-exhaustive. For the question now is in what way the understanding makes use of concepts. However, before he goes on to explain the understanding's use of concepts in judgements according to specific rules, Kant reminds us that thinking can be in accordance with the formal rules of cognition defined by the transcendental logic while not being true with respect to its content. For example, the proposition "Every composite substance in the world consists of simple parts" (A 434/B 462) meets the formal requirements of building judgements. Nevertheless, according to Kant this claim is one of the "empty sophistries" (A 63/B 88) to which the understanding is in danger of falling victim. For that reason, in the first part of transcendental logic, the "transcendental analytic", Kant presents his positive theory of the determination of "the origin, the domain, and the objective validity of ... cognitions" (A 57/B 81) as a "logic of truth" (A 62/B 87). It is only in the second part of the transcendental logic, the "transcendental dialectic", that he demonstrates the many ways in which the understanding goes wrong when disregarding the conditions of the possibility of cognition as established by transcendental analysis.[5]

Categories and judgements

Kant's theory of the understanding is particularly ambitious because of the claim according to which transcendental philosophy "is occupied not so much with objects but rather with our mode of cognition of objects insofar as that mode of cognition is possible *a priori*" (A 11/B 25, trans. mod.). The Kantian theory of the understanding is a transcendental theory because it maintains that we can have *a priori* knowledge of how we cognize the world. From this it follows that the transcendental theory of the understanding deals with *a priori* concepts that are informative with respect to our cognition of the world.

The next step, which Kant carries out in the transcendental doctrine of judgements, is to explain how judgements provide the logical frame for thinking. Kant writes:

> We can … trace all actions of the understanding back to judg-
> ments, so that the understanding in general can be represented as
> a faculty for judging. For according to what has been said above it
> is a faculty for thinking. Thinking is cognition through concepts.
> (A 69/B 94)[6]

We have already seen how the characterizations of the understanding as the faculty of thinking and the faculty of concepts are related. The question now is why we should, moreover, conceive of the faculty of concepts as the faculty for judging. Another crucial question is how it is possible to identify the *a priori* concepts that serve as the conditions of *a priori* cognition.

Kant begins to answer these questions with the methodological observation that in order to identify the *a priori* concepts of the understanding we should proceed along the lines of an "analysis of the faculty of the understanding itself" (A 65/B 90) since sensibility as the source of empirical cognition cannot help. Because the understanding is rational, the search for its *a priori* concepts must be systematic, rather than haphazard. To secure the systematicity of the "discovery of all pure concepts of the understanding" (A 66/B 91) Kant proceeds to determine the logical procedure the understanding follows when making use of concepts: "the understanding can make no other use of … concepts than that of judging by means of them", that is, by organizing concepts according to "functions" (A 68/B 93). "By function", Kant continues, "I understand the unity of the action of ordering different representations under a common one."

So in transcendental philosophy "judgement" does not mean evalu-ation or criticism; nor is it merely a linguistic term. By "judgement" Kant refers to "the mediate cognition of an object" (A 68/B 93). It is "mediate" because, as we have already seen, concepts are discursive and therefore unable to refer to objects immediately. For example, the judgement "Some chairs are wooden" formulates an indirect cognition because it employs the general concept "wooden", which refers to the concept "chair", which finally refers to the representation of particular objects in perception.

51

The indirectness of conceptual cognition is the reason that the judgement itself must be understood as a unity of concepts whose structure is determined by certain principles. Kant classifies these unifying principles as "functions": "All judgments are accordingly functions of unity among our representations" (A 69/B 94). This idea, which is not as complicated as it sounds, can be reformulated in the following way: concepts are general representations because they are discursive. Therefore they refer to objects only indirectly. Since the unity of concepts constitutes judgements, judgements are indirect cognitions. For a judgement to express cognition its unity cannot be chaotic, but rather must be well formed. The basic principles of well-formed judgements are functions of unity. So in order to determine how the understanding can achieve cognition through employing concepts in judgements, all the "functions of unity in judgments" (A 69/B 94) – all the functions by means of which the understanding unifies concepts to form judgements – must be specified.

Kant believes that the specification of the "logical function of the understanding in judgments" (A 70/B 95) relies on classical propositional logic. For "[i]f we abstract from all content of a judgment in general, and attend only to the mere form of the understanding in it, we find that the function of thinking in that can be brought under four titles, each of which contains under itself three moments" (*ibid.*). There is ongoing debate concerning exactly how the so-called table of judgements can be established, and how its completeness can be guaranteed (see Allison 2004: 135–46). Nevertheless, Kant believed that by abstraction it would be possible to arrive at a table of pure logical forms of judgement that govern the use of concepts by the understanding. Here are the four titles, each containing three moments (*ibid.*):

1. Quantity
   Universal ("All S are P")
   Particular ("Some S are P")
   Singular ("One S is P")

2. Quality
   Affirmative ("S is P")
   Negative ("S is not P")
   Infinite ("S is not-P")

3. Relation
   Categorical ("S is P")
   Hypothetical ("If S then P")
   Disjunctive ("Either S or P")

4. Modality
   Problematic ("S is possibly P")
   Assertoric ("S is in fact P")
   Apodictic ("S is necessarily P")[7]

From the point of view of more recent formal logic this table has many flaws. Although there can be no doubt that the table presents numerous problems (see Dicker 2004: 57–9), one should bear in mind that Kant is not very interested in the table of pure logical forms of judgement, since these forms belong to general logic, which abstracts from all content of cognition.

In the transcendental logic, as we already know, Kant is, rather, interested in the pure concepts of the understanding that do not abstract from all content. Like the pure logical forms of judgement, these concepts are *a priori* forms of thinking. However, unlike the logical functions, these pure concepts of the understanding, or categories, refer to a content that is given to them *a priori*. What kind of content is this? Since there are only two sources of knowledge, the only possible candidate for providing this content is pure sensibility. Concepts are discursive representations, and therefore depend on content that is given from elsewhere. So the content that the pure concepts of the understanding refer to *a priori* is the "manifold of sensibility … which the transcendental aesthetic has offered … in order to provide the pure concepts of the understanding with a matter, without which they would be without any content, thus completely empty" (A 76–7/B 102).

Kant next uses the table of the logical functions of judgement as a heuristic device to establish the table of the categories as pure concepts that refer *a priori* to the manifold of sensibility (A 82/B 106):

1. Quantity
   Unity
   Plurality
   Totality

3. Relation
   Inherence and subsistence (substance and accident)
   Causality and dependence (cause and effect)
   Community (reciprocity)

2. Quality
   Reality
   Negation
   Limitation

4. Modality
   Possibility
   Existence
   Necessity

One might wonder why Kant moves on from the logical functions of judgement to the pure concepts of the understanding. Are the logical functions by themselves not sufficient for explaining the possibility of cognition? The answer is clearly no. For general logic cares only about the formal correctness of cognition, not about its truth. Take the following example: "Either squares are round, or they are triangular. They are not triangular. Therefore they are round." From a purely formal point of view, this deduction, following the disjunctive function of judgement, is logically correct. However, from the point of view of content, this reasoning is obviously false. This is why it is transcendental logic, rather than general logic, that contributes to the determination of the truth of cognition.

Another important question must be asked here. If general logic is about the formal correctness of cognition, and transcendental logic is about its truth, are they independent or are they somehow related? It is crucial for Kant's transcendental theory of the understanding that transcendental logic depends upon general logic. Kant defends the thesis that it is possible to derive the table of the categories from the table of the logical functions of judgements.

The procedure that is supposed to show how the table of the categories can be derived from the table of the logical functions in judgement is called the "metaphysical deduction" (B 159).[8] Kant regards it as obvious that the two tables are analogous, since in both cases the understanding basically carries out the same activity. With respect to logical functions the understanding connects concepts according to logical rules; with respect to the categories the understanding synthesizes a manifold of sensibility according to rules of synthesis. In both cases the understanding follows the same idea of unity.

Kant is much clearer on this important point in the *Prolegomena* than in the first *Critique*:

> The given intuition must be subsumed under a concept that determines the form of judging in general with respect to the intuition ... a concept of this kind is a pure *a priori* concept of the understanding, which does nothing but simply determine for an intuition the mode in general in which it can serve for judging.
> (*PFM* 4:300)[9]

So categories are simply logical functions of judgements, but understood as determinations of intuition. They are *a priori* concepts that represent the pure synthesis of a given manifold. Hence, categories are richer than the pure logical functions, since they refer *a priori* to a given manifold of sensibility. As such they determine *a priori* how we must cognize a given manifold. To put it another way: whatever might be doubtful about cognition, it cannot be doubted that it is governed by the logical functions of judgement, and, moreover, that the given manifold in the process of cognition is synthesized by means of categories.

The problem now arises whether we are justified in using the categories as rules of synthesis for all kinds of cognitive content, or whether the objective use of the categories is restricted to a certain type of content. Kant answers this question in the transcendental deduction of the categories.

Transcendental deduction: apperception and imagination

The transcendental deduction of the categories in the first *Critique* (B 116–69) is one of the most debated pieces not only within Kant's work but in the entire history of philosophical literature.[10] It is controversial mainly because of its claim that it is possible to prove *a priori* that the use of the categories can be objectively justified only if the manifold of the synthesis in cognition is a manifold of our sensible intuition in space and time. Additionally, the argument of the deduction proves to be very complex and most challenging for the reader.

The transcendental deduction proceeds in two steps: it demonstrates, first, that the categories are *a priori* rules for the synthesis of a manifold of sensible intuition in general; and, second, that the categories are objectively justified only if the given manifold of intuition is not only sensible but also a manifold of spatiotemporal intuition (cf. Henrich 1969). To give an example: the claim that "The soul is a non-extended substance" is a meaningful statement following the categorical func-tion of judgement ("S is P"). However, it does not qualify as cognition because it cannot be objectively justified. The reason is that the predi-cate of the claim, "non-extended substance", can never be an object for the human mind, since the human mind can intuit only objects that are extended in space and time. So the general goal of the transcendental deduction is to reveal the conditions under which categories can refer to objects.

Kant begins the first step of the argument by pointing out that intu-ition is only given a manifold that does not contain "unity" since "we can represent nothing as combined in the object without having previ-ously combined it ourselves" (B 130). Cognition, however, requires the "combination" of the manifold. All combination, Kant argues next, is made possible through the "representation of the synthetic unity of the manifold". Since this "synthetic unity" is not given in intuition but established by the understanding, it must precede the "combination" itself and is therefore *a priori* (B 129–31).

The deduction now proceeds to determine the "ground of the unity", which according to Kant is the "I think", for "[t]he I think must be able to accompany all my representations" (B 131). With respect to cog-nition, the "I think" is the basic principle, because in order to repre-sent something it must be possible for the "I think" to be conscious of that which is represented – the "I think" must be able to accom-pany it in thought. Moreover, the "I think" is "apperception", or self-consciousness, which guarantees the unity of thought in representation. It is the unifying principle of the synthesis of the given manifold. The synthesis is spontaneously produced by apperception because, as we just saw, the unity or combination of representations is not given from elsewhere.

Kant calls the "I think" that establishes unity among representations the "transcendental unity of self-consciousness" (B 131). It has two aspects: as the original consciousness of its own identity it is the "analytic unity of apperception", for in order to be able to self-ascribe combined representations the "I think" must remain a single, identical point of reference of thought.[11] But this unity presupposes synthesis, so that the "analytic unity of apperception" is made possible by the "synthetic unity of apperception" (B 136). For example, if a cognizer runs through an argument step by step, in purely logical terms she must remain the identical cognizer throughout her cognitive processing while, at the same time, the possibility of a finalized cognition presupposes the synthetic unity of thought, the argument as a synthetic whole. The synthetic unity among given representations is thus the "synthetic unity of apperception" (B 139) since the "I think" must be able to accompany all representations.

Now judgement "is nothing other than the way to bring given cognitions to the objective unity of apperception" (B 141). At this point the categories come into play: since the possibility of cognition depends on synthetic unity, the combination of manifold representations presupposes rules that govern such unification. The rules that establish this kind of synthetic unity are nothing but the categories as the "functions for judging, insofar as the manifold of a given intuition is determined with regard to them" (B 143).

So what we know *a priori* is that in order to "think any object" we must necessarily think it "through categories" (B 165). This is the result of the first step of the argument of the transcendental deduction. It shows that since a given manifold of representations in an intuition cannot be cognized other than as a synthesized manifold, and since synthesis requires rules of combination, categories employed by the understanding, or pure apperception in judgements, the "manifold in a given intuition ... stands under categories" (B 143). However, this first step of the deduction shows only that sensible "intuition in general" (B 148), rather than specifically human spatiotemporal sensibility, stands under categories. Therefore a second step becomes necessary in order to demonstrate that for the human mind the categories have objective reality only if they are applied to "objects of experience" (B 146), that is, to objects of spatiotemporal intuition.

The argument of the second step is a necessary specification of the argument of the first step, since it is possible to imagine rational beings that have a kind of sensible intuition that differs from human intuition in not employing space and time as forms of intuition. Since the only possible objects of our sensible intuition are things in space and time, the categories cannot legitimately be applied to objects of a non-human kind of intuition. If they were, they would be nothing but "empty concepts of objects" (B 149) like the "empty sophistries" (A 63/B 88) of traditional metaphysics.[12]

A central element of the proof of the second step is the "imagination". Kant defines the imagination as "the faculty for representing an object even without its presence in intuition" (B 151). Unlike in the first-edition version (A) of the transcendental deduction, the imagination in the second-edition version (B) comes close to the understanding itself, in so far as it exercises the synthesis of the manifold of intuition according to the categories by combining the sensible given in order to yield, for example, an image in perception. The imagination is Janus-faced, though, in that it belongs to sensibility as well as to the understanding. In so far as it gives

> a corresponding intuition to the concepts of understanding … [it] belongs to sensibility; but insofar as its synthesis is still an exercise of spontaneity … and can thus determine the form of sense *a priori* in accordance with the unity of apperception, the imagination is to this extent a faculty for determining the sensibility *a priori*.
>
> (B 151–2)

And as such it belongs to the understanding. Kant finally concludes that the transcendental synthesis of the imagination is necessarily governed by categories, and that the objective reality of the categories is restricted to human sensible intuition, which is spatiotemporal intuition. Kant summarizes the second step as follows:

> Consequently all synthesis, through which even perception itself becomes possible, stands under the categories, and since experience is cognition through connected perceptions, the categories are conditions of the possibility of experience, and are thus also valid *a priori* of all objects of experience. (B 161)

One might add, however, that the validity of the categories never extends beyond experience.

Schemata and principles of the pure understanding

The transcendental deduction is an enormous philosophical achievement, since it demonstrates how it is possible for the categories to give us *a priori*, objective knowledge of the world. But the deduction is not sufficient for completing the project of transcendental philosophy, that is, the project of determining the *a priori* conditions of the possibility of experience. What we know by means of the transcendental deduction is that the objective validity of the categories is restricted to the sensible manifold of spatiotemporal intuition. "But the peculiar thing", Kant adds,

> about transcendental philosophy is this: that in addition to the rule (or rather the general condition for rules), which is given in the pure concept of the understanding, it can at the same time indicate *a priori* the case to which the rules ought to be applied.
>
> (A 135/B 174–5)

So transcendental philosophy does not restrict itself to the general demonstration that the categories have objective validity, but extends its claims to the specific *a priori* conditions under which the pure concepts of the understanding may be applied. The task of applying the categories falls to the "power of judgement" as the "faculty of subsuming under rules, that is, of determining whether something stands under a given rule (*casus datae legis*) or not" (A 132/B 171). For it is one thing to know that categories refer to objects *a priori*, yet another to know how given objects are actually determined by the pure concepts of the understanding.

The "transcendental doctrine of the power of judgment" shows how the sensible manifold of spatiotemporal intuition is subsumed under categories. It has two parts: in the first part, the "schematism of the pure understanding", it examines "the sensible conditions under which alone pure concepts of the understanding can be employed". In its second part it determines "those synthetic judgments that flow *a priori* from pure concepts of the understanding under these conditions and ground all other cognitions *a priori*" (A 137/B 175).

The two parts of the "transcendental doctrine of the power of judgment" fulfil two functions. The first part specifies how the manifold of intuition must be constituted in order for the power of judgment to subsume it under categories. Each "schema" (from Greek *skhēma*: figure, form) represents the *a priori* conditions of sensibility to which the use of its corresponding category is restricted. Since it mediates between concept and intuition in order to bridge the gap between understanding and sensibility, the schema is homogeneous with respect to the intellectual on the one hand, and the sensible on the other (A 138/B 177).[13] The second part of the "transcendental doctrine of the power of judgment" generates the "principles of the pure understanding" by connecting each category with the *a priori* sensible condition of its application. This conjunction does not merely yield more concepts, but rather principles representing *a priori* synthetic judgements that are the most general conditions of experience. Since these operations can be traced back to the pure understanding as the "faculty of rules", Kant calls the understanding itself the "source of the principles" (A 158/B 197–8). So the systematic structure of the overall argument looks like this: the table of the logical functions of judgements grounds the table of the categories, which grounds the transcendental schemata, which grounds the principles of the pure understanding. Accordingly, the logical functions prefigure the categories, whereas the categories make possible the schemata that in correspondence with the table of the categories ground the principles.[14]

Due to its complexity, Kant's argument might seem obscure. But a concrete example can clarify his view. Consider the category of substance. In order to see how the understanding ultimately yields the principle of substance, which Kant calls the "first analogy", by connecting the category of substance with its schema, we must return to the table of judgements. The third class of this table is entitled "Relation", and its first moment is the categorical function of judgement, the "relation of the predicate to the subject" (A 73/B 98). Simple predications such as "Humans are mortal" always have the logical form "*S* is *P*". The table of the pure concepts of the understanding tells us that "substance" is the category corresponding to the categorical function of judgement conceived as a determination of intuition. Accordingly, by means of the category of substance the understanding unifies a given manifold of intuition such that there is a subject that must be considered as substance and predicates pertaining to it, as in the judgement "Peter is bald-headed".

The category of substance itself informs us about neither the kind of intuition that is applicable, nor how it must be applied. The only thing we can find out through the analysis of the category of substance is that if we apply it to a manifold of intuition this manifold must be organized according to the subject–predicate structure. For this reason it seems possible to apply the category of substance to all kinds of objects, and to formulate judgements such as "Matter is composed of non-extended simple parts" and "The human soul is immortal". Although these judgements are not contradictory, the question is whether or not they are true, which depends in part upon whether or not we are justified in referring the category of substance to objects such as "non-extended simple parts" or "soul". But as we already know, the transcendental deduction tells us that the objective use of the categories is restricted to the sensible manifold of spatiotemporal intuition. Consequently, we are not justified in applying the category of substance to these objects, which by definition are not spatiotemporal.

The transcendental schema of the category of substance makes this explicit: "The schema of substance is the persistence of the real in time, that is, the representation of the real as a substratum of empirical time-determination in general, which therefore endures while everything else changes" (A 144/B 183). The schema crucially tells us that in order to be justified in applying the category of substance to a manifold of intuition, and to determine an object as subsisting and bearing predicates, that object ("the real") must fulfil the sensible condition of temporal persistence; it must persist *in time* through any changes of its properties. Note that it is not sufficient to reduce the schema to just "persistence of the real", for in this case we could claim to be able to cognize any potentially persisting object – including angels, devils or spiritual beings – as a substance. However, souls, angels and spiritual beings are not possible objects of experience, and thus they are merely objects of thought rather than cognition.

By conjoining the category of substance with the pure sensible condition of its application, the transcendental schema, Kant obtains the "first analogy" or the "Principle of the Persistence of Substance": "In all change of appearances substance persists" (A 144/B 183; cf. Allison 2004: 236ff.; Guyer 1987: 215ff.). According to Kant, we must conceive of this principle as an *a priori* synthetic judgement, since the category of substance itself does not tell us anything about "appearances", that is, objects in space and time.[15] It is only after we have added the pure sensible condition, to which the human mind is necessarily restricted, to the category of substance, that we obtain this principle of the pure understanding, which says that we can cognize objects as persisting substances only if they are objects in space and time. This result – and the analogous results that obtain for the other principles of the understanding – make intelligible Kant's overall claim that "[t]he conditions of the possibility of experience in general are at the same time conditions of the possibility of the objects of experience, and on this account have objective validity in a synthetic judgement *a priori*" (A 158/B 197).

Although one might criticize the baroque appearance of Kant's multi-layered theory of the understanding, it is important to remember that

Kant composed the *Critique of Pure Reason* in response to the central question concerning whether metaphysics is possible as a science, and the coordinated problem of the possibility of synthetic *a priori* judgements. It is this orientation that in many respects explains the particular character of transcendental philosophy.

Notes

1. In "Concerning the Ultimate Ground of the Differentiation of Directions in Space", published in 1768, near the end of his pre-critical period, Kant already argues for the independence of sensibility and understanding, or intuition and cognition. Also see the Inaugural Dissertation, *On the Form and Principles of the Sensible and Intelligible World* (1770) and the *Prolegomena*, 4:290–91.
2. For the transcendental theory of sensibility, see Chapter 2.
3. Kant also says that the "higher faculties of cognition", namely "understanding, the power of judgments, and reason" dealing with "concepts, judgments, and inferences", are "comprehended under the broad designation of understanding in general" (A 130–31/B 169–70). This is not in contradiction with what has been said before since, according to Kant, the formation of concepts, judgements and inferences is rule governed, and the understanding is the "faculty of rules".
4. See, for example, the influence of Meier's logic on Kant's word usage (16:340).
5. On the transcendental dialectic, see Chapter 4.
6. For Kant's theory of judgement in broader context, see Longuenesse (1998) and Hanna (2009).
7. For more details concerning the table of judgements, see Dicker (2004: 53–7).
8. Unfortunately Kant does not execute this procedure in detail. See Allison (2004): 152–6.
9. This specification still reflects Kant's pre-critical distinction between logical and real use of the understanding. Cf. *On the Form and Principles of the Sensible and the Intelligible World*, §§5, 7, 8.
10. For the second edition of the first *Critique* (1787) Kant completely rewrote the transcendental deduction because he was no longer satisfied with the argument from the first edition (1781). Since the version from the second edition is usually accepted as the more sustainable one, this chapter will not consider the 1781 argument for the deduction. On the transcendental deduction of the categories, cf. Allison (2004): 159–201.
11. It is crucial to note that in this context "identity" is not to be understood as biographical identity over time. Here "identity" has a logical meaning inasmuch as it refers to the sameness of thought. On these issues, cf. Allison (2004: 163–78).
12. Recall that according to Kant cognition is possible only through the cooperation of intuition and concept. Cf. A 51/B 75.
13. Altogether Kant distinguishes between three types of schemata: the empirical schema mediates between empirical concept and empirical intuition in that it directs the imagination's synthesis of the sensible manifold of intuition such that the understanding is able to subsume any given concrete manifold (e.g. a particular chair) under a general concept (e.g. "chair"). The mathematical schema does the same with respect to geometrical objects, such as triangles. The transcendental schema mediates, most importantly, between the categories

and pure sensibility, in order to show how the application of the pure concepts of the understanding to the pure manifold of space and time is possible. Cf. A 137ff./B 176ff. On the schematism, cf. Allison (2004: 202–28).

14. Kant provides only a broad overview of the twelve schemata that correspond to the categories. Unfortunately, he is not much concerned with the "analysis of what is required for transcendental schemata of pure concepts of the understanding", which he finds "dry and boring" (A 142/B 181–2). By contrast, his presentation of the "principles" is far more detailed. Following the table of the categories, Kant groups the principles as follows: 1. Quantity: Axioms of Intuition, 2. Quality: Anticipations of Perception, 3. Relation: Analogies of Experience, 4. Modality: Postulates of Empirical Thinking in General (A 161/B 200). Each of the first two groups contains only one general principle. The third and fourth groups each contain three principles. For a more detailed analysis of the principles, cf. Guyer (1987: 183ff.).

15. On the spatiotemporality of appearances as opposed to things in themselves, cf. Heidemann (2010).

FOUR

Reason: syllogisms, ideas, antinomies

Michelle Grier

> All our cognition starts from the senses, goes from there to the
> understanding, and ends with reason, beyond which there is noth-
> ing higher to be found in us to work on the matter of intuition
> and bring it under the highest unity of thinking. Since I am now to
> give a definition [*Erklärung*] of this supreme faculty of cognition,
> I find myself in some embarrassment.   (*CpR* A 298–9/B 355)

It may seem odd that Kant's first formal introduction of reason in the
Dialectic to his *Critique of Pure Reason* proceeds with such abashed-
ness. Kant suggests that the difficulty lies in the fact that in addition to
its merely formal or *logical* use, reason purports to have a "real use":
it purportedly "contains the origin of certain concepts and principles,
which it derives neither from the senses nor from the understanding"
but which at least *seem* to be generative of some *a priori* knowledge
of objects (A 299/B 356). Kant thus suggests a division of reason into
a logical and a "transcendental" faculty, and it is apparently the possibility of the latter that needs examination. As Kant shortly thereafter
asks:

> Can we isolate reason, and is it then a genuine source of concepts
> and judgements that arise solely from it and thereby refer it to
> objects; or is reason merely a subordinate faculty that gives rise to
> given cognitions of a certain logical form, through which cogni-
> tions of the understanding are subordinated to one another?
>   (A 306/B 363)

The arguments throughout the Dialectic together provide an answer to this general question. As we shall see, however, Kant's response is subtle and complicated. Once again, it is the third (after sensibility and the understanding) and presumably "highest" faculty of cognition (reason) that is critiqued in the Transcendental Dialectic. It is there that reason, and its pretensions to metaphysical knowledge, take centre stage. Nevertheless, rather than straightforwardly beginning with a discussion of the faculty of reason *per se*, Kant instead first introduces the notion of a "Dialectic". Dialectic, we are told, refers to the "logic of illusion [*Schein*]" (cf. A 293/B 350), and by a "transcendental" dialectic Kant means to direct us towards an examination of a specific kind of illusion, a "transcendental illusion", one that gives rise to concepts and principles that allow of no direct use whatsoever in connection with experience and its objects. Such concepts and principles, which claim to extend legitimately beyond all experience, are dubbed "transcendent" (A 296/B 353). Kant thus distinguishes between the transcendental (mis) employment of a concept (such as a pure concept of the *understanding*) that is designed for use only within experience, and the "transcendent" use of the concepts (ideas) of *reason*, which carry us altogether beyond the realm of possible experience and which catapult us into the realm of metaphysics (A 309/B 366).[1] The former is characterized as a misemployment of the *understanding* and is said to consist in a mere "mistake of the faculty of judgment when it is not properly checked by criticism" (A 296/B 352). Kant has in mind here errors that flow from taking categories of the understanding, such as the pure concept of "substance", which *do* have a legitimate (immanent) use, and using them to obtain knowledge of objects in a way that abstracts from the necessary sensible conditions under which actual objects must be given. In other words, he is referring to the use of the unschematized categories as modes of knowledge. By contrast, transcendental illusion involves the use of ideas and principles generated *solely by reason* and that never allow of any direct application to objects of experience. What is at issue here are the transcendent judgements that characterize the disciplines in traditional metaphysics (rational psychology, rational cosmology and rational theology) that compel us to argue about the "soul", the "world" and "God". The purpose of the transcendental dialectic is thus to disclose the illusion in these transcendent judgements. Kant is clear in his Introduction that disclosing the illusory nature of these transcendent judgements in no way diminishes their compelling and unavoidable nature; at most, a critique of the kind offered by Kant can provide an orientation that allows us to avoid being deceived by the very concepts and principles that we allegedly cannot avoid and that ostensibly stem from reason itself.

It is thus that Kant finds himself in "some embarrassment" in defining the faculty (reason) that he deems to be the "highest". On the one hand, reason allows, it seems, of an essentially unproblematic indispensable and purely *logical* use. As we shall see, Kant identifies it with a form of syllogistic cognizing, a logical drive to unify systematically the knowledge given through the understanding. But, on the other, as previously noted, reason presents itself as also having *a real use*; it generates concepts (ideas) and principles that stem from "it alone" in an attempt to yield transcendent (*a priori*) knowledge of objects that could be in no way encountered in experience (the soul, the world, God). And herein lies the potentially embarrassing element: we are confronted with a capacity that is unavoidable and necessary, but that seduces us into the use of purely rational principles that are illusory. Kant's project is thus twofold: first, he must scrutinize and critique this allegedly "real use" of reason, and expose the illusion that generates metaphysical error. Second, he must somehow nevertheless "vindicate" reason if he is to avoid falling into a pernicious scepticism as regards the faculty of reason in all respects (see O'Neill 1992).

Kant takes the metaphysical arguments about the "world" (the so-called "Antinomies") to be particularly threatening to reason's authority. The conflicts into which reason falls when addressing questions about the world (whether it is finite or infinite in space and time, etc.) invite, on Kant's view, a sceptical response with regard to reason in general. His aim is thus to protect reason's status as the "highest faculty" by preventing the misconstrual of the principles and ideas of reason.[2] In order to do so, Kant begins by a consideration of reason in its purely formal, or logical use.

The logical function of reason, syllogisms and transcendental illusion

As above, Kant begins by characterizing reason in its merely *logical* use as a capacity for syllogistic cognizing, or a faculty of drawing inferences. It is important to note that Kant here distinguishes between "immediate" and "mediate" inferences. An "immediate" inference (an inference of the understanding) is one in which an inferred judgement "already lies" in a first proposition. One can infer "immediately", for example, from the proposition that "All humans are mortal" that "Some humans are mortal", and one can do so without any other "mediating" judgement. Inferences of reason, however, are said by Kant to be "mediate", by which he means "syllogistic" (A 303–5/B 360–62). In an oft-cited example from the Introduction to the Dialectic, Kant presents the following categorical syllogism: "All humans are mortal", "Caius is a human", therefore "Caius is mortal".

As Kant notes, syllogisms such as this succeed by subsuming a concept or judgement under a rule and deducing a conclusion. In the above case the rule (major premise) is the statement that "All humans are mortal". Thus "being human" is the condition in the major premise that allows us to draw the conclusion; and since "Caius" falls under the condition stated in the universal rule (major premise), it is the term that when subsumed under the condition announced in the major premise ("All human beings are mortal") *gives us a reason* for asserting the conclusion.[3] In this, reason functions by "connecting" the judgements delivered to it from the understanding in order to systematize and unify knowledge. The essential point for our purposes is that by identifying reason as a capacity for drawing "mediate" inferences in this way, Kant is making an important connection between the formal procedure of reason and a quest for ever more general "*conditions*".

It might seem that the story stops here; syllogistic reasoning is an inferential function possibly applicable to any judgement. For any judgement, we might seek to identify the universal that justifies the conclusion. But Kant goes further than this, for he claims that reason is by its procedure compelled to continue in its attempts to ascertain the *ultimate* condition for any judgement. More specifically, the universal rule (or major premise) in the syllogism *itself* demands an explanation or explanatory grounding. And by this logic we are led to enquire into the condition for *that* condition, and the condition for *that* one, and so on:

> Reason in its logical use seeks the universal condition of its judgment (its conclusion), and the syllogism is nothing but a judgment mediated by the subsumption of its condition under a universal rule (the major premise) ... This rule is once again exposed to this same attempt of reason, and the condition of its condition thereby has to be sought (by means of a prosyllogism) as far as we may.   (A 307–8/B 364–5)

The upshot is that Kant takes reason to be unable to stop at anything less than the *complete set* of all conditions. In Kant's words, reason demands the "unconditioned". It is thus that Kant claims that the "maxim" governing the logical or formal use of reason is: "Find for the conditioned knowledge given through the understanding the unconditioned whereby its unity is brought to completion" (A 307/B 364).[4]

Again, the above prescription expresses reason's *logical* function, that of ordering the judgements given through the understanding in such a way as advances the ever-increasing systematization of already-given knowledge. As we have seen, however, Kant wants to suggest that the very function that characterizes reason leads by its own internal logic, as it were, to the extension of this systematization under the goal of *completeness* in our explanations. Although it might be objected that any *particular* project of knowledge acquisition and systematization need not proceed in accordance with such a universalizing requirement, Kant clearly takes the above maxim to represent an epistemological ideal that undergirds our collective theoretical activities. Thus, despite the fact that an individual theoretician may not feel herself explicitly committed to such a lofty goal (to find the absolutely "unconditioned"), Kant's view is that human reason *in general* operates in the arena of a progressive, and cumulative movement towards a "whole" of knowledge:

> If we survey the cognitions of our understanding in their entire range, then we find that what reason quite uniquely prescribes and seeks to bring about concerning it is the *systematic* in cognition … This unity of reason always presupposes an idea, namely that of the form of a whole of cognition. (A 645/B 673)

The idea of the form of a whole of cognition or knowledge is held by Kant to be an *a priori* idea that serves as a "rule" for the understanding and guides our theoretical endeavours (cf. A 646/B 674). Reason thus reflects a more general "point of view", one guided by an interest in the advancement of human knowledge more generally. This accords with Kant's characterization of reason as a "faculty of principles". In Kant's own words:

> Understanding may be regarded as a faculty which secures the unity of appearances by means of rules, and reason as being a faculty which secures the unity of rules of understanding under principles. Accordingly, reason never applies itself to experience or to any object, but only to the understanding, in order to give to the manifold knowledge of the latter an *a priori* unity by means of concepts, a unity which may be called the unity of reason, and which is quite different in kind from any unity that can be accomplished by the understanding. (B 359)

The above passage makes it clear that syllogistic reasoning is distinguished from the understanding first in that it plays a role that is completely *formal*, having to do *not* with the generation of knowledge claims, but only with the systematization of already-received judgements. In accordance with this, Kant refers to the prescription to seek the "unconditioned" for the knowledge given through the understanding as a merely "logical maxim", or a formal "precept" or a "subjective law for the orderly management of the possessions of the understanding" (A 306–9/B 363).[5] The essential point is that, as it stands, this maxim of reason lacks "objective validity"; it does not ground any "real use" of reason, one that might yield any direct knowledge of objects *per se*.[6]

Although the internal logic of reason's interests might express an imperative to further theoretical knowledge in general in light of the idea of the "unconditioned", what it does *not* do is justify the traditional assumption that there is any particular mind-independently given "unconditioned" entity or state of affairs that could possibly be known by us. Indeed, according to Kant, the "unconditioned" is not an object ever given to us as finite discursive knowers; Kant's well-known view is that our knowledge is limited to objects that can be given only under the subjective conditions of space and time (in "intuition"). The "unconditioned", however, is not such an "object". There is nothing that could be *intuitively given* that corresponds to the unconditioned. It is this that fuels Kant's repeated assertions that the demand for explanatory completeness ought to be understood merely as an injunction *to seek* further completeness of knowledge, without issuing from any knowable ultimate ground. Reason is a capacity that, without generating new knowledge of its own independently of the understanding and sensibility, nevertheless organizes our increasing knowledge into systems under the idea of a whole of knowledge. And yet Kant does not stop here either. According to him, in its own efforts reason necessarily falls victim to the illusion that the unconditioned *is* "there" (objectively, mind-independently) to be found, and that we can attain knowledge of it. In Kantian terms, we slide from the purely formal or logical *prescription to seek* the unconditioned to an assumption that the unconditioned is *given* (potentially to us) and is thus a reasonable target, a possible object of speculative knowledge. Thus, for Kant, we move from the above epistemological demand (to *find* the unconditioned) to the metaphysical assumption that "if the conditioned is given, the whole series of conditions ... which is itself unconditioned, is also given" (A 308/B 364).[7]

According to Kant, the above constitutes the "supreme principle of pure reason" (A 309/B 366), and he wants to say that its assumption is somehow unavoidable, inevitable. It is also, however, said to be the locus of the very transcendental illusion under examination in the Transcendental Dialectic. Kant locates this transcendental illusion in the tendency to mistake a "subjective necessity of the connection of our concepts" (that presumably demanded by the prescription to seek the unconditioned) for "an objective necessity in the determination of things in themselves" (A 297/B 354). The idea here is that reason takes the purely formal and subjective rational requirement for completeness of knowledge to map onto an objectively necessary feature of objects themselves. Put another way, we assume that our requirements for a whole of knowledge correspond to some objectively given complete unity or "whole" that *can be known*. Unfortunately, in sliding into the assumption that the unconditioned *is given*, we shift from an epistemological recommendation to a metaphysical principle about reality. We assume that our epistemological (subjective) requirements are warranted by the real existence of an objectively given and systematic (really existing) unity (see O'Neill 1992: 284).

One of the most perplexing aspects of Kant's account has to do with his claim that the "supreme principle of pure reason", that is, the principle that states that the unconditioned is *given*, is not an arbitrary or dispensable assumption. Indeed, according to Kant, it is a *necessary* postulation. He contends that the logical prescription to seek the unconditioned necessarily commits us to (presupposes) the corresponding metaphysical or "transcendental" principle. Consider the following:

> It is, indeed, difficult to understand how there can be a logical principle by which reason prescribes the unity of rules, unless we also presuppose a transcendental principle whereby such a systematic unity is *a priori* assumed to be necessarily inherent in the objects ... In order, therefore, to secure an empirical criterion [of truth] we have no option save to presuppose the systematic unity of nature as objectively valid and necessary.   (A 651/B 679)

Why should we be committed to the metaphysical principle? That is, even if we go along with Kant and agree that the logical procedure of reason commits us to an ongoing *prescription to seek* the "unconditioned", *why* should Kant think that this in turn *requires* an assumption that the so-called unconditioned is actually *given*? This seems an odd position to take, especially since the "unconditioned" is by his own account *not given*. Indeed, the unconditioned could *never be* given to us. In answer to the above question, Kant's position seems to be that the very coherence or rationality of reason's procedure has built into it the necessary assumption that the unconditioned *is given*. Such an assumption seems on Kant's view to be necessary in order to deploy the formal demand for systematicity in relation to the objective contents of the understanding. It thus grounds at least the *appearance* of reason's "real use", and it apparently is thought to do so by providing reason with a regulative goal that orients us in relation to our theoretical enquiries. On a more intuitive level, he seems to think that the project of reason in its logical capacity operates in light of the background assumption that the unconditioned we seek must really exist.[8] And indeed, it would appear to make no sense to seek the unconditioned unless we also thought that it was there to be found.[9] As Kant says:

> This unity ... although it is a mere idea, has been pursued so eagerly in all ages that more often there has been cause to moderate than to encourage the desire for it ... Yet ... everyone presupposes that this unity of reason conforms to nature itself; and here reason does not beg but commands. (A 653/B 681)

The ideas of reason

It is the demand to seek ultimate conditions, together with its attendant assumption that these are *given*, and theoretically knowable, that allegedly leads reason to posit the so-called "ideas" of pure reason. More specifically, Kant argues that reason is led to the postulation of objects that satisfy our demands for completeness. According to Kant, the ideas of reason present as *a priori* modes of knowledge that "so far transcend the bounds of experience that no given empirical object could ever coincide with them" (A 314/B 371). Kant identifies a number of ways in which reason seeks to think the unconditioned relative to various endeavours. As we have seen, he identifies the idea of the form of a whole of cognition or knowledge as a guiding (regulative) idea of reason. Later on, in the Appendix to the Dialectic, he will cite other "ideas" ("pure earth", "pure air" etc.) that, he will argue, are postulated in conjunction with reason's systematizing and unifying efforts in regard to the natural sciences. Such ideas function, when properly used, as ways of guiding and regulating our empirical enquiries (cf. A 646/B 674). The essential point is that reason can be *justified* in the sense that its function (even under the guidance of the illusory assumption that the unconditioned is given) can be shown to play a positive, albeit merely regulative, role in our theoretical activities.[10] Having said this, Kant is, in the Dialectic, particularly concerned with the three official "ideas of pure reason" (the soul, the world and God), which provide the objects for the corresponding three traditional branches of rationalist metaphysics he is concerned to critique (rational psychology, rational cosmology and rational theology). In *these* cases, however, he wants to argue, reason's otherwise essential role leads us to metaphysical error.

Kant's derivation and justification for the "ideas" of reason is notoriously controversial.[11] For our present purposes, the essential point is that Kant takes the ideas of reason to be generated under the direction of the rational demand for complete explanations, so that each of the ideas is construed as unifying knowledge by viewing it in relation to some unconditioned ground. It is well known that Kant takes each of these three ideas (the soul, the world, God) to be ways of thinking the unconditioned, or ways of securing the complete, systematic unity of thought required by reason (see Wood 1978: 17–18; Pippin 1982: ch. 7). Thus Kant thinks that reason is led, by its own formal demands and by the correlative assumption that the unconditioned is given, to postulate certain "objects" that satisfy our demands. In order to make sense of this claim, Kant once again appeals to the formal (syllogistic) procedure of reason in general. What he suggests is that the ideas are generated by applying the forms of syllogistic inference to the "synthetic unity of intuitions under the direction of the categories" (A 321/B 378). In essence, Kant claims that the three "transcendental ideas" relating to the special doctrines of metaphysics are "generated" by the three forms of relation in syllogisms. Since there are according to Kant three forms of relations among judgements (the categorical, the hypothetical and the disjunctive), there will be three "ideas" generated by syllogistic inferences from these to the unconditioned.

> All transcendental ideas can therefore be brought under *three classes*, the *first* contains the absolute (unconditioned) *unity* of the *thinking subject*, the *second* the absolute *unity* of *the series* of *conditions of appearance*, the *third* the absolute *unity* of the condition of *all objects of thought* in general.   (A 334/B 391)

The problem, as we have seen, is that although Kant takes the ideas of reason to be subjectively necessary postulations, he does not take the ideas to have any objective reality, for despite the fact that they are representations to which reason is inevitably led in its quest for completeness, they lack objective reality. To put things more simply, the ideas of reason do not, on Kant's view, function as representations of any real "object", and certainly not any object that could ever be known by us. For one thing, the alleged objects of such ideas transcend all the conditions of knowledge under which objects could ever be given to us or known. It is because of this that he refers to the ideas of the soul and the world and God as mere "pseudo-objects". It is precisely the illusion that leads us to think that the ideas have objective reality that generates the dialectical arguments of traditional metaphysics.

Perhaps the most dramatic example of the perplexities into which reason falls is found in the "Antinomies", that section in the *Critique* in which Kant considers the arguments about the idea of the "world", or the cosmos, taken as a whole. Such an idea, as we shall see presently, allegedly represents the unconditioned in relation to which we want to explain the entire series of all events and objects in the spatiotemporal world. Once again, the problem has to do with the allegedly unavoidable assumption that the unconditioned is actually given.

> Take the principle, that the series of conditions (whether in the synthesis of appearances or in the thinking of things in general) extends to the unconditioned. Does it or does it not have objective applicability? What are its implications as regards the empirical employment of the understanding? Or is there no such objectively valid principle of reason, but only a logical precept, to advance toward completeness by an ascent to ever higher conditions and so to give to our knowledge the greatest possible unity of reason? Can it be that this requirement of reason has been wrongly treated in being viewed as a transcendental principle of pure reason, and that we have been overhasty in postulating such an unbounded completeness in the series of conditions in the objects themselves? (A 309/B 366)

Kant's aim in the section on the Antinomies (as in the rest of the Dialectic) is to show that in fact we *have* been overhasty in this regard, for his considered view is that we have no epistemological "right" to move beyond the limits of possible human experience and to make assertions about objects that could never be given to us. To do so is to violate the strictures of knowledge already outlined in the Transcendental Analytic. With respect to the Antinomies in particular, Kant's aim is to show that our efforts in this regard embroil us in a set of dialectical oppositions, and they do so because we have been inextricably led by reason to think that we can have knowledge of the world-whole. To this topic we now turn.

The idea of the world

Kant takes the arguments in the Antinomies to be particularly representative of the problems that stem from reason's demand for the unconditioned. His view, as we shall see, is that the arguments of the Antinomies all represent in one way or another an attempt to acquire knowledge about the nature and constitution of the "world". Because of this it is important to get clear about the idea of the world, and the way in which it is arrived at. Kant's claim here, as with the other ideas, is that the topic in question (in this case the "world"), rather than being an actual object of knowledge, amounts to a mere *idea* generated in accordance with reason's demand for the unconditioned. Kant claims (A 498/B 526) that we arrive at the idea of the "world" by means of the following (dialectical) syllogism:

1. If the conditioned is given, the entire series of all conditions is likewise given.
2. Objects of the senses are given as conditioned.
3. Therefore, the entire series of all conditions of objects of the senses is already given.

Kant's suggestion is that the demand for the unconditioned condition for the entire series of appearances, together with the assumption that it is *given*, generates the idea of the world. Assuming that the unconditioned ground of all objects of the senses is given, reason is led to the idea of the world, understood as the sum total of all *appearances* and their conditions (A 420/B 448). Kant argues throughout the Dialectic that the syllogism, which generates the idea of the world, is necessary and unavoidable, and he later on suggests that the idea will play an essential subjective or regulative role in our attempts to systematize knowledge and bring it to completion (A 669/B 697; A 671/B 699).

Although unavoidable, Kant tells us that the syllogism by means of which we arrive at the idea of the world is nevertheless "dialectical", or fallacious. According to him, the syllogism is guilty of the fallacy of *ambiguous middle* (A 500/B 528). Whereas the major premise (which amounts to the supreme principle of pure reason, the assumption that the unconditioned is given) uses the term "the conditioned" in what Kant calls a "transcendental sense", the minor premise and conclusion assume an empirical use of the same term. By this Kant means simply that the major premise (if the conditioned is given, the entire series is given) asserts at most something about "objects in general", that is, objects considered in abstraction from the intuitive conditions under which they must be given (space and time). But the minor premise slides over into an appeal to objects taken specifically under these spatio-temporal conditions (that is appearances), and it is only because of this that the idea of the world, as the sum total of all *appearances*, is arrived at in the conclusion.

Kant therefore asserts that the idea of the world is uniquely problematic. Unlike the other ideas of reason (the soul and God), which are entirely transcendent (they refer to illusory "pseudo-objects" that are altogether outside of the spatiotemporal framework), the "world" is posited as an object that is at the same time both supersensible and allegedly empirical (A 479/B 509). Rather than being an idea of a purely transcendent object, that is, the idea of the world is an idea that takes the thought of an allegedly immanent (spatiotemporal) object beyond all possible experience.[12] The result is an idea that can be thought either as an intelligible or as a spatiotemporal object. Indeed, as we shall see, it is precisely this feature of the idea of the world that leads to the particular sets of antinomial disputes, for with respect to each problem there seem to be two distinct ways of responding: one that satisfies purely intellectual requirements, and another that appeals to the requirements of intuition. Thus, in speaking of the specific cosmological debates, Kant tells us that for each problem addressed (the finitude versus the infinitude of the world, freedom versus causality, etc.) one can adopt one of two different approaches. The first of these is referred to by Kant as reflecting a "dogmatic" (Platonic) perspective, while the second reflects an "empiricist" (Epicurean) commitment (A 472/B 500). Moreover, each of these leads to the thesis or antithesis arguments, respectively.

Each of these approaches embodies a different way of thinking the totality of conditions (A 471–2/B 499–500). Again, as we shall see, the thesis positions involve thinking of the unconditioned as an intelligible ground of all appearances, such as some first beginning to the entire series. The antithesis positions, on the other hand, will proceed by thinking the unconditioned as the total set of all appearances. Neither side to the dispute, according to Kant, can resolve the conflict. Although the thesis positions seem to satisfy the rational demand for the absolutely unconditioned, they can do so only by providing explanations that abstract from anything that could be given in space and time. In other words, they catapult us into an intelligible realm. By contrast, the so-called empiricist or Epicurean responses, while refusing to go beyond the spatiotemporal realm, err by assuming that whatever holds within space and time is true universally. As we shall see, this strategy fails by taking what are merely subjective forms of our human sensibility (space and time) to be universal ontological conditions for everything whatsoever.

The result is that for each of the cosmological questions, formally valid arguments can be produced that appear to succeed in refuting the opponent's arguments. Reason thus finds itself in a stalemate, vacillating between two powerful alternatives neither of which can bring the matter to a real close. Because of this, the faculty of reason itself comes into question. Indeed, the conflict of "reason with itself" leads, if left unresolved, to the "euthanasia of pure reason" (A 407/B 434). Clearly, at the heart of the controversies is the mutual acceptance of the above "dialectical syllogism". Each side assumes that "there is a world", understood as the sum total of all appearances, and that this idea refers to a real object of speculative knowledge. Indeed, he claims that "as long as we persist in assuming that there is an actual object corresponding to the 'world', the problem of the antinomies 'allows of no solution'" (A 482/B 510).

The antinomial conflicts

It is this more fundamental diagnosis of the confusion underlying the confrontation of "reason with itself" that allows Kant to critique the particular conflicts that characterize rational cosmology.[13] Kant identifies four antinomies of pure reason, but he divides them into two different sets: the *mathematical* and the *dynamical*. The first two (mathematical) conflicts have to do with the relation between either the world-whole itself or objects *in* the world and space/time. The first antinomy addresses the controversial question about whether the sensible (spatiotemporal) world is finite or infinite in space and time. The "thesis" position contends that the world is finite. For our present purposes, we may limit our comments to the temporal portion of the argument. Briefly, the view is that the world must be finite in time (must have some first beginning). If it did not, then there would be no completion of the process by means of which the world is given. Since, however, the cosmological debate presupposes the idea of the world, understood as the total set of all appearances and their conditions, and moreover presupposes that this world-whole is *already given*, the denial of a first beginning is utterly inconsistent with the existence of the world under consideration. As Kant puts it, a beginning of the world is taken by the thesis to be a necessary condition of the very existence of such a world (A 427/B 455).

Although the thesis argument compels this conclusion, the argument of the antithesis is that any first beginning is equally incoherent. To set a first beginning in time is to presuppose some pre-mundane (empty) spatiotemporal framework. The antithesis denies the coherence of this on the grounds that any coming to be in time must presuppose some antecedent state that accounts for (provides the condition for) this very "coming to be". Here the claim is that empty time (or space) cannot account for any state out of which an event or beginning (a change in state) could possibly take place. Thus, whereas the thesis contends that the finitude of the sensible world is required to think it as a "whole", the antithesis argues that any thought of the world as *spatiotemporal* requires thinking it as coextensive with (infinite) space and time. The debate thus clearly reflects the problems associated with the very idea of the world, understood as a spatiotemporal or sensible object that is given in its *totality*.[14]

Similar problems are generated by the next antinomy, which may be discussed more briefly. The second mathematical antinomy regards the issue about the ultimate constitution of objects *in* the world. According to the thesis, such objects (composite substances) must ultimately be composed of absolutely simple parts. Briefly, the conceptual claim is that any "composite" is by definition a composite of the individual self-subsistent beings that "make it up". After all, composition is an external relation that holds between pre-existing parts. The antithesis argument counters by noting that if composition is an *external* relation, then it presupposes space. Moreover, whatever is given in space is extended, and therefore composite. Thus any allegedly "simple" substance existing in space would itself have to be composed of parts. With this the antithesis denies that there could ever be anything that is absolutely simple ever given to us. Here the claim is that spatiotemporal objects must be infinitely divisible because space and time (mathematically) are.

Again, Kant takes each of these disputes to reflect two historically opposed positions about the relation between the world (or its objects) on the one hand, and space and time on the other.[15] What character-izes the conflicts in a general sense is this: each of the *thesis* positions seems, on Kant's view, to satisfy the demand for ultimate explanations, but they do so by demanding some absolute resting place for thought, and thus surreptitiously abstract from the spatiotemporal framework. Again, Kant takes these to be interested in finding "intelligible begin-nings" (A 466/B 494). The *antithesis* arguments, for their part, are allied by their contention that the world and objects in it must conform to the conditions or requirements of space and time. What we thus find is a dramatic set of conflicts that issue from the appeal to different norms for thinking the unconditioned: one (expressed in the theses) appeals to the norms of reason and its "subjectively necessary" and unavoidable efforts to think appearances in relation to the idea of the "whole of knowledge". The other (expressed in the antitheses) abides by the equally compelling need to apply the standards for thinking *spatiotemporal* objects. Despite the fact that each side to the dispute appears, in its own way, to satisfy the demand for the unconditioned, Kant takes the conclusions on each side to be false.

Kant's "resolution" to these "mathematical" antinomies involves two claims. The first relates to Kant's previous assertion that both sides to the dispute err by resting on the earlier dialectical assumption. More specifically, both sides have presupposed that there is a "world", and that it is an object of knowledge. It is this that is said to fuel the presumption that the "world" is either finite or infinite, for example. As we have seen, however, Kant thinks that the idea of the world is illusory (although regulatively necessary). The question then is why we might continue, on Kant's view, to be forever compelled to enter into the particular disputes. One obvious answer, given Kant's account, is that the "illusion" that leads us to the idea of the world is unavoidable and can never be eliminated; we are thus forever compelled to attempt to think the world as an object of some possible knowledge. Given the "subjectively necessary" regulative role assigned to this idea, Kant clearly wants to say that we are forever tempted by reason into the field of "cosmology":

> Transcendental illusion ... does not cease even though it is uncovered and its nullity is clearly seen ... (for example, the illusion in the proposition: "The world must have a beginning in time") ... This is an illusion [*Illusion*] that cannot be avoided at all, just as little as we can avoid it that the sea appears higher in the middle than at the shores. (A 297/B 354)

By itself, however, this does not seem to support the historical recurrence of the antinomial conflicts themselves, for Kant is *also* committed to the view that the illusion (however necessary or "indispensable" at another level) "need not deceive us" (cf. A 298/B 355; A 654/B 673). Indeed, the whole point of Kant's critique is to provide a method for avoiding the pitfalls of this illusion. Moreover, Kant's resolution seems to suggest that the two sides to the disputes are in some sense simply arguing at cross-purposes, for each appears to have an entirely different agenda and goal. The thesis arguments reflect reason's capacity to think beyond space and time, and to secure intelligible beginnings. The antithesis positions alternatively insist on following the rules for thinking things given under the conditions of space and time. Why, then, does Kant not simply argue that each of these "interests" of reason might be modified and understood in a way that avoids the semblance of any real contradiction?[16]

Kant wants to say that the reason why these competing "norms" for thinking the unconditioned seemed (before his own *Critique*) to be in direct and irreconcilable competition, and why we continue to get embroiled in the debates, is precisely because we have conflated "appearances" with "things in themselves". The essential point is that until the transcendental distinction between appearances and things in themselves is drawn (until the so-called "transcendental ideality" of space and time is recognized), both sides to the dispute are committed to the assumption that either one or the other must be correct. And indeed, Kant argues exactly this. If appearances were things in themselves, he claims, reason's illusory demand for the unconditioned would lead to both sets of conclusions, for both of these norms for thinking the unconditioned would have to be pitted against one another in the same arena.

The conflation of appearances with things in themselves, in turn, refers to what Kant calls "transcendental realism" (cf. A 491/B 519). The upshot is that, on Kant's view, the illusory (rational) assumption that the world is *given* generates two compelling and competing responses *only* because we have failed to draw the transcendental distinction between objects allegedly thought through pure concepts that abstract from the subjective conditions of space and time (things in themselves), and "objects" considered under these spatiotemporal conditions ("appearances"). Exposing the errors of transcendental realism (or, correlatively, adopting Kant's own transcendental idealism), then, allows us to avoid being *deceived* by the "illusion" that Kant thinks is both unavoidable and necessary for theoretical enquiry. Because of this, Kant (very controversially) claims that the first two (mathematical) antinomies provide an "indirect proof" for his own alternative "transcendental idealism".[17]

The dynamical antinomies

Once Kant has drawn our attention to the pernicious influence of "transcendental realism" in the first two antinomies, his efforts to resolve the second set of antinomies, the so-called "dynamical" antinomies, are fairly easy to summarize. The dynamical antinomies are the topic of the third and fourth conflicts of reason with itself. The third antinomy centres on the traditional debate between "freedom" and mechanistic causality. The thesis argues that, in addition to mechanistic causality, we must posit some first (uncaused) causal power (transcendental freedom). The idea here is that mechanistic causality is simply not sufficient to explain the world, understood as the "*totality* of all appearances".

The world, understood as such *a totality*, must be grounded in some first cause that is not itself determined by any antecedent cause (transcendental freedom). Absent this, the very idea of the world-*whole* at issue in the antinomy is incoherent. The antithesis, however, rejects this line of reasoning. According to it, the notion of a kind of causality that is itself uncaused violates the universal law of nature (causality). The claim is that every cause in the spatiotemporal world itself has to be determined by some antecedent condition in space and time.

A similar kind of impasse is generated in the fourth antinomy, where Kant showcases the "mock combat" between the arguments for some necessary being (thesis) and the denial of any such being (antithesis). According to the thesis, there must exist some absolutely necessary being (some being whose non-existence is impossible) in order to account for the empirically conditioned (contingent) series of alterations in time. In short, there must be some empirically unconditioned (necessary) being that provides the explanatory completeness for the entire series of contingent being. The antithesis, however, denies the legitimacy of moving from the contingency of particular things or events to some absolutely necessary being. Everything that is given in space and time is contingent. Any such necessary being, therefore, (if there is one) would have to be posited as something outside the sensible world, and would thus transgress the cosmological nature of the debate (that it is about the *spatiotemporal world*).

The resolution to the dynamical antinomies differs from that relating to the mathematical antinomies. Rather than arguing that both positions are "false", Kant here suggests that both positions might well be allowed to stand, so long as we clearly delineate the spheres within which the claims might be made. This option is available here, in the dynamical antinomies, because in these cases the proponents of the arguments are not simply adopting different norms for thinking the unconditioned within the same domain (the spatiotemporal world itself or objects within it); they are instead referring to alleged "objects" that could easily and consistently occupy entirely different domains. The thesis conclusions must refer to objects or states of affairs entirely outside the spatio-temporal series (a causality outside the temporal series/transcendental freedom, or a necessary being outside the spatiotemporal framework), whereas the antitheses positions refer specifically to spatiotemporal objects and their conditions. Once again, Kant's transcendental distinction between appearances and things in themselves allows for this assessment. The theses appeal to some first causality or some necessary being reflects the rational (Platonic) need to think things from the standpoint of intelligible beginnings, and so as things in themselves.

The antithesis rejoinders involve the appeal to remain within "nature's own resources" (space and time) (cf. A 451–2/B 479–80). Here one is appealing to the norms of thinking things as appearances.

It might seem that the strategy of the antitheses would, on a Kantian view, be the more acceptable. In remaining lodged in "nature's own resources", the arguments of the antitheses at least have the virtue of avoiding flights into intelligible realms. Indeed, in the "Third Section" of the Antinomy of Pure Reason (A 462/B 490), Kant identifies what he takes to be the "interests" of reason that ground the adoption of the broadly "empiricist" positions, and he notes that there is much to recommend these over those advanced in the thesis arguments:

> Empiricism offers advantages to the speculative interests of reason, which are very attractive and far surpass any that the dogmatic teacher of the ideas of reason might promise. For with empiricism the understanding is at every time on its own proper ground, namely the field solely of possible experience.
>
> (A 469/B 497)

The problem, as we have seen, is that the antithesis positions construe space and time to be universal (ontological) conditions for all things in general (and so things in themselves). In other words, in so far as the antitheses fail to recognize the "transcendental ideality" of space and time, they are equally indicative of transcendental realism, the failure to draw the distinction between appearances and things in themselves. Not only that. As a result of its commitments in this regard, empiricism itself becomes dogmatic by claiming to know that the so-called "intelligible beginnings" advanced by the thesis arguments cannot exist:

> But if empiricism itself becomes dogmatic in regard to the ideas (as frequently happens), and boldly denies whatever lies beyond the sphere of its intuitive cognitions, then it makes the same mistake of immodesty, which is all the more blamable here, because it causes an irreparable disadvantage to the practical interests of reason.
>
> (A 471/B 499)

Thus, despite the "rationalist" excesses into which the thesis positions fall, Kant takes the interests of reason *they* express (in securing some first beginning, some necessary being etc.) to be just as compelling as (or perhaps even more than) those of the "empiricist" positions, for not only do the thesis arguments seek to advance the *speculative* interests in securing the absolutely unconditioned, but they vindicate reason's *practical* (moral, religious) interests.

> We have represented the glittering pretensions of reason to extend its territory beyond all bounds of experience ... But in this application, and in the progressive extension of the use of reason, since it commences with the field of experience and only gradually soars aloft to these sublime ideas, philosophy exhibits such a dignity that, if it could only assert its pretensions, it would leave every other human science far behind in value, since it would promise to ground our greatest expectations and prospects concerning the ultimate ends in which all reason's efforts must finally unite.
>
> (A 463–4/B 491–2)

Perhaps we ought not to find ourselves in any "embarrassment" over reason after all.

Notes

1. I discuss this distinction between the transcendental misemployment of the categories and the transcendent use of reason at length in Grier (2001: esp. 101–17). I discuss the transcendental misemployment of the understanding more specifically in *ibid.*: ch. 3, 69–100.
2. Guyer notes that Kant is here most likely concerned to avoid a kind of Pyrrhonian scepticism. See Guyer (2006: 128–9).
3. For an interesting discussion of this, see Longuenesse (1998: 95). In a footnote, she introduces a "systematic connection" between "condition" and "reason". Longuenesse notes that syllogistic reasoning is a function "potentially at work" in all judgement, for the *condition* of a judgement is the term that provides a reason for deducing a conclusion, either *by subsuming or being subsumed* in a syllogism. As Longuenesse notes (*ibid.*: 97), Kant differs from the Wolffian school in so far as he thinks that synthetic judgements must have intuitions as their ultimate condition. She is right in this, of course. However, Kant seems to want to distinguish the purely rational judgements at issue in transcendent metaphysics by suggesting that they move from principles in the strict sense that the conclusion is reached *a priori without* intuition. Thus, in the Dialectic Kant will defend the supreme principle of pure reason as a *synthetic* principle that has no connection whatsoever with any intuition.
4. I discuss this "maxim" throughout Grier (2001: esp. 119–22). For other discussions of this particular maxim, see Allison (2004: 307–32); Ameriks (1992); Guyer (2006: 129–34).
5. I discuss this in Grier (2001: 119–22).
6. In a related way Kant refers to reason's principle in the Appendix to the Dialectic as a purely methodological principle (A 648/B 576). For a discussion see Guyer (1990: 30–33). I discuss this and related problems concerning the ultimate status of the logical maxim in Grier (2001).

7. I am drawing on my earlier discussion of Kant's theory of illusion in Grier (2001). See also Ameriks (1992); Allison (2004: 322–32); Guyer (2006: 129–34).

8. In Grier (2001), I try to make sense of this claim by suggesting that the second, "metaphysical", principle operates as a kind of "application condition" for the use of the logical maxim. Indeed, I suggest there that the metaphysical principle *just is* the logical maxim, viewed by reason in abstraction from the limiting conditions of sensibility and understanding (see *ibid.*: 276). Allison (2004: 329–32) also pursues this problem. As we shall see, and as is commonly noted, there are *practical* reasons that guide Kant to claim that the demand for the unconditioned is essential. See Guyer (2006: ch. 3).

9. I contend with this issue in Grier (2001: esp. chs 3, 7). See also Allison (2004: 329–32).

10. Kant does cite other ideas in the Appendix to the Dialectic. See, for example, A 665/B 693; A 687/B 715; A 696/B 674.

11. I have elsewhere attempted to make sense of Kant's derivation of the ideas of reason in Grier (2001: esp. 130–39). For discussions concerning the difficulties relating to Kant's attempt, see Kemp Smith (1962: 450); Pippin (1982: 211); England (1968: 117–20). See also Allison (2004: 313–22); Guyer (2006: 129–34).

12. See Kant's *Prolegomena to any Future Metaphysics*, 4:337–8. Thus, whereas the ideas of the soul and God are said by Kant to be "pseudo-rational", the idea of the world is "pseudo-empirical". See Grier (2001: 176).

13. I offer a much more extended discussion of the particular antinomial conflicts in Grier (2001: ch. 6). There are many very good discussions of the antinomies. See Guyer (1987: 385–415); Bird (2006: 661–724); Watkins (2001).

14. In Allison's words, "the rule or procedure for thinking the *totum syntheticum* clashes with the one for thinking an infinite quantity" (2004: 370).

15. Al-Azm (1972) traces these back to the debate between Leibniz and Newton/Clarke.

16. As I note in Grier (2001), I think that this possibility is forcefully presented by Guyer (1987). For my discussion of Guyer's claims see Grier (2001: 191–4).

17. Guyer (2006) has suggested that Kant's appeal to the transcendental distinction between appearances and things in themselves does not provide the only (perhaps not even the best) resolution to these conflicts (see *ibid.*: 144).

PART II

Practical philosophy

FIVE

Freedom: will, autonomy

Paul Guyer

Autonomy and freedom of the will

The concept of freedom is the central normative and metaphysical concept in Kant's philosophy. Freedom of choice and action from constraint by external forces but also even from one's own mere inclinations, something that can be achieved not by the elimination of inclinations, which is not possible for human beings, but by the subjection of inclination to the rule of reason and its demand for universalizability, which Kant ultimately calls "autonomy", "the property of the will by which it is a law to itself" (*G* 4:440), is the ultimate value for Kant, the only value that can be an end in itself and has a dignity beyond all price (4:435–6). Freedom of the will, the ability to initiate an action spontaneously, independently of determination by mere laws of nature, so that every human agent has the capacity to act in accordance with the moral law no matter what might seem to be predicted by her entire prior history, is for Kant only a logical possibility in theoretical philosophy but an inescapable postulate of pure practical reason, "the necessary condition of ... the complete fulfillment of the moral law" (*PracR* 5:132). For Kant, the relation between these two concepts, autonomy as our ultimate value and freedom of the will as our ultimate metaphysical property, although one assertible only on practical grounds, is intimate, to say the least – the unconditional moral law that enjoins us above all else to preserve and promote freedom of action "is merely the self-consciousness of a pure practical reason, this being identical with the positive concept of freedom" (5:29) – although his view about what to do with this identity is not stable. In the *Groundwork of the Metaphysics of Morals*, he attempts to prove that we have freedom of the will and then infers from that premise that we are obligated to achieve autonomy through adherence to the moral law, while in the *Critique of Practical Reason* he argues that our consciousness of our obligation under the moral law is "a fact of reason because one cannot ferret it out from antecedent data of reason, for example from consciousness of freedom (for this is not antecedently given to us)" (5:31), but that this fact of reason is a *ratio cognoscendi* from which the freedom of our will may be deduced (5:47–9), although only for practical purposes. There are problems with both of Kant's attempts to establish an unbreakable connection between autonomy as an ultimate norm and freedom of the will as an ultimate fact, and in this chapter, without denying that for Kant himself autonomy and freedom of the will were at bottom identical, these two concepts will be discussed sequentially. At the end of the chapter we shall see that Kant himself ultimately resolves these problems in his *Religion within the Boundaries of Mere Reason* by breaking the identity between moral autonomy and metaphysical freedom of the will.

The value of autonomy

Kant's view that autonomy is our ultimate value and the foundation of morality evolved from his earliest notes on morality in the 1760s to his final work in practical philosophy, *The Metaphysics of Morals* of 1797. There is no room to trace the pre-critical evolution of Kant's thought here; a few quotations from the lectures on ethics that he gave just before he began to publish his main works on moral philosophy can give the flavour of his thought.[1] The lectures locate the essence of morality in the exercise of free choice in a way that neither undermines the possibility for the continued exercise of one's own free choice nor conflicts with the possibility of the exercise of free choice by others. Here Kant says that the "necessary law of free choice" is nothing other than the "conformity of free choice with itself and others" (*MPCol* 27:254), and that "the essential ends of mankind" are nothing other than the "conditions under which alone the greatest use of freedom is possible, and under which it can be self-consistent" (27:347). Kant states that "the inner worth of the world, the *summum bonum*, is freedom according to a choice that is not necessitated to act. Freedom is thus the inner value of the world". He observes that in so far as freedom "is not restrained under certain rules of conditioned employment" or "restricted by objective rules", then "it is the most terrible thing there could ever be" (27:344), but then explains that the rule that is sought is nothing other than the self-consistency of freedom, that is, the rule to use of freedom on one occasion only in a way that is compatible with its continued possibility on other occasions.

Kant does not use the same language in the *Groundwork*. Nevertheless, it is freedom for both the agent who acts in accordance with it and freedom for all whom her actions concern that is preserved and promoted by the categorical imperative, and thus the intrinsic value of freedom is the normative foundation of Kant's mature moral philosophy. In Section I of the *Groundwork*, Kant proposes to determine the content of the moral law from "common rational moral cognition", in particular by analysis of the common assumption that there is nothing "good without limitation except a *good will*" (G 4:393) and then analysis of "the concept of *duty*, which contains that of a good will though under certain subjective limitations and hindrances" (4:397). Kant's analysis of duty is then that actions merit esteem only when they are done "not from inclination but *from duty*" (4:398), that since they cannot derive their merit from inclination, morally estimable actions also cannot derive their merit from the purpose to be attained through them or through their objects, and then that since "an action from duty is to put aside entirely the influence of inclination and with it every object of the will ... there is left for the will nothing that could determine it except objectively the *law* and subjectively *pure respect* for this practical law" (4:400). From this Kant derives his first formulation of the categorical imperative, that is, the fundamental principle of morality as it presents itself to creatures like us who can experience the moral law as a constraint:

> Since I have deprived the will of every impulse that could arise for it from obeying some law, nothing is left but the conformity of actions as such with universal law, which alone is to serve the will as its principle, that is, *I ought never to act except in such a way that I could also will that my maxim should become a universal law.* (4:402)

This argument depends precisely on the assumption that morality consists in freeing ourselves from the domination of inclination; that the moral agent must act only on maxims that could be universal laws is then presented as the only alternative to acting out of inclination. The key premise of Kant's argument is that "Only what is connected with my will merely as ground and never as effect, what does not serve my inclination but outweighs it or at least excludes it altogether from calculations in making a choice – hence the mere law for itself – can be an object of respect" (4:400). Morality commands that we act only on maxims that could be universal laws because what it takes to have a good will and act from duty is that we free ourselves from domination even by our own inclinations, and acting only on such maxims is the way to do this.

The argument of Section II of the *Groundwork* is more complicated than that of Section I, but it culminates with an affirmation of the dignity of autonomy, that is, the dignity of acting only in accordance with a law given by our own pure will and never merely from mere inclination (4:440, 444), which shows that Kant's underlying thought remains the same: morality consists in freeing ourselves from the domination of inclination. In Section II, Kant proposes to replace "popular moral philosophy" – not to be confused with the commonsensical but sound conceptions of good will and duty of the previous section – with a genuine "metaphysics of morals", by which he means here a derivation of "the moral law in its purity and genuineness" from entirely *a priori* concepts (4:390).[2] The pure metaphysics of morals of *Groundwork* II is to take the form of an analysis of the concept of rational agency. The first step of this analysis is the recognition that although "Everything in nature works in accordance with laws", "Only a rational being has the capacity to act *in accordance with the representation* of laws"; but if the will of such a being is not determined "infallibly" by reason, if it has non-rational motives – inclinations, that is – then the laws in accordance with the representation of which such a being recognizes it should act will strike it as "necessitating" or as "imperatives" (4:412–13). Kant then argues that there are two main types of imperatives, "hypothetical" and "categorical", the former representing "the practical necessity of a possible action as a means to something else that one wills" and the latter representing "an action as objectively necessary of itself, without reference to another end" (4:414). Hypothetical imperatives are divisible into two further kinds, the "problematic" "imperatives of skill", which tell us that some particular course of action is the necessary means to some particular end that we may or may not have, and the "assertoric" "imperatives of prudence", which inform us of means to the general end of happiness that we all naturally have, but which are not really genuine imperatives at all but only "counsels", because the end of happiness is irremediably indeterminate (4:415–18). But what is crucial is that hypothetical imperatives always merely prescribe the means to the gratification of inclination (although means we might not like, which is what makes them imperatives), whether a particular inclination in the case of a problematic imperative or the indeterminate set of inclinations the collective satisfaction of which, we think, would constitute our happiness (4:418–19). To act solely on hypothetical imperatives would thus be to allow ourselves to be dominated by our inclinations,[3] and, conversely, to act on the categorical imperative is the way to free ourselves from the domination of inclination.

Kant next asks "whether the mere concept of a categorical imperative may not also provide the formula containing the proposition which alone can be a categorical imperative". He says that we cannot know what a hypothetical imperative will contain merely from the concept of such an imperative, because its content depends on a condition given by an inclination and empirical knowledge of what it would take to gratify that inclination. But the content of the categorical imperative follows immediately from its concept,

> For, since the imperative contains ... no condition to which it would be limited, nothing is left with which the maxim of the action is to conform but the universality of a law as such; and this conformity alone is what the imperative properly represents as necessary. (4:420–21)

That is, since the categorical imperative is not dependent upon the desire to gratify some inclination, nothing is left for it to require but the universalizability of one's maxim, and conversely, to act only on universalizable maxims is the way to ensure that one is not acting merely in order to gratify some inclination, thus to prevent inclination from dominating one. Thus Kant reaches the formula of universal law (FUL). Kant's derivation of the content of the categorical imperative from its concept is essentially the same as his earlier argument that if the concept of acting from duty excludes acting from mere inclination, then acting on duty requires acting only on maxims that can be universal laws. As before, the assumption that morality requires freedom from domination by inclination is what ultimately motivates the recognition of the categorical imperative as the fundamental principle of morality.

Kant insists that his initial analysis of the concept of a categorical imperative is not yet meant to demonstrate that it is "a necessary law *for all rational beings* always to appraise their actions in accordance with such maxims as they themselves could will to serve as universal laws" (4:426), let alone that it is binding on *us* human beings to so will. To address the first but not the second of these outstanding questions, he says that we need to take a further step into the metaphysics of morals. This step consists in a further analysis of the concept of rational agency, or what it is for a rational being to have a will. Kant's claim here is that a rational agent acts not only in accordance with its own representation of a law, but must also have an end for the determination of its will connected to such a law, and that if the law is to be "universally valid and necessary for all rational beings", then so must this end be; in other words, rational agency requires a necessary end rather than the merely contingent ends suggested by inclination (4:428–8). If the law were already accepted on some independent ground, this would not follow, but Kant's idea is rather that the validity of the law can be established only by showing that adherence to it is in fact the necessary means to a necessary end. This is what he means when he says that if "there were something the *existence of which in itself* has an absolute worth, something which as *an end in itself* could be a ground of determinate laws, then in it, and in it alone, would lie the ground of a possible categorical imperative". Kant then asserts – "Now I say" –

> that the human being and in general every rational being *exists* as an end in itself, *not merely as a means* to be used by this or that will at its discretion; instead he must in all his actions, whether directed to himself or also to other rational beings, always be regarded *at the same time as an end*.   (4:428)

This leads to the second main formulation of the categorical imperative, "*So act that you use humanity, whether in your own person or in the person of any other, always at the same time as an end, never merely as a means*" (the "formula of humanity as an end in itself", or FHE) (4:429).

Since Kant has been insistent that the moral law cannot be derived from a "*special property of human nature*" but only from the pure concept of rational being in general (G 4:425), he cannot mean by "humanity" in FHE a property peculiar to *homo sapiens* as a biological species, but can only mean by it a property of rational agents as such, although one that we may be acquainted and concerned with only in human form. So what does Kant mean by "rational being" or its manifestation as "humanity", and in what sense can it ever be an end in itself? This is a vexed question in recent scholarship, with suggestions ranging from the equation of rational being or humanity with the capacity to set any end whatsoever to its equation with the achievement of a good will itself (see Dean 2006). The latter suggestion seems both circular – if the good will is defined as respect for the moral law, how can the content of the moral law then be derived from nothing but the concept of the good will? – and unduly restrictive – Kant makes it clear that we have duties to those who have not achieved a good will (which may be any and all of us at some or all times in our lives) (see Wood 1999: 132–9). The former suggestion, however, seems confirmed by a number of things Kant says:

in the *Groundwork* he says that "Rational nature is distinguished from the rest of nature by this, that it sets itself an end" (4:437), and in the Introduction to the Doctrine of Virtue in the *Metaphysics of Morals* he says that "The capacity to set oneself an end – any end whatsoever – is what characterizes humanity (as distinguished from animality)" (*MM* 6:392; see also 6:387). Reflection on both what the capacity to set oneself an end involves and on Kant's illustrations of FHE suggests a synoptic interpretation that incorporates both of these proposals. If the capacity to set oneself an end is to be distinguished from mere animality, then it must mean something different from having an end imposed upon oneself by mere inclination; rather, it must mean the capacity to choose an end *freely*, even if that end may be *suggested* by inclination. Thus if freedom from domination by inclination is achieved only through adoption of the moral law, then humanity as the capacity to set an end freely must include the capacity to achieve a good will. But Kant's examples also make clear that rational being or humanity also includes that aspect of rationality that is expressed by what Kant calls the principle of the *hypothetical* imperative that "Whoever wills the end also wills (insofar as reason has a decisive influence on his actions) the indispensably necessary means to it that are within his power" (*G* 4:417), or in other words ordinary means–end rationality. Thus rational being or humanity includes the capacity to set ends freely and to pursue them in accordance with the requirements of both means–end rationality and universalizability (see O'Neill 1989b).

The complexity of the requirement is evident in Kant's treatment of the examples of specific duties that he discusses once again after his introduction of FHE (as he had previously after his statement of FUL). Kant's aim with these examples is to confirm his own interpretation of the moral law by showing that it gives rise to paradigmatic instances of all the four commonly recognized classes of duties, perfect and imperfect duties to self and others (*G* 421n). The four examples are the proscription of suicide (a perfect duty towards oneself), the proscription of false promises (a perfect duty towards others), the prescription of the cultivation of one's own potential talents (an imperfect duty towards self), and the prescription of beneficence towards others (an imperfect duty towards others). Suicide "in order to escape from a trying condition" is proscribed because to commit suicide merely in order to avoid pain would be to use one's own person "*merely as a means* to maintain a tolerable condition up to the end of life" (4:429), but also, as Kant explains in his lectures, because it is to perform an act that considered in isolation seems free but in fact "throws away [one's] own freedom", that is, destroys the *existence* of a free agent and thus the possibility of any further free choices and acts by that agent (*MPCol* 27:342–3).[4] False promises are prohibited because by manipulating someone into accepting your promise without giving him accurate information about your real intentions you deprive him of the opportunity to consent to your action and make your end his own freely; in other words, you deprive him of the opportunity to *exercise* his humanity in freely setting his own ends. In choosing not to cultivate your potential talents, you make what may seem to be a free choice when it is considered in isolation, but it is in fact a choice to deprive yourself of the means that the cultivation of your talents would afford to the rational pursuit of your freely chosen ends; thus you undercut the possibility of pursuing your freely chosen ends in a *rational* and *effective* manner. And by rejecting the maxim of helping others, you demonstrate that you do not regard their ends as worthy of fulfilment because they have been freely chosen; thus you do not regard them as ends in themselves whose ends are worthy of fulfilment just because they have been *freely chosen by ends in themselves*. (You also undercut the effectiveness of your own free choices just as much as you do when you choose not to cultivate your talents, because if you were to will the universalization of your maxim of non-beneficence you would also deny yourself the assistance of others when you need it to realize your own ends; G 4:423.) Treating humanity as an end in itself whether in your own case or that of others thus requires a comprehensive programme of preserving freedom and the possibility of its rational exercise: preserving the existence of free agents, preserving the possibility of their exercising their free choice, preserving their ability to pursue their free choices in accordance with the canon of means–end rationality, and preserving their ability to pursue their free choices in accordance with the moral requirement of universalizability itself. Thus the status of humanity as an end in itself reveals that freedom itself is the fundamental value in Kant's mature moral philosophy.

Since the assertion that humanity is an end in itself is supposed to be the ground of any possible categorical imperative, one might expect Kant to offer a sustained argument for it. In fact, he simply says that he here offers "this proposition as a postulate" and will supply grounds for it in the third section of the *Groundwork* (4:429n). That section presents the *Groundwork*'s argument for the existence of freedom of the will, so discussion of it will be reserved for a later section of this chapter. Kant concludes Section II of the *Groundwork* by explicitly connecting the categorical imperative as expounded thus far to the concepts of "autonomy" and the "realm of ends". The "principle of the *autonomy* of the will" is the principle that, as a rational being that is an end in itself, every agent must be treated not merely as the subject of universal law but also as the legislator of universal law, and also that "every human will" must be regarded "as *a will giving universal law through all its maxims*" (4:432); in other words, freedom must be preserved throughout the domain of human agents and all of their choices of maxims: each agent must be regarded as legislating, that is, as freely assenting to, the system of rules that governs them all, and each rule in this system must be consistent with the others; that is, the freedom to act on each rule must preserve the freedom to act on all rules. This requirement as well as FHE's requirement that the freely chosen particular ends of oneself and others must be treated as ends for oneself and others because they have been freely chosen by agents who are ends in themselves are then summed up in the "formula of the realm of ends" (FRE), that "all maxims from one's own lawgiving are to harmonize into a possible realm of ends as a realm of nature" (4:437). A "realm of ends" is "a whole of all ends in systematic connection (a whole both of rational beings as ends in themselves and of the ends of his own that each may set himself)". In acting so as to bring such a realm into existence – transforming it from a mere idea into "a realm of nature" – "we abstract from the personal differences of rational beings as well as from all content of their private ends" (4:433), that is, our reason for promoting it is not based on our own inclination towards particular other persons or their particular ends; our reason for promoting it is simply their status as ends in themselves and the fact that as such they have freely chosen their particular ends. But what this status then requires us to do is to preserve their freedom of choice and action and to promote the freely chosen ends of each, in so far, of course, as doing that for any is consistent with doing that for all (thus only freely chosen ends that are themselves moral as consistent with the freedom of all fall under this obligation).

Kant's ultimate normative ideal in the *Groundwork* is thus a system in which every human being is treated as a free agent and to the extent possible the freely chosen ends of each are promoted by all. It is thus a system of pervasive freedom. Kant works out the implications of this ideal for embodied human beings existing on a single globe in his *Metaphysics of Morals* of 1797. There Kant divides our duties into duties of right, which are those of our duties towards others that, although duties to preserve freedom, are consistent with the possibility of coercive enforcement, and duties of virtue, all of our duties towards self as well as others that are not consistent with coercive enforcement but can be enforced only through our own virtue, that is, the strength of our commitment to the moral law. There is no room to discuss the details of Kant's theory of rights and virtues here.[5] We must conclude that the normative content of Kant's practical philosophy, what it proscribes and prescribes throughout the domains of both rights and ethics, is thus the preservation of the existence and the possibility of the exercise of freedom in the choice of ends and the promotion of the effective pursuit of those freely chosen ends by both oneself and others. Now of course the question arises as to how Kant argues for freedom as our ultimate value. As already noted, in the *Groundwork* he lets the unconditional value of humanity as an end in itself stand as a "postulate" while he develops its normative implications, and promises that he will return to the proof of this postulate in the final section of the work. There he attempts to prove that we have freedom of the will. So let us now follow him and turn to that issue.

Freedom of the will

Kant addressed the problem of freedom of the will throughout his career, and his position on it seems to have undergone both substantive and methodological changes. In his earliest work Kant argued against the "liberty of indifference", the position that a "person, even though all the grounds ... determining the will in a particular direction have been posited, is nonetheless able to choose one thing over another, no matter what", that such a thesis would reduce actions to "chance" and undermine the possibility of responsibility,[6] and held instead that free action is action determined by an "inner principle of self-determination" rather than an external cause but is not undetermined (*NE* 1:405). But by the time of *Religion within the Boundaries of Mere Reason* (1792 and 1793), Kant argued that freedom of the will can only be understood as an "inscrutable", that is, inexplicable choice between two alternative inner principles – the moral law on the one hand and the principle of self-love on the other hand (more precisely, the choice concerns which of these principles to subordinate to the other) – a choice that is inscrutable because it occurs at the noumenal level, rather than at the phenomenal level of experience, where everything can be explained but only by means of causal laws in accordance with which subsequent events are after all fully determined by prior events. In other words, in the end Kant seems to have accepted the liberty of indifference, although at the noumenal rather than the phenomenal level.

Kant seems to have been forced into this substantive reversal by a problem that challenges his approaches to the freedom of the will in both the *Groundwork* and the *Critique of Practical Reason* in spite of a key methodological difference between his treatments of the issue in those two works. But before we turn to those works, a comment upon Kant's treatment of the freedom of the will in the *Critique of Pure Reason*, the first work in which he returned to the issue since the *New Exposition*, is necessary. In the first *Critique*, Kant addressed the problem in the Third Antinomy of Pure Reason, where he argued that the contradiction between the thesis that at the origin of all series of causes and effects there must be one (or at least one) cause that is not itself the effect of something else and the antithesis that we can never experience a cause that is not itself the effect of yet another cause could be resolved only by transcendental idealism, which restricts the validity of the antithesis, thus complete causal determinism, to the realm of appearances, and at least leaves open the *possibility* that at the level of things in themselves there can be acts of pure spontaneity that have effects but no causes.

In the *Groundwork* and the second *Critique*, Kant clearly wants to establish the *reality* of freedom of the will. But he seems to undergo a major methodological reversal between these two works, in the *Groundwork* attempting to prove that we are bound by the moral law from a prior proof of the reality of freedom of the will but in the *Critique of Practical Reason* attempting to prove the reality of freedom of the will from our prior conviction of the reality of the moral law. In the *Groundwork*, Kant had held that the first two sections were strictly analytical, deriving the content of the categorical imperative first from the common concept of duty and then from the philosophical concept of a categorical imperative itself, but left it to the third section to prove that the categorical imperative so derived is actually binding for us human beings. His note in Section II that the proposition that rational nature exists as an end in itself is only a "postulate" the grounds for which will be provided in Section III suggests that this argument will turn on proving that we actually are rational beings, and so it does. But it takes the particular form of attempting to prove that because we are rational we are both free from determination by "alien causes" such as mere inclinations, which are only phenomenal, and instead at the noumenal level determined by the moral law. This form of proof, however, raises the problem that if freedom of the will and being determined by the moral law are equivalent, then immoral action cannot be the product of the free will, and thus we cannot be held responsible for it.

Kant starts by stating that freedom of the will can be defined negatively as freedom from the determination of the will by alien causes, but that since the will is itself a form of causality it must be positively defined by "a causality in accordance with immutable laws but of a special kind; for otherwise a free will would be an absurdity" (4:446).

He then says that since "Natural necessity was a heteronomy of efficient causes", freedom of the will can be nothing "other than autonomy, that is, the will's property of being a law to itself", that is, "the principle to act on no other maxim than that which can also have as object itself as universal law". In other words, the causal law of the free will can only be the moral law, "hence a free will and a will under moral laws are one and the same" (4:447). But Kant says that all this remains mere analysis, and it must still be proven that we actually have free will, from which it will then follow that the moral law is the causal law of our will. He explicitly rejects the idea that we can merely presuppose that we have a free will (4:448–9), for this would leave us open to "a kind of circle from which, as it seems, there is no way to escape", namely that we take ourselves to be free "in order to think ourselves under moral laws" but think of ourselves "as subject to these laws" only "because we have ascribed to ourselves freedom of the will" (4:450).[7] In order to escape from the threat of this circle, Kant turns to transcendental idealism. Maintaining his initial stance that the argument of the *Groundwork* starts from common sense, Kant remarkably claims that even "the commonest understanding" recognizes that sense perceptions are only the appearances of things in themselves whose real nature remains unknown to us in their appearances. He then adds that everyone will also accept that "the human being cannot claim to cognize what he is in himself through the cognizance he has by inner sensation", and "beyond this constitution of his own subject, made up of nothing but appearances, he must necessarily assume something else laying at their basis, namely his I as it may be constituted in itself" (4:451). However, Kant next claims that human beings are not condemned to ignorance of their underlying nature by the strictly phenomenal character of inner sense, because "a human being really finds in himself a capacity by which he distinguishes himself from all other things, even from himself insofar as he is affected by objects, and that is *reason*", which is "pure self-activity". Because of this self-activity, "the human being can never think of the causality of his own will otherwise than under the idea of freedom, for independence from the determining causes of the world of sense (which reason must always ascribe to itself) is freedom", and "With the idea of freedom the concept of *autonomy* is now inseparably combined, and with the concept of autonomy the universal principle of morality" (4:452). Thus Kant infers that inner sense and with it our subjection to ordinary causal laws is only a matter of appearance, that our true character is revealed by the self-activity of our reason, which in turn proves the freedom of our will, which itself proves that the moral law is the real law of our will, thereby breaking the threatened circle (4:453).

There are methodological and substantive problems with this argument.[8] The methodological problem is that Kant simply asserts that we find self-active reason in ourselves, that we do not merely perform theoretical inferences and formulate general principles of practical reason by means of some natural mechanism that could be empirically explained, but that reason is genuinely spontaneous; and this seems to amount to a bare assertion that we have freedom of the will rather than a proof that we do. And Kant cannot rescue himself from the charge that he is making an unsubstantiated theoretical assertion by claiming that he is only inferring freedom from practical grounds as the condition of the possibility of our obligation under the moral law, because he has on his own account not yet proven that we are bound by the moral law – he is attempting to prove that by first proving that we have freedom of the will, but seems to be begging that question after all.

The substantive problem, as earlier suggested, is that if the moral law is really the causal law of our will at its deepest, noumenal level, then it seems impossible to explain how we could ever perform immoral actions. Kant clearly does not recognize that his argument gives rise to this substantive problem, for he immediately goes on to describe human action as a struggle between the world of sense, with its inclinations, and the world of pure reason, governed by the moral law (4:453–4), but human action could not be such a struggle if it were both a phenomenon fully grounded in our noumenal reality and that noumenal reality were actually governed by the moral law as the immutable form of its own special causality.[9] Kant seems to have recognized the methodological problem with the *Groundwork*'s argument from freedom to the moral law but not its substantive problem, however, for in the *Critique of Practical Reason* he reverses his methodological tack. Kant's methodological reversal in the second *Critique* is to argue from our consciousness of our obligation of the moral law as a "fact of reason" that "forces itself upon us of itself as a synthetic *a priori* proposition that is not based on any intuition" nor can be reasoned "out from any antecedent data of reason" (*PracR* 5:31), and then to argue that the "inscrutable faculty" of the freedom of the will can be deduced from the moral law "in place of the vainly sought deduction of the moral principle" from an antecedent proof of the freedom of the will (5:47).[10] In other words, the *Groundwork*'s ambition of proving that we are subject to the moral law is abandoned; that is now taken for granted, and instead Kant's hope is that "the *moral law*, of which we become immediately conscious (as soon as we draw up maxims of the wills for ourselves) ... inasmuch as reason presents it as a determining ground not to be outweighed by any sensible conditions and indeed quite independent of them, leads directly to the concept of freedom". His argument then follows:

> We can become aware of pure practical laws just as we are aware of pure theoretical principles, by attending to the necessity with which reason prescribes them to us and to the setting aside of all empirical conditions to which reason directs us. The concept of a pure will arises from the first, as consciousness of a pure under-standing arises from the latter.   (5:29–30)

But although the direction of Kant's proof is formally reversed, its underlying assumptions are not really different from those of the argument in the *Groundwork*: Kant's key assumptions are that the necessity of the moral law implies that it comes from a pure faculty of reason, like the self-active faculty of reason in the *Groundwork*, and that the purity of reason proves the purity of the will, its determination not by the "mechanism of nature" but by the moral law of pure practical reason. But this assumes the identity of pure practical reason and the will, and thus once again raises the substantive problem of how the free will could ever choose to act otherwise than in accordance with the moral law.

Following his statement of this argument, Kant claims that "experience also confirms this order of concepts in us", in other words, he turns to common sense for confirmation of his position. His argument here is that just as anyone will admit that he could control his inclination to enjoy an immoral pleasure if he were threatened with death if he did so, so will anyone admit that he could refuse to incriminate an innocent person even if threatened with death if he does not, because, even without venturing to assert whether he *would* do what is right, "He judges … that he can do something because he is aware that he ought to do it and cognizes freedom within him" (*PracR* 5:30). That is, Kant argues that from our recognition of what we ought to do combined with the principle that if we ought to do something we can do it, we infer that we are always free to do what the moral law requires even if we cannot be sure that we will do it. This argument would give Kant a way out of the substantive problem created by his identification of free will with pure practical reason, because "ought implies can" does not imply "ought implies does", and thus leaves open the possibility that we shall not do what we ought to do; as Kant himself makes clear, we do not infer that we shall do something from the fact that we know that we can do it. But, apart from the fact that Kant has not suggested any argument for the principle that "ought implies can" itself, this principle has not been part of his basic argument for freedom in the second *Critique*, only part of its "confirmation" from experience. And Kant continues both to identify the moral law with the causal law of the noumenal self and to maintain that the noumenal self is the sole ground of the phenomenal self or "empirical character" (see esp. 5:95–8), thus he does not take advantage of the opening left by the "ought implies can" principle.

In *Religion within the Boundaries of Mere Reason*, however, Kant does assert complete freedom of the will under the aegis of the principle that "ought implies can" and thus reverts to a conception of freedom of the will as an inscrutable liberty of indifference, although safely transposed to the noumenal level. The point of *Religion* is to reinterpret the central doctrines and institutions of Christianity along lines dictated by Kant's own view that morality is grounded in pure practical reason alone. The argument begins with an interpretation of the Christian notions of original sin and grace: Kant's view is that the idea of original sin inherited from ancestors can only be a symbol for the radical evil innate in each human agent, where that in turn means that the possibility of doing evil by subordinating the moral law to the principle of self-love is the inevitable concomitant of our genuine freedom to choose to subordinate the principle of self-love to the moral law. Grace may then be interpreted as the gift of freedom itself, our power to conform to the moral law and initiate our own conversion from evil to good if we have previously chosen evil over good (as Kant assumes we all have done), as well as any assistance beyond our own powers that we might need to complete our conversion. The crucial points for Kant are that if we are "imputable" or responsible for evil, then we must freely choose to be evil, but that the freedom to do that in turn entails that we must also be able to choose to be good, and that any cooperation we might need in becoming completely good can come only after we have ourselves made the maximal possible effort to be so – grace cannot be understood as election or predestination for goodness or salvation from evil independently of our own merits. Kant makes the first point when he argues that if a propensity to the inversion of the principle of self-love over the moral law does lie in human nature, then this propensity

> must ultimately be sought in a free power of choice, and hence is imputable. This evil is *radical*, since it corrupts the ground of all maxims; as natural propensity, it is also not to be *extirpated* through human forces, for this could only happen through good maxims – something that cannot take place if the subjective supreme ground of all maxims is presupposed to be corrupted. Yet it must equally be possible to *overcome* this evil, for it is found in the human being as acting freely. (RBR 6:37)

What Kant means is not that the choice of evil as one's fundamental maxim, the general policy of subordinating morality to self-love, can only be overcome by divine intervention, but that it can only be overcome by a reversal of fundamental maxim in an exercise of one's own freedom that is not empirically explicable and is therefore inscrutable. That moral conversion cannot begin with a divine act external to the agent but must begin with an inscrutable act within the agent, which can at most be completed by cooperation from outside the agent, is made clear in this further passage:

> According to moral religion (and, of all the public religions so far known, the Christian alone is of this type), it is a fundamental principle that, to become a better human being, everyone must do as much as it is in his powers to do; and only then, if a human being has not buried his innate talent ... if he has made use of the original predisposition to the good in order to become a better human being, can he hope that what does not lie in his power will be made good by cooperation from above.   (*RBR* 6:51–2)

Kant does not introduce any new arguments for transcendental idealism or for the existence of freedom of the will in *Religion*, rather taking both our binding obligation under the moral law and the principle "ought implies can" for granted, invoking the latter principle immediately before the previous passage – "If the moral law commands that we *ought* to be better human beings now, it inescapably follows that we must be *capable* of being better human beings" (6:50) – and no fewer than six other times (6:41, 45, 47, 49n, 62, 66). Without worrying about his objections four decades earlier to the liberty of indifference, in *Religion* Kant takes advantage of the room left by the principle that "ought implies can" to impute to us the possibility of inexplicably choosing to convert from evil to good even if we have previously, and equally inexplicably, chosen to be evil instead of good.[11]

Conclusion

What makes it possible for Kant finally to ascribe to us the freedom of the will to choose either good or evil is that he no longer attempts either to derive autonomy from the freedom of the will by treating the moral law as the causal law of the noumenal free will or to derive freedom from our consciousness of the moral law by identifying the pure will with pure practical reason as the source of the moral law. If these argumentative strategies are dropped, then the persuasive force of Kant's moral philosophy depends upon accepting both the "fact of reason" and the principle "ought implies can", that is, accepting that humanity must be treated as an end in itself and can only be so treated by acting in accordance with the moral law and that it is within our power to so act. Kant's idea that humanity must be treated as an end in itself and never merely as a means has gained wide acceptance in modern moral thought and philosophy, even if there continues to be debate over both the origin and the application of this fundamental value. However, whether only transcendental idealism can justify the claim that it is always within our power to act as morality demands or whether a conception of freedom of the will adequate for our sense of moral responsibility can be constructed without recourse to transcendental idealism is a difficult question, but will have to be left unanswered here.[12]

Notes

1. See Immanuel Kant, *Vorlesung zur Moralphilosophie*, Werner Stark (ed.) (Berlin: Walter de Gruyter, 2004), based on a transcription by Johann Friedrich Kaehler from the summer semester of 1777, and *Moral Philosophy*, transcribed by Georg Ludwig Collins in the winter semester 1784–5 (*MPCol*), in Kant, *Lectures on Ethics*, Peter Heath and J. B. Schneewind (eds) (Cambridge: Cambridge University Press, 1997), 37–222.
2. This sense of the phrase "metaphysics of morals" is different from that Kant uses in the 1797 work of that name, where it means the *application* of this pure moral law to ourselves in light of certain basic empirical circumstances of our existence, above all the inescapable fact of our embodiment, thereby giving rise to our concrete duties.
3. The choice between ends that we like and means that we do not will itself be a matter of mere inclination unless morality speaks against or in favour of one or the other.
4. Kant does consider the possibility that suicide might be justifiable when there is in fact no way to preserve one's own future freedom but one's own suicide might encourage others to preserve theirs by resisting a tyrant, the case of Cato against Caesar. See *MPCol*, 27:370, and *The Metaphysics of Morals: Doctrine of Virtue*, §6, 4:423. This shows that Kant need not consider duties as prohibitions or prescriptions of actions-types as such, but of actions in certain sorts of circumstances and for certain sorts of ends, all of which need to be specified in the maxim of an action to be tested for duty. See O'Neill (1975: 34–42) and Korsgaard (2009: 14–15).
5. For fuller discussion, see Gregor (1963) and Guyer (2006: chs 7, 8).
6. Kant, *New Elucidation of the First Principles of Metaphysical Cognition*, 1:402, in Walford (1992: 26).
7. For discussion of the threatened "circle", see especially Brandt (1988) and Quarfood (2006).

8. I have discussed these problems in detail in Guyer (2007).
9. Some commentators have attempted to liberate Kant from this problem by arguing that he has only proven that the noumenal will is a *determinability* or *capacity* to be governed by the moral law; see for example Engstrom (2002: 295–8). Perhaps Kant should have said this in the *Groundwork*, but his claim that reason must be "a causality in accordance with immutable laws but of a special kind" (*G* 4:446) is clearly incompatible with this rescue attempt.
10. The reversal in the direction of Kant's argument has been widely noted; see especially Henrich (1975) and Ameriks (1981; 2000b: ch. VI, 189–233). The "fact of reason" is also discussed in Beck (1960: 166–70) and Rawls (2000: 253–72).
11. For Kant the original decision in behalf of evil is actually inexplicable for two reasons: first, evil cannot be seen as a simple matter of following natural predispositions towards self-preservation, sexual congress and so on, because in Kant's teleological perspective, natural predispositions are predispositions to the good that have to be actively perverted if they are not actually to lead to the good (e.g. *Religion*, 6:28), and, secondly, all noumenal choices, whether for good or evil, are inexplicable because causal explanation is confined to the phenomenal surface of human action. Allen Wood's anthropological interpretation of the sources of radical evil has to be tempered with the recognition that for Kant empirical factors can at most be occasions for evil but not sufficient conditions for it; see Wood (1999: ch. 9, esp. 283–91).
12. For my own view of this matter, see Guyer (2008).

SIX

Practical reason: categorical imperative, maxims, laws

Kenneth R. Westphal

Introduction

Kant's *Groundwork of the Metaphysics of Morals* inaugurated an approach to moral philosophy so original it is designated "Kantian Ethics", including work prizing fidelity to Kant's own views and work inspired primarily by his views. Kant's moral philosophy advocates a distinctive fundamental moral principle and develops a unique system of moral principles, centring on the key terms "practical reason", "law", "maxim" and "categorical imperative".[1]

Kant worked with the traditional classification according to which "moral philosophy" is a genus, with two proper, coordinate species: theory of justice [*Rechtslehre*] and ethics [*Tugendlehre*]. Twentieth-century anglophone moral philosophers, however, commonly regard ethics as the primary discipline, demoting social, political and legal philosophy to a mere corollary to ethics. The oddity of this recent conception is highlighted by the fact that central ethical issues about individual action and virtue can be nothing but theory, if even that, without a significant degree of public peace, security and stability, which require principles and institutions basic to theory of justice. This reminder underscores why Kant's *Groundwork* must be considered within the corpus of his major writings in practical philosophy, *The Critique of Practical Reason*, *The Metaphysics of Morals* and much of his *Religion within the Bounds of Reason Alone*, along with his several essays on ethics and politics.[2] More importantly, Kant knew first hand that whoever inaugurates a new kind of systematic enquiry must begin with an initial conception of the proposed system, which is inevitably revised and improved through its development (*CpR* A 834/B 862). This holds true of Kant's mature, properly Critical moral philosophy, first enunciated in the *Groundwork* but only completed in much later works.

Flanking the present chapter are chapters on Kant's *Groundwork*, doctrine of justice and doctrine of virtue. This chapter considers the centrality of moral principles in Kant's moral philosophy, their distinctively "Kantian" character, why Kant presents a "metaphysical" system of moral principles and how these "formal" principles are to be used in practice. These points are central to how Kant thinks pure reason can be practical. These features have often puzzled anglophone readers, who have a pervasively empiricist orientation.

Kant's opposition to moral empiricism

Practical principles aim (at a minimum) to indicate how to act rightly, in everyday life and in uncommonly problematic circumstances, by distinguishing moral right from wrong, good from bad and permissible from impermissible. If we stipulate, as Kant does, that a purely rational agent is one who decides how to act solely on the basis of rationally justified moral principles, then moral principles, in conjunction with information about circumstances of action, simply describe how such an agent behaves (cf. *MMV* 6:383). For such a being, moral principles are normative because they define or specify right action, as distinct from wrong or merely permissible (optional) action. Yet for a pure rational agent, normative moral principles are not *imperatives*, because *ex hypothesi* that kind of agent acts only as morality requires. Notoriously, of course, human beings can and do depart from what morality requires. For us, normative moral principles are also imperatives because such principles indicate how we ought to behave, even if we fail to behave ourselves (6:379–80).

This prescriptive character of morality, both as norms and as imperatives, is one reason why Kant holds that moral principles cannot be identified or justified by empirical methods alone. Famously Hume argued that normative conclusions do not follow from factual premises alone ("is" does not imply "ought"), not at least without the intervention of a sentiment (cf. Hume 2000: 302), which as a class Hume contrasted sharply with reason. Whether such sentiments are regarded as necessary for drawing normative conclusions, or instead as the sole and sufficient basis for drawing such conclusions (Hume espouses both views in various passages), Kant is suspicious about the purported roles of sentiments or other affective states in moral *reasoning*, especially that involved in identifying and justifying basic moral principles.

Kant's reasons for caution are highlighted by Mill's counterpart empiricist view in *Utilitarianism*:

> If the end which the utilitarian doctrine proposes to itself were not, in theory and in practice, acknowledged to be an end, nothing could ever convince any person that it was so. No reason can be given why the general happiness is desirable, except that each person, so far as he believes it to be attainable, desires his own happiness. (Mill 1963–91: 10:234)

This passage begins with the issue of justifying the principle of utility to particular individuals, and then makes a perhaps stronger statement about what can justify the principle of utility as such. In both regards Mill appeals to a (presumed) empirical fact, that each human being does desire his or her own happiness. Both Hume and Mill appeal directly and ineliminably to affective states, including sentiments and desires, to identify and to justify basic moral principles, and these affective states are also linked, in their views, with our motives for action (cf. Williams 1980). Accordingly, one of Kant's concerns about empiricist moral theories is: what are we to make either of the truly apathetic – those who lack affect altogether, whether by nature, socialization or practice – or of those whose affects lead them to act contrarily to what we ordinarily and uncontroversially regard as minimum moral standards? If, say, typical human affects strongly favoured murder and mayhem, could such affects identify, justify or motivate such actions as morally right? Can moral empiricism reject such scenarios without rescinding empiricism?[3] These questions are not arguments, yet they highlight Kant's concern that the specification of right action, our obligations so to act and our motivating reasons for so acting must not be hostage to something so varied and variable as human sentiments: our affects, sentiments and motives require moral assessment as much as do our decisions and behaviour (cf. *G* 4:444; *PracR* 5:158). Apt feelings are of course central to proper and to virtuous action, in part because they are central to proper appreciation of morally salient features of our circumstances of action (see Herman 1993: 73–93; 2007). However, whether feelings *are* appropriate is not adequately specified by *feelings* of appropriateness. These issues vitiate much of Hume's ethical theory, as he realized in his unjustly neglected theory of justice (see Westphal 2010a).

These issues also vitiate contemporary neo-Humean constructivist moral theories that follow the model of Hume's ethical materials and strategies. If affective states, moral intuitions or shared commitments are taken as the *basic* materials for constructing a moral theory, the principles identified and justified on such bases can aspire to no more than generality holding across a group of agents who happen to be like-minded about those basics (cf. *PracR* 5:58–9). In principle no such constructivist theory can provide resources for assessing and rationally resolving moral disputes between groups of agents who disagree about those basics, or about the proper forms of construction for moral theories based upon them. In principle such forms of constructivism are ill designed to avoid or to resolve problems about moral conventionalism, relativism or *petitio principii* (see Westphal 2010a, 2010c).

Social-contract models for identifying or justifying basic practical norms confront a basic problem: because contract models can only appeal to reasons or grounds that potential contractors avow, they are incapable of addressing anyone who disregards or denies important features of his or her circumstances, obligations or entitlements. Hence such models are powerless against the socially obstinate, namely egoists, who are to social philosophy what radical sceptics are to epistemology. The prospect of correcting someone's understanding – or rather misunderstanding – of society and of him- or herself in relation to it directly challenges the radical contractarian strategy because grounds for correcting anyone's understanding of relevant matters may suffice to justify social principles and practices, regardless of anyone's contractarian agreement. More precisely, the prospect of providing sufficient reasons to justify certain principles and practices of social interaction regardless of anyone's express recognition of those reasons would render contractarian agreement redundant, revealing it to be a dispensable epicycle on a more fundamental non-contractarian justificatory analysis, such as Kant's (see O'Neill 2000b; Westphal 2010b).

If Kant's search for a fundamental moral principle, universally valid across all rational agents, may look quaint or quixotic, we must refresh our appreciation of the problems confronting the entire modern natural law tradition – and confronting us worldwide today – of identifying sufficient, multilaterally justifiable principles of conduct governing public life, both domestically and internationally, which, when institutionalized, provide the minimum sufficient, legitimate (morally justifiable) principles and institutions required to solve fundamental problems of social coordination and thus to establish peace and to enable prosperity, while acknowledging fundamental substantive disagreements between our various understandings of a good or pious life (see Schneewind 1991).[4] Concretely, these problems confronted modern moral philosophers in controversies over international maritime trade, religious schisms and the Thirty Years War in Europe.[5] These kinds of very real problems can easily escalate into irreconcilable conflicts of interest and bi- or multilateral *petitio principii*, as Kant knew (*PracR* 5:63).[6] These are among Kant's reasons for developing a distinctive, carefully qualified kind of moral rationalism (5:70–71).

The objects of pure practical reason

If the concerns just sketched are to be addressed, then pure reason must be practical: reason itself must be able to specify morally legitimate aims and actions, and not merely calculate the most effective ways of attaining ends to which we are antecedently committed (*PracR* 5:62). This is not, quixotically, simply to neglect or omit our ends, but rather to require us to act towards our ends only in so far as such ends and the actions taken to achieve them are morally legitimate. Kant aims to show, *pace* Hume, that reason is not simply the calculative slave of the passions (Hume 2000: 266). This independence of reason from our particular ends is fundamental to Kant's sense of the "autonomy" of reason (5:42).[7]

Kant recognizes that to suppose that pure reason can be practical in this sense is strange and unparalleled (5:31). To develop this prospect, he enquires whether the concept of the morally right can be specified by examples of (purported) morally good objects; or can morally good objects only be specified by use of an independent, antecedent concept of what is morally right (5:62)?[8] If the concept of right is specified by examples of (purported) morally good objects, questions directly arise about how we identify such objects, adequately and reliably, and distinguish them from others that are morally indifferent or morally bad, along with questions posed above about how to achieve sufficient agreement, in theory and in practice, about which objects are which.

Kant uses a version of Socrates' question to Euthyphro, whether the pious is loved by the gods because it is the pious, or whether the pious is the pious because it is loved by the gods (*Euthyphro*, 10a), to underscore the priority of our conception of what is morally right over any and all examples of what (purportedly) is morally good. Kant contends that conceiving the divinity as the paragon of moral perfection presupposes rather than defines our concept of moral perfection, and that we can only recognize the holiness of the Christian saviour by using our prior and independent concept of moral perfection (G 4:408–9).

This summary of Kant's reasons for seeking a basic *a priori* principle of morality suffices to explain some important points of Kant's analysis of an "object of pure practical reason" (*PracR* 5:57–71). An "object" of practical reason is something to be obtained by free action. By definition *pure* practical reason omits all corporeal desires, motives, urges, inclinations or preferences and all consideration of the agent's capacities and resources for achieving ends. An object of pure practical reason, accordingly, is one obtained by free action, regardless of any physical or physiological constraints on capacity or feasibility, and of any merely elective goals or motives of action. Hence the sole question regarding whether something is an object of pure practical reason is whether it is possible to will to achieve or to bring about this object (were the agent capable of so doing). This question has only two answers: necessarily the moral good is an object of pure practical reason; necessarily the morally evil is not.

The definition of pure practical reason, Kant's severe reservations about moral empiricism and his aim to avoid *petitio principii* about the most basic principles of moral obligation, together entail that the most basic practical principle must concern the form, rather than the matter (i.e. the particular objects or ends) of the will's determining ground (*PracR* 5:27). Any such principle must be a rational rather than an empirical principle because it can be neither defined nor justified by empirically given ends, desires or motives.

Furthermore, any will that can determine how to act solely on the basis of such a principle must be negatively free from the influence of such empirical factors and positively free both to decide how to act, and to act, regardless of such factors (cf. *PracR* 5:25, 28–9, 42, 65).[9] Because a pure will omits all such empirical factors, it can only determine how to act by using a *concept* of how properly to act; any such concept must be a principle, and indeed a law, because at issue here are the necessary objects of a pure will, the good and the evil as such. Hence no considerations pertaining only to individual, actual agents pertain to a pure will. Thus this principle of action must be a practical law holding of all free rational agents as such.

A law, Kant claims, has only two aspects: its matter, that is, the objects or states of affairs to which it pertains, and its legislative (law-like) form. Because the will as pure practical reason prescinds from such objects, only the legislative form of a practical law can provide the ground upon which the will can determine how to act, provided the will incorporates this ground into its own maxim (*PracR* 5:29). A maxim is an individual agent's principle of action ("I shall so act ..."), in contrast to the universal form of a practical law ("All are so to act ..."); in this regard maxims are "subjective", in contrast to practical laws, which are "objective" because they hold for all rational agents as such (5:19).[10] Kant's basic criterion for the moral status of maxims is whether one's maxim is suited to the universal form of practical legislation and thus can serve as a universal law. This is Kant's Fundamental Law (*Grundgesetz*) of Pure Practical Reason:

> So act that the maxim of your will could also always count as a principle of universal legislation.　　　(*PracR* 5:30; my trans.)

Obviously, this is a variant of Kant's Formula of Universal Law (*G* 4:221). This principle is a criterion for maxims, that are agent-specific ("subjective"), and is stated in imperative form. Hence this *Grundgesetz* is fundamental in regard to any agent's deliberation about how rightly to act.

Kant's fundamental criterion of right action as such (that is, objectively) is announced only in his *Metaphysics of Morals*; this is Kant's Universal Principle of Right:

> An act is *right* if it, or if according to its maxim, one's freedom of will can coexist with everyone's freedom in accord with a universal law.　　　(*MM* 6:230)[11]

Kant's view is consistent, although we must attend to the specific roles and aims of his various principles. In particular, we must be careful with his repeated claim, early and late, that "the" categorical imperative is "the" (sole) fundamental principle of his practical philosophy, if the categorical imperative is taken to be his criterion for testing maxims and is thus taken to contrast with his Universal Principle of Right. What is objectively right and wrong, Kant contends, is specified by the moral law; the most fundamental criterion for specifying the moral law is his Universal Principle of Right. The basic criterion for agents to use in deliberation is his Fundamental Law of Pure Practical Reason, or, as it is often designated, the formula of universal law of the categorical imperative. These principles specify right action in the form of strict or perfect duties (*G* 4:421n). Secondary to this fundamental specification of right action is the further specification, among right actions as such, of broad or meritorious duties (whether self- or other-regarding). These are the topic of Kant's *Doctrine of Ethics*. The better wisdom is to recognize that when claiming that "the" categorical imperative is the fundamental practical principle, Kant often uses "categorical imperative" to designate a close-knit family of principles, based upon the objective Universal Principle of Right and its complementary, subjective or first-person criterion, the Fundamental Law of Pure Practical Reason.[12]

The structure of Kant's practical philosophy

How can focusing on the universal legislative form of law discriminate among obligatory, permissible and forbidden actions? Kant answers by noting that the relevant laws are norms by use of which a free rational will can determine how to act. Willing is a species of causality; the objects of the will are goals to be achieved by acting (*PracR* 5:65). Consequently, judging the moral status (forbidden, permissible or obligatory) of the alternative courses of action available in any situation requires considering what kind of rational will the agent is, morally salient features of the agent's situation and of the consequences and implications of available courses of action. These modal categories of possible free acts (forbidden, permissible, obligatory) provide "the transition from practical principles as such to the practical principles of morals" (5:67). This "transition" is not simply a restriction of scope, focusing on a specifically moral subset of practical principles. The main point of Kant's transition is to move from the purely *a priori* principles of morals considered so far to more specific principles required for a doctrine of morals. This doctrine is, in a specifically Kantian sense, metaphysical. "Metaphysics" in general, Kant holds, is "a system of *a priori* knowledge from concepts alone" (*MM* 6:216). If these concepts are *a priori*, their analysis provides a general metaphysics; if a specific, contingent, empirical concept is also included, the analysis provides a "specific" metaphysics pertaining to that concept. In this regard, Kant's *Critique of Pure Reason* provides a "general metaphysics" of nature. His *Metaphysical Foundations of Natural Science* (4:470) provides a "specific" metaphysics of nature by *a priori* analysis of the contingent concept "matter". Kant's "general" metaphysics of morals is contained in the *Critique of Practical Reason* and in the Preface and Introduction to the *Metaphysics of Morals*. His "specific" metaphysics of morals results from *a priori* analysis of the contingent concept of our finite, human form of rational agency, as developed in his *Doctrines of Justice* and of *Virtue*.

In both the *Groundwork* and the *Metaphysics of Morals* Kant insists that his pure rational principles of practical reason require "practical anthropology" to be applied to us as human beings, to generate specific moral injunctions or permissions (*G* 4:388, 412; *MM* 6:216–17). This practical anthropology is a "proper appendix" to Kant's practical philosophy (*MMV* 6:469); it provides the contingent, determinate concept of our species of finite human rational agency, including pervasive features of our worldly context of action. Although Kant never composed this "appendix", his examples and analyses of our moral obligations provide much information about it (see O'Neill 1989a: 74, 105–6, 114–15, 121, 133–4; Herman 1993: 122, 203–6, 235; Louden 2002; Westphal 2002).

Kant's frequent insistence that moral imperatives are categorical rather than hypothetical expresses his view that our moral obligations are not conditional upon whatever we happen to want to do; they do not depend upon our contingent motives or ends. It is not at all Kant's view that our moral imperatives are unconditioned by our circumstances of action and our capacities to act; famously Kant contends that no one can be obligated to do whatever she or he is incapable of doing; "ought implies can", whereas "cannot" implies "cannot be obligated to" (*PracR* 5:30, 125).

Kant's universalization tests use the principle governing instrumental reasoning, the Principle of Hypothetical Imperatives: "Whoever wills the end, also wills (insofar as reason has decisive influence on his actions) the indispensably necessary means to it that are within his power" (*G* 4:417). This principle requires considering what *we can will*. It thereby serves to introduce relevant practical–anthropological information about our capabilities and our circumstantial resources into Kant's tests.

Kant's universalization tests

In the first instance, Kant's universalization tests provide criteria for the moral status (obligatory, permissible, prohibited) of an agent's maxim.[13] A maxim is a principle on which an individual acts, for example, "In order to get ahead in the world, I will only deceive people when I am sure not to be detected", or, more positively, "In order to be able to borrow money again, I will repay my present loans on schedule". A maxim can be schematically formulated as: "I will do x if y in order to z", where x holds a place for an act description, y for a description of a kind of agent confronting specified circumstances and z for a description of an end, purpose or reason for acting. Kant has two tests for our maxims that are to be used in sequence, commonly called the "Contradiction in Conception" and the "Contradiction in the Will" tests. The Contradiction in Conception test determines whether a certain kind of contradiction infects simply conceiving of a certain kind of act; this test specifies strict duties or prohibitions. The Contradiction in the Will test determines whether maxims found permissible by the first test can also be consistently *willed*; it specifies broad or meritorious duties. In neither test is the relevant "contradiction" merely logical.

Kant first presents these tests in the first person, for any agent considering prospectively how rightly to act *now*. These tests can also be used retrospectively to evaluate past actions. They thus provide criteria of right (wrong, permissible) acts, and a basis for determining an agent's moral credit in view of whether the agent acted rightly *because* so acting is right. This is the topic of Kant's discussion of "moral worth" in the *Groundwork*, though it is often overlooked that Kant and Mill agree on this basic distinction between assessing the rightness of acts and assessing the moral virtue of the agent.[14]

The Contradiction in Conception test determines whether there is a contradiction between a maxim and its universalized counterpart. Kant's test relies upon a very specific kind of universalization, one often misunderstood or neglected by his critics. The Contradiction in Conception test uses the first two of the three descriptions comprised in a full maxim; it omits the description of the agent's ends, purposes or reasons. This test works with two partial maxims; schematically these are the schema of a maxim of action, "I will do x if (agent + circumstances) y", and its universalized counterpart maxim, "Everyone will do x, if (agent + circumstances) y". By assuming the fiction, expressed in Kant's formulae of the categorical imperative, that an agent's will is universally legislating, as if for the entirety of nature, an agent can confront two intentions: an intention expressed in his or her own (first-person, "subjective") maxim and an intention expressed in its universalized counterpart, constructed by an agent in his or her putative membership in a universal realm of ends, as legislating for all agents. As noted, willing rationally to do something requires willing sufficient means for success. Using means partially distinguishes willing from mere wishing; using sufficient means partially distinguishes rational from irrational willing. Empirical information about sufficient means is relevant to testing the acceptability of maxims, for the conditions under which we as rational agents must act and how we are able to act belongs to the information about our finite kind of rational agency.

A certain wrinkle must be accommodated to avoid obvious and trivial counter-examples. Strictly, this step is not expressly made by Kant, although the relevant kinds of reciprocity are central to his account of the rights of acquisition, use and possession.[15] The wrinkle arises in cases of optional actions involving coordination among various agents (see O'Neill 1975: 75–7; Herman 1993: 138–43). Consider the maxim, "When I reach a door at the same time as another, I shall always pass through second". If universalized, this maxim would have neither party willing to pass through the door first, resulting in an indefinite, comical standoff. Using Kant's universalization test twice over avoids such silly problems. The first step is to test the agent's maxim against its universalized counterpart; the second is to test the *negation* of the agent's maxim against *its* universalized counterpart.

In two cases, this paired use of Kant's Contradiction in Conception test finds for permissible (optional) maxims: if the intention expressed in one's maxim is consistent with that expressed in its universalized counterpart, *and* if the intention expressed by the negation of one's maxim is consistent with *its* universalized counterpart, then the original maxim is permissible. Likewise, if the intention expressed in one's maxim is *in*consistent with that expressed in its universalized counterpart, *and* if the intention expressed by the negation of one's maxim is *in*consistent with *its* universalized counterpart (this occurs in cases of optional coordination maxims), then the original maxim is permissible.

If instead the intention expressed in one's maxim is consistent with that expressed in its universalized counterpart, *but* the intention expressed by the negation of one's maxim is *in*consistent with *its* universalized counterpart, then the original maxim is obligatory.

If the intention expressed in one's maxim is *in*consistent with that expressed in its universalized counterpart, *but* the intention expressed by the negation of one's maxim is consistent with *its* universalized counterpart, then the original maxim is prohibited.

Mill charged that Kant's *Metaphysics of Morals* fails to demonstrate any contradiction, whether logical or physical, by using the criterion of the categorical imperative, instead succeeding only in demonstrating that the consequences of certain acts are such as none "would choose to incur" (Mill 1963–91: 10:207, cf. 249). His objections have been echoed repeatedly since. However, neither logical nor physical impossibility, nor actual consequences of these sorts pertain to Kant's tests. Kant's test is a test of *kinds* or *types* of acts, based on their intentions (as expressed in maxims), not directly of particular acts or their actual consequences. Expectable consequences of kinds of acts are important to Kant's universalization tests, although only under the expressly hypothetical *fiction* of *universal* action by all upon the same maxim to perform the same kind of act. A host of criticisms of Kant's universalization tests seeks to devise maxims that, though stated "universally", in fact only pertain to one agent (or perhaps very few agents). Such "tailored maxims", as they are often called, do not generate counter-examples to Kant's universalization tests because they fail to engage in the kind of universalization Kant's tests require. (Merely inserting a universal quantifier somewhere in an act description does not satisfy *Kant's* universality requirement.) In considering the preconditions of my own act and of the same kind of action committed by everyone, I consider what is involved in *willing* my act together with the same kind of act by all agents, for I *intend* these preconditions in intending to act rationally at all. In considering whether I can consistently will the "universalized counterpart" of my maxim, I am considering whether I can consistently will or intend the preconditions for the same kind of act by all – consistent, that is, with my intention to commit the act expressed in my maxim.

Kant's universalization tests determine whether performing a proposed act would involve treating any other person only as a means, and not at the same time also as a free rational agent. The key point of Kant's method for identifying and justifying moral duties and proscriptions is to show that sufficient justifying grounds for a proscribed act *cannot* be provided to all concerned (i.e. affected) parties. Conversely, sufficient justifying grounds for omitting positive moral obligations cannot be provided to all concerned parties. By contrast, morally legitimate kinds of action are ones for which sufficient justifying reasons *can* be given to all concerned parties, also on the occasion of one's own act. Kant's basic criterion of right action is *modal*. The modality of Kant's basic criterion is nicely formulated by O'Neill: "When we think that others *cannot* adopt, a fortiori *cannot* consent to, some principle we cannot offer them reasons for doing so" (O'Neill 2000b: 200; cf. Westphal 1997: §§4, 5). "Adopt" here means to be able to follow consistently the very same principle in thought or action on the same occasion as one proposes to act on that maxim. This is an issue of capacity and ability, not a psychological claim about what someone can or cannot bring him- or herself to believe or to do. The possibility of adopting a principle thus differs fundamentally from "accepting" one, in the senses of "believe", "endorse" or "agree to". Kant's tests rule out any maxim that cannot possibly be adopted by others on the same occasion on which one proposes to act on that maxim. The universality involved in Kant's tests includes the agent's own action, and extends (hypothetically) to all agents acting the same way at that time and over time. What we can or cannot adopt as a maxim is constrained by the form of behaviour or its guiding principle (maxim), by basic facts about our finite form of rational agency, by basic features of our worldly context of action and most centrally by whether maxims of the proposed action cannot be adopted by others because that action neglects or overrules their rational agency. Kant's Contradiction in Conception test directly rules out maxims of coercion, deception, fraud and exploitation. In principle, such maxims *preclude* offering to relevant others – most obviously to victims – reasons sufficient to justify *their* following those maxims (or the courses of action they guide) in thought or action, especially as the agent acts on his or her maxim (O'Neill 1989a: 81–125).[16] This is signalled by the lack of the very possibility of consent, which serves as a criterion of illegitimacy. Obviating the very possibility of consent on anyone's part obviates the very possibility of offering sufficient justifying reasons for one's action to all concerned parties. Any act that obviates others' possibility of acting upon sufficient justifying reasons cannot itself be justified, and so is morally impermissible.

Because any maxim's (or course of action's) passing his universalization tests requires that sufficient justifying reasons for that maxim or action *can* be given to *all* concerned parties for acting on that maxim on that very occasion, Kant's universalization tests embody at their core equal respect for all persons as free rational agents, that is, as agents who can determine what to think or to do by rationally assessing the merits of the case.[17] This links Kant's formulae of "the" categorical imperative; specifically it links his formulae of universal law (FUL) and of the law of nature (FLN) with his formulae of humanity as an end in itself (FH), of autonomy (FA) and of the realm of ends (FRE).[18] Ruling out maxims that fail this universalization test establishes the minimum necessary conditions for resolving the fundamental problems of conflict and social coordination that generated the central concern of modern natural law theories with establishing normative standards to govern public life despite deep disagreements among various groups about the substance of a good or pious life.[19]

Kant contrasts strict or perfect duties with broad or imperfect duties as duties of justice in contrast to duties of virtue, and as duties regarding overt actions in contrast to duties regarding maxims (*MMV* 6:388). In the *Groundwork* (4:440, 4:421n) Kant expressly reserves the proper division of duties to his then-projected *Metaphysics of Morals*. Duties of justice typically involve omissions of proscribed actions, which can be enforced because any violation of the proscription is wrong and, because it involves an overt outward action, at least in principle it can be prevented by external constraints. Behaviour rather than intention is primary in (most) duties of justice. In contrast, duties of virtue typically involve positive actions, for example to assist others; if such duties were unrestricted, fulfilling them would be self-destructive of the agent. Accordingly, Kant contends that duties of virtue are broad or imperfect because they require us to adopt a maxim to act on such duties while allowing latitude for agents to determine when and to what extent to fulfil them (cf. *MMV* 6:390).

Kant's distinction between outward and inner duties is, however, different from his distinction between strict duties of justice and broad duties of virtue. Two examples make this plain: both murder and lying involve not only outward action but also intention; killing someone is manslaughter, so doing with the intent to kill may count as murder, except in cases, for example, of legitimate self-defence. Likewise lying is distinct from both misspeaking and from stating falsehoods if one is ignorant about the point at issue, whereas lying involves the intent to deceive one's audience. The proscriptions upon murder and lying are strict duties, although they also involve the agent's character and intentions. Accordingly, Kant begins the *Doctrine of Virtue* by establishing the possibility and legitimacy of duties towards oneself, before analysing the character and grounds of the duty not to lie and of our obligations to assess and to improve our own moral character (*MMV* 6:417–20, 429–31, 437–42, 444–47, respectively).

Duties of virtue are based on the facts that human beings are purposive (we do not merely behave; we act in order to achieve various ends), mutually interdependent and sociable, and that we have only finite capacities and resources for obtaining our ends. Duties of virtue are determined by the "Contradiction in the Will" test. The Contradiction in Conception test considers two of the three components of any maxim, the descriptions of the act and of agent and circumstances. The Contradiction in the Will test considers the third component, the description of the objects, ends or purposes of the action. The relevant maxim schemata are the Schema of a Maxim of Ends:

I will do or omit what is needed to z.

Its universalized counterpart is:

Everyone will do or omit what is needed to z.

The Contradiction in the Will test determines whether purposes embodied in intentions previously tested by the Contradiction in Conception test are, as matters of virtue, proscribed, obligatory or permissible. In conjunction with the principle that willing an end involves willing sufficient means to achieve that end, these points generate several duties of wide obligation. These are shown to be duties because, if one has ends, then one wills sufficient means to those ends, which often include the cooperation of others.

Conclusion

Kant develops a theory of moral judgement, guided by his basic principles and universalization tests. He does so, in part, because using rules ineliminably requires judgement (*CpR* B 171–4); consequently, no moral algorithm, metric or fully determinate decision procedure is forthcoming.

Here, as elsewhere, we must attend to Mill's observation: "There is no difficulty in proving any ethical standard whatever to work ill, if we suppose universal idiocy to be conjoined with it" (1963–91: 10:224). The phrase "moral judgement" has regained prominence in contemporary anglophone moral philosophy, although often without due consideration of the logical forms of thought and judgement.[20] These considerations are often neglected by Kant's critics. Obviously, full understanding and appreciation of Kant's principles and methods require further development and examples of their use. Kant's examples, however, are often only illustrative and cannot be understood properly without appeal to Kant's systematic moral philosophy, as presented in his *Metaphysics of Morals*.[21] Indeed, Kant's mature moral philosophy presented there *is* the proper explication and exemplification of his principles of pure practical reason and their proper use in identifying and justifying our moral obligations.

Notes

1. Kant's principle is not without precedent. See Hruschka (1987) and Riley (1986).
2. Also pertinent are large sections of the Dialectic of the *Critique of Pure Reason*.
3. In this connection it is important to reject the common notion that empiricism has a monopoly on the empirical; much of Kant's decidedly anti-empiricist and anti-rationalist theory of empirical knowledge in the *Critique of Pure Reason* is sound (see, e.g., Westphal 2004, Bird 2006); there Kant first develops his sophisticated accounts of rational judgement and justification, which are extended and further refined in subsequent works. The important point here is that Kant's Critical philosophy is the first to provide a sound alternative to Hume's verification empiricism ("Hume's fork"), in part by recognizing that strict logical deduction suffices for justification only within formal or (as Kant thinks of them) analytic domains (*scientia*), so that rational justification in substantive (non-formal, non-analytic) domains, including morals, requires more than logical deduction, although it is not, for that reason, restricted to merely empirical justification (*historia*). These results stand independently of Kant's transcendental idealism and sharply distinguish his Critical philosophy from empiricism and rationalism, both historical and contemporary.
4. This point was the downfall of pre-Modern natural law theory, which presumed general agreement about the good, pious life; it recurs in Finnis (1980).
5. For further discussion, see Westphal (1997: §§4, 5; 2010c). Although neglected by Christian natural lawyers, the Crusades were another important earlier case in point.
6. The classic statement of the problem of *petitio principii* and the problems avoiding it in justificatory reasoning is the Pyrrhonian dilemma of the criterion (Sextus

Empiricus 1934: 2.4.20; cf. 1.14.116–17). The Pyrrhonian dilemma of the criterion is much more subtle and fundamental than Chisholm's "problem of the criterion", which has recently been discussed, for example, by Sinnott-Armstrong (2006: 15), who mistakes Chisholm's "problem" for the Pyrrhonian "dilemma". On the differences between these two problems, see Westphal (1998: §0).

7. That ethical egoists reject the autonomy of reason (in this sense) does not, of itself, show that Kant's project is ill conceived or mistaken; nor does the logical consistency of ethical egoism show that Kant's justification of a more robust moral philosophy fails. To suppose that it does is to presume the deductivist ideal of justification (*scientia*), to which Kant's critical philosophy develops a cogent alternative in the non-formal domains of knowledge and morals. (See also *MMV* 6:386 and Westphal 2010b.)

8. Kant's question should not be assimilated to Ross's (1930) question about which has priority, the right or the good, and to his consequent distinction between moral "teleology" and "deontology". Ross's distinction obscures rather than illuminates Kant's view (*PracR* 5:63–4; cf. Herman 1993: 208–40).

9. Both decision and execution belong to the will; merely conceiving of an action or merely wishing to act (that is omitting any means or efforts to achieve an end) specifies no concept of *will*. Kant's analysis raises concerns about trans-causal freedom and about his appeal to transcendental idealism to defend its possibility. However, Kant's analysis of the autonomy of rational judgement suffices to justify the freedom of rational judgement, in cognition and in morals, without appeal to transcendental idealism (see Westphal 2004: §61; 2010d), or to Kant's purported "Fact of Reason" (*PracR* 5:31–2, on which see Wolff 2009). Kant's analysis also justifies important cautions against the appeal by moral philosophers to belief–desire models of individual action (Westphal 2010b: n8).

10. Maxims are "subjective" in this sense because they are first person; they are not restricted to agent-centred reasons.

11. This passage from Kant's Introduction to *The Metaphysics of Morals*, §C, belongs neither to *Doctrine of Right* nor to *Doctrine of Virtue*, although it pertains to both. The Universal Principle of Right specifies strict duties, most of which belong to justice, some to ethics. (All references designated *MM* are to Kant's Preface or Introduction to the *Metaphysics of Morals*.)

12. It is common to complain that Kant is often technical without being precise; more germane is the observation that Kant often develops distinctions or terminology only to the extent required by his immediate discussion, although his terminological flexibility underscores that his issues and analyses are more important than his terminology.

13. This section is directly indebted to O'Neill (1975; 1989a).

14. See *G* 4:398–9, 401, 411; *PracR* 5:127–9, 147–8, 151, 159–60; cf. Mill (1963–91: 10:219–20n). For discussion of Kant's account of moral worth, see Herman (1993: 1–22).

15. See Westphal (1997; 2002); the latter summarizes (and in one regard improves) the previous detailed analysis.

16. A maxim such as one by which you and I agree now that "I shall exploit you at one time and you me at another" may satisfy minimal requirements on the generality of reasons for action (namely, that a reason for one agent can also be a reason for others), but such examples only underscore that such generality does not suffice for Kant's specific universality requirement, which expressly

rules out making an exception for oneself from an otherwise universal rule (*G* 4:424, 440n; *MMR* 6:321).

17. Those who think moral justification can dispense with this condition ought carefully to rethink the Pyrrhonian dilemma of the criterion. The embeddedness of equal respect for all persons as free rational agents within Kant's universalization tests shows that the fallacy in Kant's argument for the incommensurable worth or "dignity" of free rational agency (*G* 4:434–5) does not have the dire consequences for his moral system that "Kantian consequentialists" (Kummiskey 1996) seek to exploit, in part because a key premise in the consequentialist appropriation of Kant's theory is Ross's distinction between "deontology" and "teleology", which ill suits Kant's moral theory.

18. These formulae are identified, documented and designated by Paton (1947: 129–98). Kant's test raises issues about how to determine our responsibilities towards those who are mentally compromised. For discussion of patient autonomy and related matters, see Manson & O'Neill (2007).

19. For further discussion, see O'Neill (2003a), Westphal (2010c).

20. Like Kant, Sellars examines the logical forms of thought, the sense of which he finds, prior to Kant, in Ockham's disciples and in Leibniz, though it is "almost totally lacking in Descartes and his British successors" (1968: 35).

21. For a careful study of Kant's own examples of using the tests of the Categorical Imperative, see Schnoor (1989); a précis is provided in Westphal (1995: §2). Several of Kant's examples presuppose various social, political or legal norms, the identification and justification of which belong to his *Doctrine of Justice*. For a relevant example of Kant's Contradiction in Conception test, see Westphal (2002).

SEVEN

Moral obligation: rights, duties, virtues

Georg Mohr and Ulli F. H. Rühl

Terminology: morals – right – ethics

It is quite common to speak of "Kantian Ethics".[1] Kant himself uses this terminology in the Preface to the *Groundwork of the Metaphysics of Morals* (1785) where he distinguishes between physics as the science of the laws of nature and ethics as the science of the laws of freedom (G 4:387). In the *Groundwork*, following the ancient philosophical tradition, Kant uses the terms "ethics" and "doctrine of morals" [*Sittenlehre*] synonymously.

But in *The Metaphysics of Morals* (1797) Kant abandons the long-standing terminological equivalence between "ethics" and "morals". To prevent misunderstandings of his philosophical views, it is crucial to appreciate this shift in his terminology. At the beginning of the second part of the *Metaphysics of Morals*, Kant explains:

> In ancient times "ethics" signified the *doctrine of morals* (*philosophia moralis*) in general, which was also called the *doctrine of duties*. Later on it seemed better to reserve the name "ethics" for one part of moral philosophy, namely for the doctrine of those duties that do not come under external laws (it was thought appropriate to call this, in German, the *doctrine of virtue*). Accordingly, the system of the doctrine of duties in general is now divided into the system of the *doctrine of right (ius)*, which deals with duties that can be given by external laws, and the system of the *doctrine of virtue (Ethica)*, which treats of duties that cannot be so given; and this division may stand. (MM 6:379)

In the terminology of 1797, "morals" is a general term referring to all "duties" or "obligations", whether legal or ethical. The adjective "moral" is equally general, meaning "related to duty or obligation". Kant employs this term in a number of specific contexts: the "moral law" is a principle from which duties are derived; an action has "moral worth" if it is done "from duty"; man is a "moral being" endowed with freedom, capable of experiencing and responding to obligation (6:280–81); and "moral personality" is the "freedom of a rational being under moral laws" (6:223).

"Morals" – also referred to as "morality" or the "doctrine of morals" – are treated by the "System of Duties in General", which provides the philosophical justification and derivation of all universally valid duties. The "System of Duties in General" is differentiated into "Duties of Right" and "Duties of Virtue" (6:242, 375, 379). These philosophical distinctions are reflected in the organization of the *Metaphysics of Morals*, in which Kant systematically distinguishes between right and ethics. *The Metaphysics of Morals* consists of a doctrine of rights (*Metaphysical First Principles of the Doctrine of Right*) and a doctrine of virtue (*Metaphysical First Principles of the Doctrine of Virtue*). The "doctrine of right", which in contemporary terminology is called the "philosophy of law", provides the philosophical justification and derivation of universally valid legal duties. The "doctrine of virtue" is concerned with universally valid ethical duties.

The concept of duty, according to Kant, contains the concepts of necessitation and constraint (6:379). Kant treats the concept of duty as part of a theory about the autonomy of finite rational beings. Autonomy means self-legislation and self-determination. Its principle is the "Fundamental Law of Pure Practical Reason". According to this theory, acting from duty is acting from self-constraint and self-necessitation.

The concept of law does not appear in the *Groundwork of the Metaphysics of Morals* or in the *Critique of Practical Reason*. In his works before 1797, Kant does not explicitly address the relation between law and ethics, or the relation between the foundations of these two subdisciplines of practical philosophy. The crucial question is whether Kant intends the "moral law" – the "fundamental law of pure practical reason" (5:30) or categorical imperative – to be the supreme principle of ethics *and* law. If so, then the "universal principle of right" (6:230–31) is derived as an extension of, and hence is dependent upon, the moral law. Since the categorical imperative "as such only affirms what obligation is" (6:225), and duties of right as well as duties of virtue are both types of obligation, it would seem to follow that the law, as a system of duties of right, depends on the categorical imperative just as much as ethics, as a system of duties of virtue, does. Furthermore, there seems to be explicit textual evidence for this interpretation:

> [W]e know our own freedom (from which all moral laws, and so all rights as well as duties proceed) only through the *moral imperative*, which is a proposition commending duty, from which the capacity for putting others under obligation, that is, the concept of right, can afterwards be explicated.   (6:239)

However, as recent research on this issue shows, even the *Metaphysics of Morals* does not provide an unequivocal answer to this question.[2]

Perfect and imperfect duties

Kant does not introduce the right–ethics division in the *Groundwork* or the *Critique of Practical Reason*, even though he might have been expected to do so, since those works include illustrations of violations – the false promise (*G* 4:422) and the deposit (*PracR* 5:27) – that concern duties of right.

However, the division between enforceable law (right) and personal virtue (ethics) was already an established topic within practical philosophy in the period of rationalism and the Enlightenment. It was traditional to distinguish between duties that are enforced by external constraint, and duties where this is not the case. It is instinctively plausible, for example, that the fulfilment of a contractual obligation can be coercively enforced, whereas an ethical duty to be charitable cannot. Duties that correspond to a coercive right, as in the case of contracts, are referred to in Kant's terminology as "perfect duties". If there is no right corresponding to a duty, as in the case of charity, Kant calls this an "imperfect duty".

Kant's distinction between enforceable perfect duties and unenforceable imperfect duties may have *prima facie* plausibility, but a systematic moral philosophy must provide criteria to justify this intuitive classification. The specification of these criteria is of crucial importance for the whole system of the *Metaphysics of Morals*. For these criteria not only determine the extent to which a single human being can put other people under obligation within the state of nature, and thus establish basic individual rights, but also set limits to the state's legitimate interference with individuals after the transition from the state of nature to a civil condition.

But Kant does not immediately provide the criteria that distinguish between enforceable duties of right and unenforceable duties of virtue. First, he introduces a number of conceptual distinctions. He distinguishes not only between perfect and imperfect duties, but also between duties to others and duties to oneself. The division of duties within the *Doctrine of Virtue* (MM 6:240) is based on this pair of distinctions.

Kant changes his definition of "perfect" and "imperfect duties" in the transition from the *Groundwork* to the *Metaphysics of Morals*. Kant originally assumed, somewhat arbitrarily and with reservations, that perfect duties were characterized by allowing no exception in the interests of inclination (*G* 4:421n). This would imply that imperfect duties, in contrast, must allow exceptions in the interest of inclination. But this implication seems to be incompatible with Kantian moral philosophy. In the *Metaphysics of Morals*, Kant rejects this distinction, and instead characterizes perfect duties as "narrow" and imperfect duties as "wide" (*MM* 6:390). Narrow duties define precisely the action that must be performed, whereas wide duties leave the agent latitude for complying with the law in a variety of ways. For example, the duty of beneficence specifies neither who would have to donate to whom, nor how high a given donation should be. Kant takes into account that human resources to help others are subject to real constraints, and hence that conflicts between competing duties are possible. Kant mentions as examples the conflict between "love of one's neighbour in general" and "love of one's parents" (6:390), and the conflict between one's own happiness and the happiness of others (6:393). In these cases individuals have the liberty to decide how to fulfil their obligations.

Juridical and ethical laws

The *Metaphysics of Morals* also differentiates between "juridical" and "ethical laws" (6:214). These are subcategories of moral laws (laws of freedom) that Kant contrasts to laws of nature. The division between juridical and ethical laws is introduced alongside a number of other important terminological distinctions.

The distinction between *law* and *incentive* is fundamental (6:218). All lawgiving consists of two elements: (1) a law, which represents the objective ("theoretical") cognition of the duty's content; (2) an incentive, which provides the subjective ("practical") determining ground to act in conformity with the duty. Juridical and ethical laws are distinguished in virtue of having different types of incentive: "That lawgiving which makes an action a duty and also makes this duty the incentive is *ethical*. But that lawgiving which does not include the incentive of duty in the law and so admits an incentive other than the idea of duty itself is *juridical*" (6:219). Since ethical lawgiving has the "idea of duty" as its incentive, it can only be based on self-necessitation and self-constraint; such lawgiving must be internal. Juridical lawgiving permits other incentives, including "external constraint" (6:220). Kant thus writes: "Ethical lawgiving (even if the duties might be external) is that which *cannot* be external; juridical lawgiving is that which can also be external" (*ibid*.). Ethical lawgiving *cannot* be external because it makes "internal actions duties" (6:219). Internal actions include the adoption of motives ("incentives") and aims. The performance of such internal actions, including acting out of respect for the law, is not externally enforceable. In contrast, obeying juridical law requires merely the performance of "external actions" (6:214), which can be observed and enforced.

Ethical lawgiving does require, like juridical lawgiving, that the agent perform an external action. But in contrast to juridical lawgiving it requires additionally that the idea of the duty be the incentive to act in conformity with the law. Ethical lawgiving is thus more ambitious than juridical lawgiving, since not only must the duty be fulfilled by means of an external action in conformity with it, but also the idea of the duty itself must be the incentive to perform the action. The morality of an action consists in meeting both of these conditions (6:219). According to Kant, an action in conformity with duty has "moral value" only if the sufficient motive of the action is respect for duty itself, rather than the desire to earn a reward or enhance one's reputation. For example: helping a person in time of need has moral value only if it is performed out of respect for the duty to help. Although helping a person for other reasons is still beneficial, such action has no moral value.

Juridical lawgiving is concerned only with the external performance of the given action, while the motive is irrelevant. It is not important *why* a legal duty is fulfilled, only *that* it is fulfilled. The conformity of an action with juridical duty is called *legality* (*ibid*.). Since juridical lawgiving should be externally enforceable, it can only command the performance of external actions "irrespective of the incentive" (*ibid*.).

The fulfilment of duties of right also has an ethical aspect, even though juridical lawgiving cannot command that a person be virtuous. Kant illustrates this point with the example of a contractual obligation (6:219). Ethics commands that a contractual duty must be fulfilled, even in circumstances when this duty of right cannot be externally enforced (e.g. because the creditor has no proof of the transaction). Fulfilling a legal duty is itself not commendable, but it is virtuous when a person performs the obligation out of pure respect for the idea of the duty, while knowing that he could not be coerced to do so (6:221).

For this reason, one has to distinguish within the system of the *Metaphysics of Morals* between the universal duty of virtue in the singular, which applies to the performance of all obligations, and particular duties of virtue in the plural, which are the specifically ethical obligations treated in the *Doctrine of Virtue*. The general obligation to be virtuous, even in the performance of duties of right, consists of the "universal ethical command: 'act in conformity with duty *from* duty'" (6:391). This ethical obligation to act out of respect for the law applies to all particular duties and constitutes a universal duty to be virtuous.

Despite all this terminological clarification, it remains unclear exactly how duties of right are different from duties of virtue. At first it seemed as if duties of right were addressed to external actions, while duties of virtue were addressed to internal actions. But this proved not to be the case, since duties of virtue always command the performance of external as well as internal actions. For example, to fulfil the duty of beneficence it is not enough merely to wish to help others (one must actually help). But if the external action does not distinguish duties of right from duties of virtue, then what is the distinguishing feature?

Ethics as the system of the ends

Not until the *Doctrine of Virtue* does Kant finally emphasize that the fundamental distinction between right and ethics is that right is based on a formal principle and ethics is based on a material principle.[3] For ethics the "concept of an *end that is in itself a duty*" is fundamental: "ethics can also be defined as the system of the *ends* of pure practical reason" (6:381). By contrast, as Kant states within the *Doctrine of Virtue*, the doctrine of right deals with discretionary ends. Depending on their inclinations or interests, people set themselves discretionary ends and the duty of right, as expressed in the general principle of right (6:230, §C), serves as a criterion to determine whether the chosen ends are acceptable:

> The doctrine of right dealt only with the *formal* condition of outer freedom (the consistency of outer freedom with itself if its maxims were made universal law), that is, with *right*. But ethics goes beyond this and provides a *matter* (an object of free choice), an *end* of pure reason which it represents as an end that is also objectively necessary, that is, an end that, as far as human beings are concerned, it is a duty to have.   (6:380)

Thus Kant distinguishes in the *Doctrine of Virtue* between right and ethics by means of the distinction between "form" and "matter". Ethics as a doctrine of virtue provides human beings with an *a priori* determination of moral ends. The subject matter of ethics is the ends one is obligated to adopt. Kant identifies precisely two overarching ends of pure practical reason: *one's own perfection* and *the happiness of others* (6:385). This material doctrine of ends serves as the basis for the particular duties of virtue that Kant considers in detail within the "Doctrine of the Elements of Ethics". Since ethics, in the sense of a doctrine of virtue, is based on "the concept of an end that is in itself a duty", it is now clear why Kant believes that ethical lawgiving *cannot* be external: "I can indeed be constrained by others to perform actions that are directed as means to an end, but I can never be constrained by others to *have an end*: only I myself can *make* something *my* end" (6:381). Setting oneself an end is an "internal act of the mind" (6: 239). Therefore it is impossible to coerce someone into setting himself an end; only the person himself can do so. The performance of the external action that realizes the end can be enforced, but adopting an end is in principle unenforceable.

The concept of right and the universal principle of right

In the *Metaphysics of Morals* Kant develops a philosophical doctrine of right from principles of pure reason, which he clearly distinguishes from jurisprudence as a science of historically and geographically contingent positive law (6:229, §A). The philosophical doctrine of right is concerned only with the elements and structural principles that are conceptually necessary to constitute a legal system. Kant's doctrine of right is *a priori*, and thus a species of metaphysics, claiming to provide knowledge from concepts alone. Jurisprudence as mere empirical legal expertise can refer only to what happens to be lawful in a certain place at a certain time. A metaphysical doctrine of right must determine "what the universal criterion is by which one could recognize right as well as wrong" (6:229).

The preceding discussion of the distinction between right and ethics has revealed only that right is concerned with external actions. The setting of ends is an internal action that is excluded from right. Nonetheless, this point does not yet definitively exclude ethical obligations from the purview of the law, since the external aspect of an action commanded by virtue can definitely be enforced. For example, although nobody could be forced to set the perfection of his own body and soul as an end, it is possible to make exercise, nutrition or education compulsory.

In the "Introduction to the Doctrine of Right" (6:229ff.) Kant presents the rational concept of right and the universal principle of right (UPR). It is the task of the concept of right to distinguish from among the totality of imaginable duties the actual duties of right. Additionally, the concept of right must determine the extent to which one person can impose an obligation upon another person. The UPR is supposed to provide the rational criterion by which one could recognize right and wrong. Kant expresses the concept and the principle of right as follows:

1. Concept of Right: "Right is ... the sum of the conditions under which the choice [*Willkür*] of one can be united with the choice of another in accordance with a universal law of freedom" (6:230, §B).
2. Universal Principle of Right: "Any action is *right* if it can coexist with everyone's freedom in accordance with a universal law, or if on its maxim the freedom of choice of each can coexist with everyone's freedom in accordance with a universal law" (6:230, §C).

The concept of choice can be understood in the sense of freedom of action. Kant assumes in the *Doctrine of Right* that human beings can set themselves discretionary empirical ends and realize them through external actions: "What end anyone wants to set for his action is left to his free choice" (6:382). It is the task of law to adjust the freedom of action so that the choices of many people are mutually compatible. By right the law should address only those actions that encroach upon the freedom and action of other people. Right has to do "only with the external and indeed practical relation of one person to another, insofar as their actions, as deeds, can have (direct or indirect) influence on each other" (6:230). The concept of right hence picks out of the totality of imaginable duties those duties that we have *towards others*. Only duties to others can be duties of right. All duties towards self – with a single exception: the right of humanity in our own person (6:236) – are duties of virtue or ethics, and as such are excluded from legal enforcement.

Not all duties towards others are duties of right, however. Some duties towards others are duties of virtue. The duties of right towards others thus need to be distinguished from the duties of virtue towards others. Kant accomplishes this by pointing out that the concept of right does not refer to "the mere *wish* (hence also to the mere need) of the other ... [but] to the other's *choice*" (6:230). It is ethics, not law, that commands one to adopt the happiness of another as an end. To foster the happiness of another, one must know, acknowledge and fulfil the other person's empirical wishes. So within the doctrine of virtue the empirical wishes of others are a source of obligation. But this is not the case within the doctrine of right. Duties of virtue are oriented towards "the end of human beings", whereas legal duties are oriented towards "the right of human beings" (6:240). This makes clear that right does not take the wishes of others into account. The law concerns itself only with explicitly executed declarations of intention; whatever the parties were imagining, hoping or wishing for is legally irrelevant. Kant illustrates this principle of civil law by giving an example concerning a transaction: "it is not asked, for example, whether someone who buys goods from me for his own commercial use will gain by the transaction or not" (6:230). Only the external action is legally relevant, which in the case of the transaction consists in the executed declaration of intent. The motives and purposes of the parties to the transaction are rightfully excluded from the scope of the law.

Right and authorization to use coercion

The transition from self-obligation to the enforcement of duties by means of coercion is the central problem of Kantian legal philosophy. Kant asserts the legitimacy of such coercion in two short theses: "Right is connected with an authorization to use coercion" (6:231). And, even more strongly, "Right and authorization to use coercion ... mean one and the same thing" (6:232).

Kant's justification of this analytic connection of right and the authorization to use coercion is abstract and logically formal: hindrance of an action that is in conformity with the UPR is wrong by definition. Therefore elimination of the unlawful hindrance is necessary to restore a state in conformity with right. Coercion and hindrance are logically related as the negation of the negation; they are connected "by the principle of contradiction" (6:231). Kant summarizes this view in a single sentence in the introduction to his *Doctrine of Virtue*: "The supreme principle of right is therefore an analytic proposition" (6:396).

Kant's thesis concerning the analyticity of right and the authorization to use coercion has to be explained and specified in several ways (see Kaufmann 1997; Guyer 2002: 48–54; Willaschek 2009). Analytic judgements are those in which the predicate is implicitly contained in the subject (*CpR* B 10). The analyticity of a sentence can be tested by negation of the predicate. If such negation results in a contradiction, then the original judgement is analytic. If Kant's thesis concerning the analyticity of the connection between right and the authorization to use coercion were true, then it should pass this test. It is quite obvious, however, that the sentence "there is right without the authorization to use coercion" does not contain a contradiction (Kaufmann 1997: 73). Right without the authorization to use coercion is not a self-contradictory concept like "married bachelor". In fact, Kant himself recognizes a type of "right without coercion" that he calls the sphere of equity (6:234). He reconciles this by distinguishing between right in a narrow or strict sense and a right in a wider or loose sense: "An authorization to use coercion is connected with any right in the *narrow* sense" (6:233).

Strict right

"A strict right can also be represented as the possibility of a fully reciprocal use of coercion that is consistent with everyone's freedom in accordance with universal laws" (6:232). Here Kant develops a rational test for legitimate coercion. Coercion is legitimate only if one can conceive it to be (1) a fully reciprocal coercion that is (2) consistent with everyone's freedom in accordance with universal laws. The criterion for conceivability is the UPR: coercion is "conceivable" only if it eliminates hindrances to the free choice of rightful actions.

The concept of strict right is an idealization. Kant provides another example of such a conceptual idealization in the *Groundwork*: action motivated purely by duty, in contrast to action that is merely in conformity with duty. Whether there has ever existed a truly pure motive – *pure* because no other (pathological) motivation is mingled with it – is a question that even Kant judges sceptically (6:447). Action done purely from respect for duty is an idealization. One could call it a *perfectly internal* ethics. A radical thinker might then ask himself what would be the conceptual opposite of a purely and perfectly internal ethics. It should be a purely and perfectly *external* right. Kant conducts this thought experiment, conceiving of a purely external right in §E of the *Doctrine of Right*:

> Strict right, namely that which is not mingled with anything ethical, requires only external grounds for determining choice; for only then is it pure and not mixed with any precepts of virtue. Only a completely external right can therefore be called *strict* (right in the narrow sense). (6:232)

Strict right depends upon coercion, which seems at first to be incompatible with freedom, and so to be incompatible with right itself. But

Kant's thought experiment resolves this apparent paradox. Coercion can be rightful, but only when it is employed to overcome unlawful hindrances to the use of freedom. If this condition is met, then a system of purely external right, within which duties of right are enforced by coercion, is conceivable in Kant's sense.

Intelligible possession

The key concept in Kant's legal philosophy is that of *intelligible possession*, which is established in §§1–7 of the account of "Private Right" in the *Metaphysics of Morals*. A methodologically strict deduction of the concept of intelligible possession is carried out in the Exposition (§4), Definition (§5) and Deduction (§6). Kant defines the concept by stating, "a right is already an intellectual possession of an object" (6:249).

It is a widespread assumption that *property*, rather than intelligible possession, should be the concept at the centre of Kantian legal philosophy. If this were the case, then "Private Right" should be devoted to establishing the concept of property. But the assumption is incorrect.[4] Kant's legal philosophy is developed *a priori* from the fundamental concept of "having a right", which immediately involves intelligible possession. Private property and civil society are derivative subcategories of these more fundamental concepts.

Metaphysical philosophy of law must proceed by means of cognition from rational concepts alone. Kant begins in §§1–7 of "Private Right" with the most elementary distinction between the rational concepts of *mine* and *yours*. David Hume had already emphasized the need to clarify the ordinary talk of mine and yours: "Why this must be mine and that yours; since uninstructed nature surely never made any such distinction?" (1973: 195). In sensual perception, external objects are spatially (and chronologically) located in relation to persons, either closer or further away. Sensual perception does not reveal whether an external object is mine or yours. From the perspective of empirical science, mine and yours do not exist. Mine and yours are classifications that belong only to our thinking, rational concepts that exist only in the intelligible world. Nonetheless, mine and yours have practical reality for us.

In §1 Kant develops the fundamental distinction between mine and yours in three steps: mine/yours – having – possession. The relationship between these steps can be clarified by posing and answering a series of three questions: (1) What does it mean that an external object is *mine* (or *yours*)? It means that I *have* that object. (2) What does it mean that

I *have* an external object? It means that I *possess* it: "The subjective condition of any possible use is *possession*" (6:245). (3) What does it mean that I *possess* an external object? The crucial insight is that the concept of *possession* has two meanings: *physical possession* and *intelligible possession*. By physical (empirical) possession Kant means the actual power over an object. One is in actual power over something when holding it in one's hand, sitting on it, or being able to defend it by use of physical force. Physical possession can be perceived through the senses. In contrast, merely intelligible or rightful possession is imperceptible.[5] It is possession without direct physical control of the object. Kant explains: "something *external* would be mine only if I may assume that I could be wronged by another's use of a thing even *though I am not in possession of it*" (*ibid.*).

What can it actually mean to prove the practical reality of the rational concept of intelligible possession? Practical philosophy is concerned with the moral reasons for action. Subjective moral reasons Kant calls *maxims*; objective moral reasons are called *laws*. The objective moral reasons resulting from practical laws are called *duties*. The rational concept of intelligible possession has practical reality when it corresponds to a duty. Kant establishes such a duty in §2: the right to possession corresponds to the obligation of other people to refrain from using whatever is possessed. The permissive law of practical reason allows each person "to put all others under an obligation" (6:247) to refrain from using his or her possessions.

Kant argues for the permissive law of practical reason by transforming the concepts of physical possession and intelligible possession into two maxims, which he tests against the principle of right (6:246).[6] The "realist" maxim that makes ownership contingent upon physical possession proves to be contrary to right, because it would result in useful objects becoming ownerless whenever their owners lose the actual power of dominion. Consequently, the limitation of rightful possession to physical possession would be, in Kant's view, "a contradiction of outer freedom with itself" (*ibid.*). Rightful possession must therefore include intelligible possession, and thus the "Postulate of Practical Reason with Regard to Rights" leads from the test of maxims to the permissive law and the obligation to refrain from using the possessions of others (*ibid.*).

Kant comments on his method in §7 (6:253–5). Because he undertakes a purely rational deduction of the concept of right, the resulting rights have a universal validity that obtains even in the state of nature. But in the absence of a civil constitution, the application and enforcement of rights is only provisional. The transition from the state of nature to civil society guarantees and secures the rights that reason has already validated:

> Any guarantee, then, already presupposes what belongs to someone (to whom it secures it). Prior to a civil constitution ... external objects that are mine or yours must therefore be assumed to be possible, and with them a right to constrain everyone with whom we could have any dealings to enter with us into a constitution in which external objects can be secured as mine or yours.
>
> (6:256; see also 6.312)

The argument for the rational necessity to recognize and respect the right to intelligible possession thus leads ultimately to a duty to enter into a civil constitution. This duty even generates an authorization "to constrain everyone ... to enter with us into a constitution" (6:256). The idea of the social contract thus serves as the measure of the legitimacy of the state, although Kant regards actually signing such a contract to be superfluous (6:315).

Legal punishment

Kant's legal philosophy, as one part of the *Metaphysics of Morals*, tries to develop universal and necessary criteria that provide *a priori* justification of legitimate principles of right. Kant thus seeks to demonstrate that there is a non-contingent measure of just legal punishment that is independent of empirical considerations. This is possible to the extent that institutions of right and their principles can be derived as practical applications of the "fundamental law of pure practical reason" (5:30). According to Kant, the right to punish can be established in this way. The elements of Kant's argument for this claim are found in various parts of the Doctrine of Right. The most important sections are §§D–E of the Introduction, which treat the analytic connection between right and the authorization to use coercion and the end of the right of a state (the first part of the public right), and §49 "General Remark E: On the Right to Punish and to Grant Clemency", in which the purpose and justification of punishment and the measure of the sentence are defined (6:331–7, §49 E), as well as the Appendix in the fifth part, with further discussions of the the concept of the right to punish (5:362–3, Appendix).

Kant considers punishment to be the necessary correlate of any violation of a practical law. The concepts of "transgression" and "deserving punishment" are "immediately connected" with one another (11:398,

Kant's letter to J. B. Eberhard, 21 December 1792). "[I]n the idea of our practical reason … the transgression of a moral law" is "accompanied" by "its *deserving punishment*" (5:37). In this context, "moral" ("*sittlich*") signifies the general concept that encompasses the more specific "juridical" and "ethical" norms that the *Metaphysics of Morals* addresses, respectively, in the *Doctrine of Right* and the *Doctrine of Virtue*.

Among the controversies concerning the theory of punishment, two questions are traditionally of central interest: what is the *purpose* that legitimates punishment as an institution? And, what is the appropriate *measure* of the sentence? In relation to these questions, the theory of retribution and the theory of prevention have competed against each other since classical antiquity. The theory of prevention emphasizes deterrence and reform. Theories of prevention use utilitarian arguments to legitimate punishment by referring to the (presumed) benefit to society or the criminal. According to such theories, the primary benefit of punishment is that its threat diminishes future violations of the law.

Kant argues directly against utilitarian theories of prevention:

> *Punishment by a court (poena forensis)* … can never be inflicted merely as a means to promote some other good for the criminal himself or for civil society. It must always be inflicted upon him only *because he has committed a crime.* For a human being can never be treated merely as a means to the purposes of another or be put among the objects of rights to things: his innate personality protects him from this, even though he can be condemned to lose his civil personality. He must previously have been found *punishable* before any thought can be given to drawing from his punishment something of use for himself or his fellow citizens. The law of punishment is a categorical imperative.   (6:331ff.)

Kant's primary criticism of utilitarian theories of punishment is that they violate the "innate personality" of human beings. According to the third formulation of the categorical imperative in the *Groundwork*, it is an unconditional duty to "use humanity as much in your own person as in the person of every other, always at the same time as end and never merely as means" (4:429). The punishment of a crime may sometimes result, legitimately according to Kant, in the loss of "civil personality" (citizenship), but the personality or human dignity that every person has as a rational being "by nature", which is "innate" to him, is unalienable (6:331ff.). Human dignity has to be respected and protected by public institutions. No law that reduces human beings to mere objects or things is legitimate. Penal law thus has to "take into account respect for humanity in the person of the wrongdoer" (6:362ff.). Although Kant describes the relation between the government and its citizens as that of a "ruler" and its "subjects", this does not affect the "innate personality" that every human being has by virtue of his humanity. It may not be touched even by the state. Therefore legal punishment cannot be justified by referring to its hypothetical pragmatic consequences. The legitimation of punishment and the criteria of justice have to lie within the normatively relevant characteristics of the criminal deed itself. According to Kant, the law of punishment is a *categorical* imperative.

Only under this normative condition can the *justice* of a penalty be guaranteed, according to Kant. The justification of punishment has to be that the criminal "committed the crime". The "guilt" of the criminal is the *conditio sine qua non* of being subject to punishment. The prospective "usefulness" of the preventive effects of punishment may be taken into account as a secondary factor. But utility can neither legitimate the practice of punishment, nor provide necessary and sufficient criteria for appropriate sentencing. The primary factor in the justification and application of punishment must be retrospective retribution, and thus Kant advocates a retributive theory.

Kant argues accordingly when considering how to determine the just *measure* of punishment. The gravity of the deed provides the measure of the penalty:

> What kind and what amount of punishment is it that public justice makes its principle and measure? None other than the principle of equality (in the position of the needle on the scale of justice), to incline no more to one side than to the other. Accordingly, whatever undeserved evil you inflict upon another within the people, that you inflict upon yourself. If you insult him, you insult yourself; if you steal from him, you steal from yourself; if you strike him, you strike yourself; if you kill him, you kill yourself. But only the *law of retribution (ius talionis)* – it being understood, of course, that this is applied by a court (not by your private judgement) – can specify definitely the quality and the quantity of punishment; all other principles are fluctuating and unsuited for a sentence of pure and strict justice because extraneous considerations are mixed into them. (6: 332)

While retribution as a general criterion for the legitimation of punishment can intuitively be related to the principle of guilt (which is still valid in contemporary German law), the *talion* principle for measuring punishment raises considerable questions. What can and should be meant by "equality" of deed and punishment? Would the consequence inevitably be "an eye for an eye, a tooth for a tooth", requiring us finally to "imagine the miscreant as one-eyed or toothless" (Hegel [1820] 1991: §101A, 128)? Kant in fact demands the death penalty for murder (6:333), castration for "rape" and "pederasty", and the "permanent exclusion from civil society" for "bestiality" (6:363). For a modern legal system this conception of retaliation is inappropriate. Kant himself seems to admit that it is not crucial (and is sometimes impossible) to punish the criminal to the exact "letter" of the law. The important thing is that whatever is "done to him" is equal to what he has done to others, at least "in terms of [the penal law's] spirit" (*ibid.*).

The commensurability of deed and punishment remains an essential topic in contemporary penal theory. Fichte and Hegel made an effort to "rationally" interpret the *talion* principle, which they thought inadmissible in its Kantian version, and tried to correct its deficiencies. Within more recent Kant interpretations attention has been increasingly called to the possibility of unifying the various aspects of the Kantian theory of punishment. Such interpretations aspire to articulate the connections between Kant's arguments related to the appropriate roles of retribution and prevention (see e.g. Byrd 1989; Hill 1997; Merle 2000).

Notes

1. The authors of this chapter would like to thank Amelie Stuart for assisting with the translation of their text from German into English.
2. Recent papers, defending opposing readings, are Seel (2009) (arguing for the dependence thesis) and Willaschek (2009) (defending the independence thesis). Further important contributions on this issue are Gregor (1963, 1993a, 1993b), Guyer (2002), Wood (2002), Ripstein (2009).
3. In this chapter we concentrate on Kant's philosophy of law in the *Doctrine of Right* and its relation to his ethics in the *Doctrine of Virtue*. Important books on the foundations and systematic elaboration of Kant's philosophy of law are Gregor (1963), Murphy (1970) and Mulholland (1990). More detailed analyses of Kant's ethics as developed in the *Doctrine of Virtue* in *The Metaphysics of Morals* can be found in Guyer (2005) and Betzler (2008).
4. See Kuehn: "In the first chapter Kant tries to explain and justify the legal concept of ownership ... Kant's question is, how is ownership possible in the first place? Or, what are the conditions that make ownership possible" (2001: 397). For more specialized scholarship on the issue, see Gregor (1988).
5. Kant also uses the concept pairs "ideal/real" and "virtual/actual" to distinguish between intelligible and physical possession (23: 211–12).
6. Concerning the "permissive law", see Hruschka (2004) and Flikschuh (2000: ch. 4).

EIGHT

Political obligation: property, trade, peace

Katrin Flikschuh

Introduction

Current work on Kant's political thought tends to divide into two kinds. There is, first, the broader, longer-established, and more inter-disciplinary work on Kant's cosmopolitanism; its primary focus is on aspects of Kant's well-known essay, *Perpetual Peace*.[1] The second, more recently emergent and on the whole more narrowly philosophical type of research concentrates on Kant's mature work, the *Doctrine of Right*, published as Part I of the *Metaphysics of Morals* in 1797 but largely neglected, for a variety of reasons, until the 1980s (see e.g. Ludwig 1988; Flikschuh 2000; Ripstein 2009; Byrd & Hruschka 2010). In the English-speaking world, work on the *Doctrine of Right* did not get seriously under way much before Mary Gregor's publication in 1991 of the first complete translation. The *Doctrine of Right* is the less accessible of these two texts: its structure of argument is often obscure and its substantive concerns seem far less radical than those of the earlier proposal for laws of international peace.[2] Indeed, the *Doctrine of Right* returns us to themes familiar from the tradition of modern social-contract theory – themes to do with property rights, political obligation, state foundation and the constitutional division of powers. By contrast with the extended sections on "Private Right" and the first section of "Public Right", entitled the "Right of a State", later sections of "Public Right" – those dealing with international and cosmopolitan right respectively – receive rather cursory treatment. Kant acknowledges the imbalance: in the preface to the *Metaphysics of Morals* (of which the *Doctrine of Right* forms the first part) he admits that "towards the end of the book [he has] worked less thoroughly over certain sections than might be expected in comparison with the earlier ones" (*MM* 6: 209). Had the author of the *Doctrine of Right* simply lost interest in the radical ideas he defended in *Perpetual Peace*, or did his more systematic engagement with the philosophy of right lead him to become more circumspect about the possibility of justice beyond the limits of the bounded state?

What, if anything, binds together these two major texts of Kant's political philosophy? Why does Kant move from a seemingly uncompromising focus on the international domain, with sharp criticism of state warfare and state power in *Perpetual Peace*, to the *Doctrine of Right*'s no less decisive focus on individual rights claims and accompanying benign view of the state as necessary enforcer of these claims? How can the one work demand a curtailment of state power and the other insist upon the juridical authority of states? Little sustained work has been done on the relationship between these two aspects of Kant's political thinking: the plea for thoroughgoing reform of state behaviour internationally and the view of the state as necessary public enforcer of individuals' rights claims at the intrastate level. Nor is it possible to make much headway with this question within the constraints of a short introductory chapter. My reflections will be general and somewhat speculative: my overall view is that Kant's underlying cosmopolitan commitments had not changed by the time he came to write the *Doctrine of Right* (a process that in any case occupied him for the better part of three decades). While his mature work reflects a much more considered conception of political morality as distinct from ethics, including an acknowledgement of the indispensable function of the state as public agent, his account even of justice within the state would ultimately be unintelligible in the absence of his abiding cosmopolitan commitments.

Elsewhere I have considered the relationship between ethics and law (Flikschuh 2010a),[3] as well as the role of the state as public agent; here I want to take the opportunity to examine a typically Kantian idea: the idea of a "system of right". For the purposes of this chapter, my focus will be on what I call Kant's interdependence thesis, that is, his claim in the *Doctrine of Right* that the concept of public right in general "gives rise" to three forms of public right: the right of a state, the right of nations, and cosmopolitan right. In so far as Kant claims that all three of these "forms" derive from the same general concept of public right, he must be thinking of the intrastate, interstate and cosmopolitan domains as conceptually interdependent. Kant nonetheless also thinks of each particular form of public right as functionally distinct from its two sister forms. The system of right specifies a set of conceptually interdependent though functionally differentiated domains of public right where each domain stands in relation to the other two in such a way as to ensure that the system as a whole is self-sustaining. Kant's system of right is, in that sense, a good example of a non-foundationalist approach to political thinking.

In the next section I offer some preliminary remarks on Kant as a systematic thinker. Then I set out the general idea of a system of right. Following that, I consider the functional differentiation between the three forms of public right against the background of their common root in the concept of right in general, focusing on intrastate and cosmopolitan right in particular. I conclude with some comments on Kant's cosmopolitanism as a methodological commitment of political thinking – a commitment that sets his position apart, I shall suggest, from dominant current forms of cosmopolitan thought.

Kant's "architectonic"

That Kant is a highly systematic thinker is not contested. There is less agreement as to the virtue of a systematic approach to philosophical thinking. The objection has often been raised that Kant's "architectonic" frequently gets in the way of his substantive arguments (see e.g. Bennett 1966; Strawson 1966). Kant's philosophical system strikes many as a labyrinth of divisions and subdivisions within and across distinct works, all of which are seen as related to one another, directly or indirectly, in some more or less obscure way, such that no individual aspect of his work can be considered independently of all the others, rendering each individual part of only limited accessibility to anyone not conversant with the whole. The domain of practical reason cannot be specified before we have explored the limits of theoretical reason, yet having delimited both we must then search for the unifying principle that connects them. The practical philosophy itself is divided, eventually, into a *Doctrine of Virtue* and a *Doctrine of Right*. The two are said to be distinct yet complementary; then there is, additionally, the philosophy of religion, which, conceivably, stands to the two parts of the *Metaphysics of Morals* as the *Critique of Judgment* stands to the first and second critiques respectively.

There are plenty of divisions within the *Doctrine of Right* itself – we encounter these long before we come to the main sections of that text. Having introduced the distinction between virtue and right in the general Introduction to the *Metaphysics of Morals* (6:211–14) Kant offers a "systematic division" of juridical duties into "inner" and "outer" duties in the Introduction to the *Doctrine of Right* before distinguishing further between positive and natural law (6:240–42). The latter comprises "innate" and "acquired" rights respectively. Natural law further divides into private right [*Privatrecht*] and public right [*Öffentliches Recht*] – the latter is thus not to be confused with positive law.

Are Kant's systematizing tendencies helpful or are they a hindrance? As noted, the objection has often been made that Kant's philosophical architectonic falls victim to its own rigorism and associated futile search for philosophical completeness. Karl Ameriks has contested this assessment: systematic thinking is essential, according to Ameriks, for Kant's unavoidably open-ended style of philosophizing, which is driven by no singular conception of a final or ultimate truth (Ameriks 2000a: 37–80). Onora O'Neill makes a similar point: given Kant's anthropocentric turn, his only available starting point is our capacity to reason – Kant's systematizing endeavours constitute, in effect, an attempt at self-orientation in thinking (O'Neill 1992; see also O'Neill 2000a: 11–28). That said, neither Ameriks nor O'Neill read Kant's nonfoundationalism in the spirit of radical human self-emancipation. The claim is not that in shedding religious superstitions and philosophical dogmatisms we have become "masters of our own fate" (Dewey, quoted in Hare 2006: 75), or that in liberating ourselves from the morality of custom we have become "autonomous and supramoral" (Nietzsche, cited in Korsgaard 1997: 297). Both O'Neill and Ameriks emphasize the underlying modesty of Kant's anthropocentric turn, expressed most clearly in the critical philosophy's stated aims to "limit knowledge in order to make room for faith" (*CpR* B xxxi; Kant 1992).

The indispensability of faith – practical and metaphysical – is a corollary of Kant's insight into human beings' constitutive finitude; Kant's system-building tendencies are a reflection of his commitment to the view that for humans as finite rational beings there are no ultimately secure premises from which to begin or final truths at which to arrive. This, as Ameriks has noted, is the crucial difference between Kant's system and that of a number of his immediate followers, who sought to improve upon the system by leading it towards the new certainties of absolute idealism. Kant resolutely refused to follow their lead: Kantian systematic thinking is always necessarily open-ended and incomplete, ending more often than not in the frank acknowledgement of our complete lack of insight into final causes and ends.

How does the system of right as it is developed in the *Doctrine of Right* stand in relation to Kant's general systematizing endeavours? The *Doctrine of Right* is an often obscure late work whose underlying elegance is initially difficult to appreciate – not least if one's paradigmatic Kantian text is the *Groundwork of the Metaphysics of Morals*.

The *Doctrine of Right* lacks the immediate and intuitive appeal of the *Groundwork*. The latter begins from "popular" acknowledgement of the concept of duty in people's lives and actions; it only then moves into progressively more abstract and demanding analysis and vindication, retaining throughout a sense of the argument's proximity to agents' actual moral experience. The *Doctrine of Right* similarly begins with the general concept of right. However, it does so not from the perspective of our intuitive everyday understanding but enquires into it as an underexplored metaphysical concept that implicitly guides specialist, legal practice and discourse. Already, these less intuitive beginnings put the *Doctrine of Right* at a relative disadvantage.

The *Groundwork* has become something like the "gold standard" of Kantian practical theorizing – everything Kant ever wrote in the domain of practical philosophy tends to be assessed with reference to terms set out in the *Groundwork*. From this perspective the *Doctrine of Right* comes as a shock. The *Groundwork* emphasizes the purity of moral maxims; it values inner moral worth over actual action outcome; its most prized discovery is the idea of morality as self-legislation. The *Doctrine of Right* abstracts from agents' inner maxims; it prioritizes external conformity with principles of right over inner moral worth; it dismisses self-legislation as irrelevant – indeed as inappropriate to the political context where principles of right must necessarily be externally – that is, coercively – enforced. The *Doctrine of Right* appears to play havoc, in short, with some of Kant's most basic moral and philosophical commitments; many commentators continue for that reason to exclude Kant's political philosophy from his moral philosophy "proper".[4]

Understanding Kant as a systematic philosopher in the manner sketched can be helpful here. Contrary to a still-widespread view, the *Doctrine of Right* does not amount to the repudiation in the political context of everything Kant cherishes and defends in his ethical writings. The work should be thought of, on the contrary, as the attempt at a systematic extension of Kant's moral thinking: the external morality of right is developed contrastively with the internal morality of ethics. This is evident from the Introduction to the *Metaphysics of Morals*, which is common to both its parts – *Doctrine of Right* and *Doctrine of Virtue*. After a couple of opening paragraphs explaining the need for a metaphysics of morals and indicating the relation of its laws to the human will, Kant lists and defines a series of "preliminary concepts" (6:221) that he regards as guiding moral enquiry in general. Among these are the concepts of obligation, of law (the categorical imperative), of the person, of a deed – these all pertain equally to *Doctrine of Right* and *Doctrine of Virtue*. Indeed, only once he has set out these common concepts does Kant introduce the "division" of the *Metaphysics of Morals* into right and virtue, outer and inner morality. The "outer" morality of right is explicated by juxtaposition with the more familiar "inner" morality of virtue. The centrality of agents' maxims in relation to virtue is contrasted with the requirement of their actions' outward conformity with law in relation to right. There is no competition between *Doctrine of Right* and *Doctrine of Virtue*; nor is there a conflict or inconsistency: the one does not deny what the other affirms. The *Doctrine of Right* complements the *Doctrine of Virtue* – it is my claim that it is the open-endedness of Kant's systematic thinking in general that makes it possible for him to extend his practical philosophy from ethics to politics through the contrastive analysis and construction of the complementary notions of inner and outer.

The system of right

The Introduction to the *Doctrine of Right* offers a preliminary exposition of the moral concept of right as specifying a formal relation between persons with regard to their capacity for freedom of choice and action (6:230). Right pertains to the formal external relation between the power of choice (*Willkür*) of one person and that of another. In a further step Kant derives the universal principle of right from the general concept of right in conjunction with a universalizing rule:

> Any action is right if it can coexist with everyone's freedom in accordance with a universal law, or if on its maxim the freedom of choice of each can coexist with everyone's freedom in accordance with a universal law. (6:231)

This principle is reformulated into the universal law of right. The latter enjoins agents to "so act externally that the free use of your choice can coexist with the freedom of everyone in accordance with a universal law" (*ibid.*). Note that in contrast to the universal principle of right, the universal law of right omits all reference to agents' maxims: the universal law specifies "strict right" – right in the narrow sense, that is, externally enforceable right.

The external enforceability of right is a function of the equal status of the external freedom claims of each relative to those of all others. If any action is right that can coexist with the equal freedom of everyone else, my freedom is limited by the equal claims to freedom of everyone else. Whether or not my action is right does then not fall within the competence of my inner personal judgement – it is, rather, a judgement that only a person or authority is competent to make who or which is in a position to determine the validity of my freedom claim *relative to everyone else's equally valid freedom claims*. The elimination of reference to agents' maxims from the universal law of right thus signals the idea of an external law-giving in relation to that law. As a law of freedom, the universal law of right is a moral law that does "lay an obligation on me". Yet as a law of *external* freedom, this moral law "does not expect that I myself should limit my freedom" (6:231) in conformity with the law's conditions; the law simply affirms that my freedom *is* limited to the condition of its conformity in action with everyone else's equal freedom, and can therefore be so limited by the relevant authority independently of my will.[5]

Again, the coercive character of right is a function of its external enforceability. Right is coercive not because it serves as a sanction upon those who fail to conform to its demands of their own volition.[6] Right is coercive in the sense that the compatibility of the freedom claims of each with those of everyone else requires a restriction of the capacity for willing of each to the conditions of universal freedom. Right coercively restricts the power of choice of each for the sake of the equal power of choice of everyone else. It is in the context of Kant's explication of the necessarily coercive character of right that we get an intimation also of its systemic conception. In §E of the Introduction Kant likens the universal law of right to the law of the "equality of action and reaction" in physics:

> The law of a reciprocal coercion necessarily in accord with the freedom of everyone under the principle of universal freedom is, as it were, the construction of that concept, that is, the presentation of it in pure intuition *a priori*, by analogy with presenting the possibility of bodies moving freely under the law of the equality of action and reaction. (6:233)

This is a fascinating if obscure passage. Before proceeding, it may be useful to recap the summary exposition thus far: we began with the concept of right in general which, as a moral concept, pertains to the power of choice (external freedom) of one relative to that of another. We derived from this concept in conjunction with a universalizing rule first the universal principle of right and then the more narrow universal law of right. We diagnosed the essentially coercive because externally enforceable character of right: if the aim of right is to ensure equality of freedom of choice for everyone, the rightfulness of the action of each is not a matter of personal, inner judgement but must issue from a source capable of making such external judgements. The universal law of right is then coercive in the sense that it imposes a restriction upon the freedom of choice of each independently of the subjective will of each. Kant now appears to "map" this universal freedom relation in space. In the above quotation we have a reference not only to the law of the equality of action and reaction – Kant additionally invokes the idea of a mathematical construction of the universal law of right in analogy with a physical law. In physics, the law of equality of action and reaction places "bodies" that would otherwise "move freely" (i.e. arbitrarily) in a determinate relation with one another, thereby imposing a coordinate order among them. The universal law of right, as a moral law of "reciprocal coercion", achieves much the same among persons whose individual freedom claims would, absent such a law, come into conflict with one another. The mathematical construction of the universal law of right is a construction in pure intuition *a priori* – it is not a construction in empirical space. The construction maps the law of reciprocal coercion in (non-empirical) space, and does so "with mathematical exactitude" (6:233); Kant invokes the contrast between a straight line and an oblique line in mathematics:

> As opposed to the one that is oblique, straightness is that position of a line towards another intersection or touching it such that there can be only one line (the perpendicular) which does not incline more to one side than the other and which divides the space on both sides equally. Analogously to this, the doctrine of right wants to be sure that what belong to each has been determined (with mathematical exactitude). (*Ibid.*)

Kant adds that the same degree of exactitude cannot be expected in ethics, where greater leeway is given to individual moral judgement. In the domain of right, by contrast, where others' equal freedom claims are at stake, we must be sure to give each exactly what is theirs. The external (spatial) character of the morality of right and its exacting demands seem thus to imply one another: only where morality is external to the wills of those subject to its demands can we model moral relations in space, and must do so given the exacting demand of this domain of morality.

The analogy between the law of right and a law of physics on the one hand, and the further analogy between the construction of right and a mathematical construction on the other hand offer striking intimations, within the Introduction of the *Doctrine of Right*, of Kant's highly systematic procedure. By the end of the Introduction we have an overall conception of right as an external morality that places claimants in a determinate and systematic relation in space such that the legitimate freedom claims of no one exceed those of anyone else, enabling all to interact and coordinate their actions with one another much in the way in which physical bodies that would otherwise move about in space arbitrarily are brought into systematic interaction with one another under the law of equality of action and reaction.

When we turn to the first main section of the text proper, entitled "Private Right", matters become more complicated. The Introduction concluded with a 'division' of rights into innate and acquired rights (6:237). Innate right, which refers to the rights of each in their own person, is stated briefly only to be set aside (6:238); the remainder of the *Doctrine of Right* purports to concern itself with the category of acquired right exclusively – rights of persons in objects external to them, including certain types of relations with other persons. The connection between innate and acquired right is obscure, and the subject of scholarly puzzlement (cf. Ludwig 1988: 102–5). In particular, it is not clear whether, given Kant's derivation of political obligation from claims to acquired right, a state would even be needed to secure innate right alone. Possibly, innate right specifies the extent of each person's private entitlement to secure others' respect for their rights in their person; alternatively, innate right may be a necessary presupposition of acquired right such that the necessity of state entry in relation to the latter entails or implies the same necessity in relation to the former. I cannot here discuss the contested relation between the two types of right, although it is as well to point out that the relation is by no means clear.

Of principal interest to our current concern is the manner in which the discussion of acquired right in Section 1, "Private Right", returns to spatial imagery. In the Introduction, we saw Kant invoke the idea of mathematical space – pure intuition *a priori* – in order to construct the universal law of right. Space there was a formal condition of the construction of the general schema of rights relations. The problem of acquired right – the claims of persons to external possessions of their choice – seems to move us into empirical space. It is in the context of his justification of property rights as a *prima facie* valid type of external freedom claim that we find Kant's well-known statement concerning the earth's spherical surface:

> The spherical surface of the earth unites all the places on its surface; for if the earth were an unbounded plane, people would be so dispersed on it that they would not come into community with

one another, and community would then not be a necessary result
of their existence on the earth. (6:262)

The reference to an "unbounded plane" carries a certain resonance with
the earlier reference to space in general, that is, non-empirical space.
Granted: the idea of the earth as an unbounded plane is the idea of
empirical space unbounded; nonetheless, space in general – space as
necessary intuition *a priori* – is similarly unbounded. If we think of the
original construction of the law of right as proceeding in non-empirical,
unbounded space, the property argument introduces the curvature of
empirical space – space as circumscribed by the spherical surface of the
earth. The property argument maps the *a priori* construction of rights
relations, conceived by analogy with the law of the equality of action
and reaction, onto empirical space. If the original construction envis-
aged rights relations as, in principle, unbounded – as extending across
possible persons in space indefinitely – the mapping of the schema
of such a relation onto the earth's limited space introduces a further
determination: rights relations between persons are relations in limited
space. The earth is precisely not an unbounded plane such that persons
could disperse in order to avoid community with one another.

It is the bounded surface of the earth and the consequent unavoid-
ability of human coexistence that grounds the necessity of states as
guarantors and enforcers of everyone's equally valid claim to external
possessions. If the earth were unbounded, we could, in each claiming
this or that object of our choice as our own, avoid potential rights
conflicts simply by stepping out of each other's ways and choices and
dispersing across the plane. Under conditions of bounded space and
unavoidable coexistence, conflicts over external possessions are similarly unavoidable. Since what belongs to each by right cannot be a
matter of personal, inner judgement, an external authority is necessary
that has the relevant authority to pronounce on what belongs to each
relative to all others: this, for Kant, is the role of the state (cf. Flikschuh
2008; Ripstein 2009; Byrd & Hruschka 2010).

The state's essential function is to act as public authority – as guar-
antor and enforcer of external rights relations as a type of relation for
the adjudication of which an external authority is required. The state
fulfils the function of the general united will – the public will – which,
in contrast to the plurality of conflicting private wills, is authorized to
impose coercive universal law on everyone equally. Kant's characterization of the state as moral agent relates to his attribution to it of a
public, juridical, rights-pronouncing will. Given its status as (artificially
constructed) moral agent, the state is an entity capable of agency and

hence capable also of incurring obligations. Kant's view of states' obligation to enter into relations of international right with each other is intimately tied to his conception of states as a type of moral agent – and this conception is intimately linked in turn with his account of the state as agent of the public will. This brings us to the third and final passage I want to flag – what I call Kant's interdependence claim – which occurs at the transition from "Private Right" to "Public Right":

> Under the general concept of public right we are led to think not only of the right of a state but also of a *right of nations (ius gentium)*. Since the earth's surface is not unlimited but closed, the concepts of the right of a state and of a right of nations lead inevitably to the idea of a *right for all nations (ius gentium)* or *cosmopolitan right (ius cosmopoliticum)*. So if the principle of outer freedom limited by law is lacking in any of these three possible forms of rightful condition, the framework of all the others is unavoidably undermined and must finally collapse.
>
> (6:311)

Property and trade within the system of right

The passage from the *Doctrine of Right* with which I concluded the previous section confirms Kant's status as the most "thoroughgoing" cosmopolitan thinker even now. It enumerates the threefold division of right in general into state-based, interstate and suprastate rights relations. The passage occurs in what I described at the outset as the least accessible work of Kant's political philosophy; it is the shorter essay, *Perpetual Peace*, which is usually seen as grounding Kant's claim to being the "lead cosmopolitan" in modern political thinking. It is tempting to assume that the passage from the *Doctrine of Right* simply offers the clearest and most succinct summary statement of Kant's cosmopolitan position in general: while it happens to be located in the *Doctrine of Right*, the passage expresses a thought already familiar from *Perpetual Peace*. I do not believe this to be the case: far from either rescinding from or merely restating his earlier cosmopolitan commitments, the *Doctrine of Right* contains the most mature philosophical exposition and defence.

We saw that it is not until the *Metaphysics of Morals* that Kant develops a systematic distinction between the inner morality of virtue and the outer morality of right. It is not until the *Doctrine of Right*, therefore, that we are offered an exposition of the concept of right followed by the derivation of universal principle and universal law of right. Only in the late work are we given a defence of the coercive morality of right and only there does Kant attempt the systematic mapping of universal rights relations onto the earth's spherical surface. The above passage containing the threefold division of forms of public right could not have been contained in any of Kant's earlier political texts: the passage affirms that it is the general concept of public right that "gives rise to" the three "forms of rightful condition" – yet before the *Doctrine of Right* Kant did not possess a clearly formulated conception of right.

The concept of right in general pertains to the capacity for choice and action (external freedom) of each in relation to that of everyone else. In the pre-civil condition, each lays claim to external freedom, including freedom of choice over external objects, against everyone else. Under conditions of coexistence in limited space, rights conflicts result. Resolution of these conflicts – exact determination of what belongs to each – requires an external enforcement authority competent to pronounce universal coercive law in relation to everyone: "From private law in the state of nature proceeds the postulate of public law: In a situation of unavoidable contact with all others, you should leave this state [of lawless freedom] and move to a juridical state, that is, the state of distributive justice" (6:307). *Public* right is thus "the totality of statutes that need to be announced to the public in order to create a juridical state" (6:311). Kant's original expression is "juridical condition". The state represents a "juridical condition" – that is, a condition in which rights relations between persons are regulated by public laws. Since the emergence of the territorial state and concomitant rise of social-contract theory, juridical condition and territorially bounded statehood have tended to be treated as virtual synonyms. To be in a juridical condition just is to be in a territorially bounded state; there is, moreover, no juridical condition beyond the state. For modern social-contract theory, the problem of justice essentially terminates in the establishment of the state. Kant's position is unusual in that he conceives of the state as the quintessential expression of a juridical condition and yet does not think of the problem of justice as terminating in the establishment of the individual state. State entry is a necessary but not sufficient condition of justice.

If we recall the foregoing analysis, it is easy to see why this should be so. Kant's exposition of the concept of right in general departs from minimal presuppositions about human agency. No particular time or place is assumed, no special interests, or needs, or forms of interaction and cooperation with particular, proximate others are prioritized. The mapping of the schema of rights relations in pure intuition *a priori* cannot discriminate between this or that locality; when Kant does apply the general schema of rights relations to empirical space it would have been arbitrary of him to restrict the scope to anything less than the earth's spherical circumference. Significantly, if unexpectedly, Kant's well-known remark regarding the earth's spherical surface occurs in the context of his property argument – those very sections of the *Doctrine of Right* that are usually deemed especially intimately tied to the account of political obligation and hence to the establishment of the individual state. Kant nonetheless thinks even our obligation to enter into particular states as grounded in our unavoidable coexistence, with *all* others, on the earth's spherical surface. Coexistence on the earth's spherical surface is un-chosen: "nature or chance" assigns each a place on the earth quite "apart from [our] will" (6:262). It is from this original right to a place on the earth that the legitimate acquisition of external objects of one's choice is then derived, together with the obligation to enter into the rightful condition specified by statehood. Kant's account is complex and highly obscure in places; I cannot enter into detailed discussion here:[7] the important point is simply the cosmopolitan premise – the earth as shared surface – of a property argument that eventually leads to state establishment.

One might well ask: if Kant's property argument is grounded in the idea of "original possession in common" of the *earth*, why have distinct states at all? Would a more consistent Kantianism not have bypassed the establishment of states? Why not just one global state?[8] Recall my opening remarks regarding Kant's systematic thinking in general. Kant's thinking is non-foundationalist: the endeavour is not to discover ultimate truths but to orient thinking without assuming particular starting points and secure premises. The non-foundationalism of Kant's systematizing endeavours is exemplified in what I call the interdependence claim – the claim that all three forms of rightful condition are derivable from (and in turn vindicate) the general concept of public right together with the claim that none of them taken individually is self-sustaining. Only the system of right as a whole is self-sustaining – and yet a system is composed of several elements that mutually support one another while remaining distinguishable from each other. My preliminary answer to the question "Why states?" or "Why not just one global state?" is that the constraints of Kant's systematic thinking in effect disallow the idea of a single, unitary, global state as ultimate solution to the problem of right. A unitary global state is contrary to the idea of a system as an internally related yet functionally differentiated hence self-sustaining composite of distinct constitutive elements. A system of right requires a plurality of states as a distinct secondary type of agents that make possible, together with the plurality of individual agents, combinations of interdependent rights relations of a kind that render the system as a whole self-sustaining.

This is a large, insufficiently specified and insufficiently defended interpretive move: I cannot here set out and defend this reading in detail but can only launch it as a possible approach from the perspective of which to appreciate the underlying continuity of Kant's political thinking as one that acknowledges both the universal scope of right and the legitimate existence of a plurality of distinct (hence particular) states.[9] Within this general conception of the system of right as consisting of a threefold division of interdependent types of rights relations that together form a complex, self-sustaining whole, I want to conclude this section by elaborating in somewhat greater detail one particularly striking aspect of functional differentiation against a background of conceptual continuity. This concerns Kant's focus on property relations at the intrastate level and his corresponding focus on trade relations at the cosmopolitan level.

Kant's grounding in the first section of the *Doctrine of Right* of political obligation in the claim of each to external possession has received increased attention recently. The distinctiveness of Kant's property argument, especially when contrasted with Locke's historically influential alternative account, is now widely recognized. Less frequently thematized is the continuity in conception between property rights at the intrastate level and what one may call obligations of "fair trade" at the cosmopolitan level. Indeed, the recent turn to Kant's intrastate property argument has led to the somewhat unfortunate tendency to treat Kant's account of political obligation as separable in principle from his cosmopolitan commitments: there is a tendency to return Kant to the fold of exclusively statist exponents of political obligation in the social-contract tradition. It is as well to note, therefore, the conceptual link between property rights and obligations of fair trade.

Substantively, trade presupposes property relations of some sort. Trade is an exchange of things among those in possession of them: absent assumptions about mine and thine I cannot trade with another. This may seem, on the face of it, a pedestrian observation; yet the fact that trade relations presuppose mutual respect for one's trading partners' property rights was generally little acknowledged during the period of liberal commercially motivated colonialism whose early beginnings Kant witnessed as a contemporary and against which much of his substantive cosmopolitan arguments were directed. Trade was regarded by Kant as a potentially juridical form of interaction with distant others: it presented a way in which peoples from different cultural backgrounds and distinct political systems could seek to establish contact with one another, thereby establishing rights relations beyond the confines of individual states or nations. Yet trade was not deemed justifiable by Kant on any terms whatsoever. To the contrary, Kant is among the few liberal thinkers of his time to condemn, rather than seek to justify, the merciless exploitation, under the pretext of civilizing them, of slaves on commercial plantations; he speaks out against the settling, again for commercial purposes, of nomadic lands under the pretext of nomads' non-legal ownership of their homelands and pastures; and he endorses the decision taken by China and Japan respectively to cease all trade with foreigners in view of the latter's aggressively mercenary behaviour (PP 8:357–9; MM 6:353–4).[10]

At the beginning of this chapter I pointed out that whereas *Perpetual Peace* and related earlier essays are known for their outspoken cosmopolitan commitments, the *Doctrine of Right* seems to return us to familiar themes in early liberal thought. Kant's focus, in particular, on the conceptual links between property rights, political obligation and state establishment might encourage the thought that the *Doctrine of Right* abandons Kant's earlier cosmopolitan concerns – these may now appear as but an appendage to his central focus on state building. Kant's interdependence claim puts paid to these worries, which are a reflection, admittedly, of the dominant trend in early liberal thinking where the tight connection between property rights and state establishment on the one hand, and the view of justice as terminating in state establishment on the other hand, encouraged a severance of the – on the face of it – obvious tie between property and trade, property rights and justice. In Kant that tie is rendered explicit and restored: the interdependence claim holds, in effect, that no proper philosophical understanding of the concept of right in general can deny either the dependence of intrastate justice on just interstate relations, nor the importance of just trade relations to a well-functioning system of property rights. My principal claim in this section has been that whereas the conceptual and substantive connection between property rights and just trade relations seems obvious once it is pointed out, it takes a systematic approach to the question of (global) justice, such as the one Kant offers us in the *Doctrine of Right*, for one to be able to make and see that – retrospectively obvious – point.

Conclusion: Kant's outdated architectonic

The aim of this short chapter has been to offer an overview of central aspects of Kant's political philosophy by means of thematizing the idea of a system of right. Kant's systematizing tendencies in general are well known: the Kantian architectonic has often been belittled, especially by those with greater confidence than Kant possessed in the human capacity to discern and establish ultimate truths. Many have deemed it a somewhat irritating obsession on Kant's part that added nothing or little to the substance and quality of his philosophical arguments. Against this view I have suggested that Kant's systematizing endeavours are best understood as a corollary of his non-foundationalist approach to philosophical thinking. When we turn with this alternative appreciation of Kantian architectonic to Kant's political philosophy, it allows us to relate themes within that part of his work that are often seen as puzzlingly unrelated: the condemnation of states' barbaric behaviour at the international level in *Perpetual Peace*, and the endorsement of states as juridical public agents in the *Doctrine of Right*. I have argued that Kant does not, in his later work, abandon his earlier cosmopolitan commitments in order to focus in on intrastate rights relations. The system of right constitutes a sustained effort to establish conceptual and substantive connections between intrastate and interstate political morality. The perhaps most dramatic and yet least widely acknowledged connection is that between intrastate regimes of property rights and interstate trade relations. Within Kant's system of right both forms of external interpersonal interaction are conceived as types of rights relations. They are non-identical, yet conceptually and substantively interconnected: trade presupposes property, and just trade is premised on respect for others' property rights. In the history of modern liberal thought the connection has tended to be ignored, and the obligations to fair trade that liberal regimes of property rights arguably entail have been denied and violated. Nor are these connections much explored or acknowledged even in the current cosmopolitan literature. And yet Kant's system of right offers a powerful model through which to analyse global rights relations as a complex whole. Far from being outdated, Kant's approach seems in many ways still ahead of the times.

Notes

1. Two very good edited volumes on *Perpetual Peace* are Höffe (1995) and Bohman & Lutz-Bachmann (1997).
2. The "spoilt" state of the first and successive editions of the *Doctrine of Right* is well known and has been a subject of periodic scholarly discussion. See, most recently, Ludwig (1988), who suggests and defends substantial revisions of the originally published texts; many of Ludwig's revisions were accepted and incorporated into the second edition of Gregor's translation. Compare Gregor (1991) and Gregor (1996).

3. The relationship between ethics and law in Kant is discussed in Höffe (1989), Willaschek (1997), Wood (2002) and Ludwig (2002).
4. These discrepancies have led Allen Wood to conclude that the *Doctrine of Right* should not be read as forming part of Kant's moral philosophy in its own right. Cf. Wood (2002).
5. For a helpful discussion see Ludwig (2002); see also Flikschuh (2010a).
6. Excellent here is Ripstein (2004).
7. For detailed analysis and discussion see Flikschuh (2000: chs 5, 6).
8. Höffe (1995), Habermas (1997) and Pogge (2002) all argue that the logical conclusion of Kant's position is a global state. A more differentiated view is taken by Kleingeld (2004). I defend a statist view in Flikschuh (2010b).
9. The highly systematic nature of Kant's approach is thematized by Ripstein (2009) in relation to intrastate rights relations. Similarly, see also Byrd & Hruschka (2010).
10. For an excellent discussion of Kant's position on colonialism see Niesen (2007).

PART III

Aesthetics, teleology, religion

NINE

Beauty: subjective purposiveness

Kirk Pillow

Kant's philosophy encompasses metaphysics and epistemology, moral and political philosophy, and also a theory of aesthetics that is closely related to these subjects. In many ways his conception of beauty as an aesthetic value stands in counterpoint to his epistemology, while sharing certain commonalities with his moral theory. The "judgement of taste", in which for Kant we find pleasure in something deemed beautiful, is the centrepiece of his aesthetics, and the focus of this chapter. Related aspects of his complex theory of aesthetics will be explored briefly towards the end.

Kant presented his aesthetic theory in the third of his three great *Critiques*, the 1790 *Critique of the Power of Judgment*. The judgement of taste is one kind of judgement situated in a broader theory of judgement carried over from his epistemology. As we know Kant holds, all experience and understanding of objects in the world around us occurs through the application of concepts that identify, when we judge well, what an object is. We know something to be a dog when we subsume it accurately under our concept "dog". Each empirical concept of this sort functions as a kind of rule for categorizing things; understanding is a matter of developing these conceptual rules, while judgement involves applying them (well). What marks the great contrast between Kant's theory of knowledge and his aesthetic theory is that he came in the *Critique of the Power of Judgment* to identify forms of judgement in which no concept is actually applied to categorize an object. He draws a distinction there between determinative judgements, in which we determine what things are through the use of conceptual rules, and what he calls "reflective" judgements (*CJ* 5:179–80).[1] Kant's epistemology concerns determinative judgements through which we know things, while aesthetic judgements are reflective, a matter of feeling rather than of cognition.

A judgement of taste is then not a matter of knowing that something is beautiful, and beauty is not a property of certain objects that can be known or identified through the application of concepts. Finding something to be beautiful is not to discover a property in the thing, but to have a subjective feeling in relation to that thing. This is Kant's first key aspect of aesthetic judgements, that they are subjective. Whereas objective judgements about the characteristics of objects determine their properties through the use of concepts, subjective judgements in aesthetics are free of conceptual rules, matters instead of a felt relation to the object, and hence subjective. This important first step differentiates aesthetic experience as a contrast to cognition and our knowledge of objects, and establishes the aesthetic as a unique subject of enquiry for Kant. Ultimately the subjectivity of aesthetic judgement will establish aesthetics as an independent source of value and human ingenuity apart from the spheres of knowledge and of moral philosophy.

Important consequences follow from the position that aesthetic appreciation is not a matter of applying concepts or of discovering some objective property in things. Kant conceives concepts as rules for understanding what things are, and the non-conceptual nature of aesthetic judgement will mean that Kant rejects any notion of "aesthetic rules" that determine in advance what will have aesthetic value, much less that would allow us to predict what is beautiful apart from what happens in the moment of appreciation. "If one judges objects merely in accordance with concepts", Kant writes, "then all representation of beauty is lost. Thus there can also be no rule in accordance with which someone could be compelled to acknowledge something as beautiful. Whether a garment, a house, a flower is beautiful: no one allows himself to be talked into his judgement about that by means of any grounds or fundamental principles" (CJ 5:215–16). Kant would not deny that cultural traditions develop norms of aesthetic value that play a role in shaping taste. But the non-conceptual subjectivity of the focused moment in which each of us finds something worth appreciating aesthetically, or does not, is not a matter of following any rules. That moment, as will be stressed again below, is a moment of *free* appreciation.

Judgements of taste are subjective judgements for Kant, and a long tradition holds in a subjectivist vein that "beauty is in the eye of the beholder", meaning that aesthetic judgement is purely subjective, a matter merely of individual taste or opinion. Kant rejects this notion, and most of his theory of beauty and taste is devoted to explaining how aesthetic judgements can have a kind of universal validity akin to something objective, despite their subjectivity. Across Kant's theory of determinative versus reflective judgements, the objective universality of concept-governed cognitive judgements, in which there is a right answer binding for all regarding whether something is a dog or not, will be matched by a "subjective universality" of non-conceptual (felt) aesthetic judgements, in which we are entitled to demand agreement from others regarding our taste in feeling something to be beautiful. Understanding how this could be, or at least how Kant makes a case for aesthetic value being something more than a matter of mere subjective opinion, is the key to grasping Kant's aesthetic theory.

Having established that judgements of taste are subjective (non-conceptual, non-cognitive matters of feeling), Kant then holds that these judgements are also *disinterested*. "Disinterested" does not mean "uninterested" or "uninteresting", but instead that aesthetic judgements are impersonal, detached from our everyday needs and desires. If we are hungry and see a banana, our "interest" in the banana is not impersonal, and our liking the eaten banana is instrumental as it satisfies our hunger. When we observe virtuous behaviour, our liking for it (a feeling of respect) is motivated by a desire to see the good realized. Aesthetic judgements, to the contrary, Kant holds, are not motivated by personal inclinations or by considerations of utility or moral value. Kant argues that there are essentially three ways in which something can be liked (*CJ* 5:205–10). First, we find something *agreeable* when it gratifies our inclinations, and there really is no arguing about what is agreeable or not. Some people like bananas, some do not; this is just a matter of mere personal tastes. Finding something agreeable is not a matter of aesthetic judgement, because this liking is interested, motivated by our inclinations, rather than being a disinterested appreciation of something. So liking a still-life painting of fruits is not an aesthetic liking if hunger is driving the liking. Second, we *esteem* something if we like how it fulfils some purpose we have in mind, or if we discern moral value in it. To like a painting because we can prop open a door with it is not an aesthetic judgement. Nor do we judge aesthetically when we like a painting because what it depicts accords with our moral sentiments or our sense of justice. These may be reasons to like a painting, but they are not aesthetic reasons, in part because they are judgements guided by interests, and also because judgements guided by interests involve applying rules and concepts, and we have seen that for Kant aesthetic appreciation is not determined by conceptual rules.

Apart from our inclination for the agreeable and our esteem for the good, Kant sees a disinterested liking or *favour* as fundamental to aesthetic appreciation. To enjoy something beautiful is not to wish to possess or consume it, or to use it for the fulfilment of some goal, or to value its moral worth. Enjoying beauty is instead a merely contemplative appreciation of something in its own right, apart from personal inclinations and desires. Importantly, Kant holds that only this contemplative appreciation of something is truly *free*, because the other kinds of liking are driven by our inclinations or are subservient to our instrumental purposes or our moral values. The disinterested appreciation of something in aesthetic judgement is a *free liking*.

If we accept the notion that aesthetic judgements are free of interest, then Kant is well on his way to being able to argue that these judgements, while subjective, are not merely personal opinions "in the eye of the beholder". For if the liking we feel for something beautiful is not derived from personal inclinations, is not a matter of what we just happen to find agreeable, and is not motivated by utilities potentially irrelevant to others, then surely the liking we feel is not peculiar to us. Surely this is a liking we are in a position to expect others also to feel. To like something aesthetically, Kant holds, is to feel a liking for it that is not peculiar to you but is instead shareable, or communicable, across a community of judging persons. The idea that aesthetic judgement is disinterested is essential to Kant's position, because disinterestedness is supposed to provide a basis for the *subjective universality* of judgements of taste. Even though aesthetic judgements are subjective matters of feeling rather than concept-governed objective judgements, they nevertheless make a claim to universality – a claim on others to agree with the appreciation – because a disinterested appreciation distances the judger from influences and conditions peculiar to herself.

To understand how a liking for something could be required or demanded of others, how in the judgement of taste a person "judges not merely for himself, but for everyone" (*CJ* 5:212), it becomes critical for Kant to explicate carefully the relationship between (i) the feeling of pleasure we have when we find something beautiful, and (ii) the judgement we make when we find something beautiful. Kant holds that if we first feel a liking for something and as a result judge it positively, this liking has to be based on our inclinations and hence a mere liking for the agreeable. That is, if pleasure is the immediate basis for the thumbs-up judgement, we have no basis for thinking that the liking derives from anything other than our purely subjective inclinations. So for the pleasure we find in something beautiful to have a communicable universality, it must be the case instead that the judgement precedes and gives rise to the pleasure. Kant conceives the judgement of taste as the basis for a pleasurable feeling, rather than being itself based on, or the result of, a feeling of pleasure. We need, then, to understand how an act of judging can give rise to pleasure in aesthetic appreciation.

Kant's answer to this relies on aspects of his epistemology and psychology relating back to the *Critique of Pure Reason*, refined for purposes of his aesthetic theory. We know that knowledge of objects for Kant involves a relationship between the mental powers of imagination and understanding. Imagination pulls together and presents the material of sensation, the content of experience, to a power of understanding that orders it under our empirical concepts. In this cognitive relationship, imagination is subservient to the rules of understanding, as is to be expected for determinative judgements about things and their properties. Imagination and understanding work harmoniously in cognition, and are well suited together to the task of knowing objects through concepts, but understanding is the predominant power. We have seen that Kant characterizes aesthetic pleasure as a free liking for something, and he similarly sees the aesthetic judgement underlying this pleasure as a free relationship of imagination to understanding, rather than one in which understanding has the upper (Kant would say "legislative") hand. He conceives aesthetic judgement as involving a "free play" of imagination and understanding in which they harmonize with each other without imagination being governed by understanding's rules and concepts (*CJ* 5:217–19).

Just what this "free harmony" of imagination and understanding amounts to, what imagination attends to in the object or how this makes for a harmony, has invited a couple of centuries (so far) of debate. We shall explore one way of interpreting this in a moment, but the overall notion is that in aesthetic experience imagination freely explores the characteristics of something, ranges over its aspects, relates them all in various ways, *plays* with the thing in an unfettered way that is not at odds with rule-bound understanding, but is equally not constrained by any predominant concept or rule. From the first *Critique* Kant retains a distinction between what he calls "reproductive" versus "productive" powers of imagination (*CpR* A 118–30). Reproductive imagination merely brings back to mind previous sensations, while a productive imagination invents new ways of relating to something, or of relating its various aspects. Productive imagination is freely creative of new avenues for experience. So in aesthetic judgement, imagination and understanding interact in this freely harmonious manner, and this judging activity gives rise to a feeling of pleasure. One could think simply that the imaginative free play is in itself a pleasurable activity, but Kant construes the judgemental basis for this pleasure more fundamentally. He observes that we find pleasure in the satisfaction of our aims (*CJ* 5:187). Accomplishing what we seek is enjoyable. We achieve our cognitive aims in the determinative, rule-governed relationship that obtains between understanding and imagination, but in fact, Kant holds, that relationship would not be possible if these powers were not able to first relate in the freely harmonious manner that obtains in aesthetic experience. The free relationship underpins the determinate one, making aesthetic judgement a part of the overall satisfaction of our cognitive aims, even if in a pre- or non-conceptual way. And so through aiding the satisfaction of our cognitive powers, the free play of imagination and understanding in aesthetic judgement gives rise to a pleasure. Aesthetic appreciation is for Kant a pleasure based on the free harmony of our cognitive powers.

The judging activity, of imagination at play with understanding, precedes the pleasure we associate with finding something beautiful. And this account is designed to reinforce Kant's position that aesthetic judgements are subjectively *universal*. He holds that a disinterested liking can make a claim on the agreement of others because it is not made from mere personal inclinations. Similarly, he holds that a pleasure derived from a fundamental structure of human cognition, shared by all judging persons, must be a pleasure that is not peculiar to anyone in particular, but instead a pleasure that anyone can be expected to feel when they let imagination play. The harmony of cognitive powers provides a universal basis for aesthetic appreciation to be communicable, that is, sharable across a community of judging subjects who are each in a position to require that others agree with their taste.

Given the disinterestedness of the judgement of taste, and its basis in a shared cognitive structure, Kant thinks aesthetic judgements carry the force of an "ought". Despite the subjectivity of these judgements, aesthetic value is not merely in the eye of the beholder, a matter of personal preferences or inclinations. When we judge something to be beautiful, we "judge for everyone" and insist that they agree with the judgement. "One solicits assent from everyone else because one has a ground for it that is common to all" (*CJ* 5:237), namely a basis in a fundamental pre-cognitive relationship between imagination and understanding. Since objective, cognitive judgements about things are communicable among judging subjects who are all equipped with the same basic capacity to understand (to judge through the use of concepts), then surely the experience of that basic "attunement" between mental powers required for all such cognition can be shared in judgement as well. Kant therefore calls the free harmony of imagination and understanding that underlies aesthetic pleasure a "common sense", giving this pleasure a claim to universality (5:238). Importantly, this claim for others' agreement about what is beautiful is not a prediction that they *will* agree, but rather a demand that they ought to. Someone whose judgement is not free of the influence of personal inclination, or who fails to let their imagination freely and creatively appreciate the thing in question, may well disagree with our judgement. But according to Kant, judging persons who cultivate disinterested aesthetic responses, and who set their cognitive powers to play in such a way as to tap into the satisfactions of a basic mental attunement common to all, *ought* to agree about what they find beautiful together.

Before raising some general questions and concerns about this view, we should explore another aspect of Kant's theory of the judgement of taste that has itself raised many questions. Kant's analysis of these judgements is divided into four "moments" or aspects; we have already covered three of them. Judgements of taste are (i) devoid of interest, (ii) embody a universal liking, and (iii) they do so because they are based in a common sense (free harmony). These are, in fact, the First, Second and Fourth Moments of his explication. The Third Moment of explicating judgements of taste presents Kant's famous characterization of beauty as a *purposiveness without purpose*. As Kant summarizes this, "Beauty is the form of the purposiveness of an object, insofar as it is perceived in it *without representation of an end*" (*CJ* 5:236).[2] What could this mean? We can first recognize that, just as there is a close relationship between the Second and Fourth Moments of Kant's explication (universal liking and the common sense), there is a close relation between the First Moment of disinterestedness and this Third Moment. We saw that when we appreciate something in a manner devoid of all interest, we judge it without reference to concepts of utility or of the moral good (in fact, without delimiting our appreciation under any concept). To conceive of something as having a purpose, Kant thinks, we must understand some concept or idea to be the basis for its being intended to have the purpose it has. To understand a mug for what it is requires knowing that its maker made the concept "holding-of-liquids-for-drinking" the basis for the character of the object. Something cannot have a definite purpose, Kant thinks, without a defining concept as its basis, its intended reason for being. But since aesthetic judgement, as we have seen, does not rely on determinative concepts when responding in a felt way to something, aesthetic judgement does not involve ascertaining what the purpose of something is. The free appreciation imagination has for something beautiful is free as much from blunt purposes as it is from concepts or any rules of understanding.

The challenge in making sense of Kant's Third Moment, then, is to understand how something we appreciate as beautiful, without attributing a definite purpose to it, nevertheless is marked by a certain "purposiveness". Kant's essential idea is that in beautiful things imagination discerns an indefinite orderedness or designedness, a well-formedness that is pleasing. Beautiful things seem to be wrought by an intentionality shaping them to some purpose, even though we do not know what that purpose might be. There is, of course, an ancient tradition of understanding beauty as well-formedness in things (e.g. unity, symmetry, balance of elements), but there is also an early modern tradition of defining beauty as the manifestation of an object's perfection in fulfilling its purpose. Kant's notion of "purposiveness without purpose" rejects this latter idea of beauty as a kind of perfection in a purpose fulfilled, while retaining indefinite designedness as an aspect of the beautiful. Related to Kant's account of the free harmony of cognitive powers in aesthetic judgement, what imagination produces in its free aesthetic play with something is an appreciation of how, in multiple ways, the beautiful thing intimates a suitability for a purpose, or suggests a designing intention in its exquisite form. To find beauty in "purposiveness without purpose" is to like the well-shaped form of something so much that it seems it could only be intentional, despite our not really attributing any fixed purpose to it. Attributing any too fixed a purpose would only cut short imagination's free appreciation by suborning it to a concept of a purpose derived from our understanding. "Purposiveness without purpose" is tightly related in Kant's theory to both the disinterestedness and the non-conceptual nature of aesthetic judgement.

The Third Moment has sparked all manner of controversy over time. I indicated above that we would see a more specific interpretation of what characteristics of an object imagination attends to when appreciating beauty. Kant sometimes writes in the Third Moment that imagination attends to the "mere form of purposiveness" (a synonym for purposiveness without purpose), but he also writes that imagination attends to the purposiveness of *form* (and I did begin to appeal to form, controversially, in the previous paragraph). Kant writes: "A judgment of taste on which charm and emotion have no influence ... which thus has for its determining ground merely the purposiveness of the form, is a *pure judgement of taste*" (CJ 5:223). In the fine arts, Kant writes, "the *design* is what is essential, in which what constitutes the ground of all arrangements for taste is not what gratifies in sensation but merely what pleases through its form" (5:225, trans. mod.). This could seem harmless enough: we discern well-shaped designedness in the form of something when we find it beautiful. But given the many links in Kant's aesthetic theory back to his first *Critique* epistemology, "form" has a pretty limiting meaning for him. The form of an object is its shape in space as perceived through sensation, its geometry in essence, with relations among fields of colour among the parts of an object perhaps admissible also as contributing to its form. And it is reasonable, after all, to suppose that imaginative appreciation of these formal aspects of something contributes to aesthetic judgement. When appreciating a beautiful landscape we take in foreground and background elements, relations of colour and shadow in the variety of natural features and their lighting, stillness and movement from passing clouds and breezes, all aspects of the shape of what we see.

But this account of imagination's free play with the purposiveness of form invites an "aesthetic formalism" in which formal elements are the *only* things relevant to aesthetic judgement. Kant himself is often understood to be the progenitor, in the Third Moment, of a strict formalism that excludes all but form from aesthetic evaluation. When appreciating beauties of nature, formalism may not seem problematic (though it is), but when aesthetic judgement trains its eye on human works of art, a strict formalism holds that *nothing* is relevant to appreciation but shape and colour. What a work of art might depict, who a portrait is a portrait of, what a work might mean, where it is located in the history of art, the environs from which it and its maker(s) arose, how it has been reinterpreted over time and the like, all become irrelevant to aesthetic judgement. Indeed, in the early and mid-twentieth century, critics adopted strict formalist views while claiming to be carrying the banner of Kantian aesthetics. In the 1910s the British critic Clive Bell championed Postimpressionism and Cubism as the arrival of pure form in art. In the 1950s American critic Clement Greenberg extolled pure painting among the Abstract Expressionists, against all representation of anything concrete, as the consummation of what art should be: nothing but form. Such views clearly capture an important element of aesthetic appreciation, but Kant's Third Moment has on occasion encouraged an imprudent indifference to everything other than shape and colour, to the many elements of content that contribute both to the rich meaningfulness of works of art and to the full challenge of engaging with them aesthetically in all their complexity.

To make matters worse, Kant attempts in the Third Moment to draw a distinction between what he calls pure judgements of taste versus "dependent" ones. The pure judgement of taste, which his entire analysis has focused on characterizing, avoids knowing an object through concepts or conceiving the purpose that makes an artefact what it is. We instead appreciate it imaginatively and freely apart from conceptual determination. Dependent beauties, on the other hand, involve understanding something through "the end that determines what the thing should be" (*CJ* 5:230), and appreciating it thereby as a fine instantiation of that purpose. Generations of scholars have observed that this characterization of dependent beauties appears to be at odds in every way with Kant's whole account of aesthetic judgement. It is hard to see how dependent beauties could be matters of beauty at all, given Kant's theory. They seem a regression to the notion of beauty as perfectibility from which we have seen Kant distance his theory. Worse yet, Kant writes as if dependent beauty is what we find mostly in human works of art, while the true beauty of pure aesthetic judgements is to be found primarily in nature. It would be most unsatisfying if the centrepiece of Kant's aesthetic theory, finding pleasure in a free harmony of cognitive play, were attainable only in relation to nature. And it would create troubling results for Kant's aesthetics if real beauty were not to be found in works of art, or if their beauty could have nothing to do with how they represent what they represent, or with their meanings, or if the subjective universality of aesthetic judgement were supportable only in our appreciation of nature. Such results would create doubly troubling inconsistencies for Kant when we consider that he, after all, proceeds in the *Critique of the Power of Judgment* to argue that works of art can be beautiful, and beautifully meaningful, and that works of art are the focus of judgements of taste in which we insist that others agree with us about aesthetic value.

These and other troubles with the Third Moment of Kant's analysis of aesthetic judgement have led many commentators practically to wish that Kant had left this part of the third *Critique* unwritten. And some commentators have sought to show that Kant's theory of aesthetic judgement can be separated from the problems with the Third Moment, and defended without reference to it, in part as a strategy to save Kant from his own formalistic tendencies (see e.g. Guyer 1979).

Other aspects of Kant's theories of beauty and of the subjective universality of aesthetic judgements have also raised concerns. We have seen that Kant holds the claim to universality in a judgement of taste, the aesthetic ought of taste, to have a basis in a common sense, a mental attunement between imagination and understanding that underlies all cognition. This common mental attunement is a requirement of cognition, as this free relation between these mental powers is the precondition for the determinative, concept-governed relation between them when understanding knows objects around us through concepts. All known objects have been known through the offices of this mental attunement, and this appears to give Kant's theory the implication that everything is beautiful. Given that the common sense must be in place to know any objects, it must presumably always be present, always communicable, and hence finding things beautiful and requiring others to agree would be an omnipresent condition. Why do we find only certain things to be beautiful, if the attunement of imagination and understanding, in the judgement that underlies the feeling of aesthetic pleasure, always obtains? We could recall that aesthetic pleasure arises only from the *free* relation when imagination plays with appreciating something, not when we are busy knowing something conceptually through a predominant understanding. Not everything is beautiful because imaginative free play does not always obtain. But then it seems that all we need do to find anything and everything beautiful is to set imagination to play, free it from conceptual determination, and *voilà*, everything becomes beautiful. That is, if imaginative free play is a voluntary activity, which its freedom would seem to require it to be, then we are always free to play away, and find beauty everywhere.

But we find only some things beautiful; only some things actually reward the imaginative effort to appreciate them aesthetically, and it is alternatively a strength or weakness of Kant's theory that he cannot account well for why some things give us aesthetic pleasure and others do not. This is a strength if one values Kant's conviction that aesthetic experience is not governed by rules that would allow us to state the characteristics in advance of those things found beautiful; but it is a weakness if that is just the sort of thing one thinks should actually be the project of a theory of aesthetics.

Not only is it not clear why imaginative free play does or does not bear fruit in particular attempts to appreciate things aesthetically; it may not even be clear, in Kant's account, *when* truly free imaginative play is occurring. At the end of the Fourth Moment of his analysis of judgements of taste, when discussing the idea of a common sense, Kant observes that "our presumption in making judgements of taste" (*CJ* 5:240) shows that we presuppose a communicable common sense that would give their "ought" a basis. But he also observes that this common basis lends validity to one's judgements "if only one were certain of having correctly subsumed under it" (*ibid.*), which means provided one knows that the pleasure one feels is indeed an aesthetic pleasure arising from the fundamental mental attunement. If instead the pleasure were merely a liking for something agreeable, if instead our judgement did not succeed in being disinterested, we would have no cause to claim that our judgement arose from a common sense and hence we would have no claim on the agreement of others. How do we know when we have judged without interest?

Kant writes:

one cannot judge that about which he is aware that the satisfaction in it is without any interest in his own case in any way except that it must contain a ground of satisfaction for everyone. For since it is not grounded in any inclination of the subject (nor in any other underlying interest), but rather the person making the judgment feels himself completely *free* with regard to the satisfaction that he devotes to the object, he cannot discover as grounds of the satisfaction any private conditions, pertaining to his subject alone, and must therefore regard it as grounded in those that he can also presuppose in everyone else; consequently he must believe himself to have grounds for expecting a similar pleasure for everyone.

(*CJ* 5:211)

The problem is that not discovering private conditions underlying my liking, or not being aware of any, does not mean that none are there. What extent of self-scrutiny is required to ensure the absence of private conditions guiding my likes and dislikes? Worse, can any extent of self-scrutiny provide enough assurance to warrant my demanding that others share my taste? That is, can Kant plausibly claim that one can be aware that one's satisfaction is devoid of interest? Kant's account of the universality claim for the aesthetic ought hinges entirely on whether we are capable of judging aesthetic matters with disinterest, along with whether we are capable of even knowing when we have done so. The crux of Kant's case for rejecting the merely subjective, "eye-of-the-beholder" tradition comes down to this: the possibility of aesthetic disinterestedness combined with the plausibility of our having confidence of when we have achieved it.

Despite the numerous challenges to which Kant's aesthetic theory is subject, the *Critique of the Power of Judgment* has been of profound importance to the philosophy art, in many respects defining the basic topics and ground rules of discussion in the field (for better or worse). Kant's many great insights into aesthetic experience sit on the page with as many vexing problems unresolved. His theory of beauty and the judgement of taste is but one feature of a rich aesthetic theory presented in the third *Critique*, and I wish to round out this chapter by briefly touching on a few key topics also found there: the sublime; Kant's notion of beauty as a "symbol" of morality; and fine art, genius and "aesthetic ideas".

The judgement of taste is actually one of two kinds of aesthetic judgement Kant treats in the third *Critique*, the other being the judgement of sublimity. The sublime was a popular subject of the era, previously treated by the English thinker Edmund Burke (1990), and Kant finds a basis in his theory of the mind for including the topic in his aesthetics. We know that, in addition to imagination and understanding, the third great mental power in Kant's scheme is reason, which for him has both intellectual and practical roles to play. While in the appreciation of beauty imagination stands in a relation to the understanding, the judgement of sublimity issues from a relation of imagination to reason. And because reason has dual powers (intellectual and practical), there are two species of sublimity, which Kant calls the "mathematical" and the "dynamical" sublimes (CJ 5:247). In the mathematical sublime, imagination attempts to take in and comprehend an experience of vastness or infinity but is frustrated by magnitudes that overwhelm its grasp. This is the awe-inspiring sublime long associated with spiritual experiences. In the dynamical sublime, we find ourselves threatened by overwhelming forces of nature; this is the awesome sublimity of earthquakes and the perfect storm. In both cases, Kant conceives the experience of sublimity as one of frustration and displeasure that ultimately gives way to a satisfaction. Imagination is humbled by vastness, our mortality is threatened by great might, but this suffering gives way to a pleasure in our value as rational beings. Imagination cannot truly grasp all at once the infinite heavens, but reason can think the idea of infinity; nature might dash us to pieces, but nothing can destroy our dignity as free moral beings. Many twentieth-century commentators were drawn to the violence and negativity of Kant's account of sublimity, but in fact for him the sublime is ultimately redemptive of clear-headed reason as the pinnacle of our humanity.

I noted from the beginning important ties between Kant's aesthetics and his moral theory, and the exaltation of reason in the judgement of sublimity bears this out. Kant goes further in the third *Critique*, arguing famously that aesthetic judgement provides a kind of training in moral judgement. The essential characteristics of the beautiful – that we like it directly, disinterestedly, freely and with a universal voice – parallel the form of moral judgements as encapsulated most purely in the categorical imperative. Kant sees an analogy between these two spheres of judgement, and he had a theory that symbols are based on analogies (CJ 5:351–3), so he advances the view that beauty is a symbol of the morally good. Just as judging beauty requires setting aside one's peculiar inclinations in order to appreciate something in a manner sharable with others, moral reasoning requires suborning one's inclinations and desires to universal principles. Through exercises of taste we resist the mere sensible charms of the agreeable in order to lay claim to an aesthetic ought, and this activity can give practice for the moral exertions of achieving freedom from inclination as a principled actor. "Taste as it were makes possible", Kant writes, "the transition from sensible charm to the habitual moral interest without too violent a leap" (5:354). As we have repeatedly seen in Kant's aesthetics, promising insights abut dubious claims, and here again Kant likely pushes the analysis too far by proposing that *only because* the beautiful refers symbolically to the morally good "does it please with a claim to the assent of everyone else" (5:353). This claim has elicited much dispute, and at least on the face of it appears to be squarely at odds with Kant's main analysis of the freely imaginative purposiveness *without* purpose enjoyed in the experience of beauty.

Finally, I briefly note that Kant does provide a philosophy of human works of art in the third *Critique*, indeed a highly influential one centred on a Romantic (or rather, Romanticism-inspiring) concept of genius as the source of artistic inspiration. Keeping true to his conviction that aesthetic experience is not governed by rules or concepts, Kant holds that when appreciating fine art "one must be aware that it is art, and not nature; yet the purposiveness in its form must still seem to be as free from all constraint by arbitrary rules as if it were a mere product of nature" (5:306). Given this requirement, Kant conceives artistic genius as a kind of natural talent "for producing that for which no determinate rule can be given" (5:307). Artistic inspiration is a matter of nature speaking through the artist, giving expression to things richer than can be captured in any formula or rule. The artist expresses what Kant calls "aesthetic ideas", which can be thought of as rich complexes of allusive content that give us more to respond to than can be summed up in words. If in his account of the judgement of taste we found an arguable formalistic bent towards appreciation of shape and colour, in his theory of fine art Kant makes meaningful content the focus of the genius' output and the locus of appreciation. He goes so far as to hold that "Beauty (whether it be beauty of nature or of art) can in general be called the *expression* of aesthetic ideas" (5:320), seeming nicely to tie together many strands of his theory. This position has, as with so many others of Kant's, invited more than two hundred years of vigorous debate. How can beauty express aesthetic ideas if we focus on formal appreciation when judging beauty? How can beauty express aesthetic ideas when aesthetic appreciation has no truck with conceptual determinations? If works of art can be beautiful by virtue of their expression of aesthetic ideas, can they also be sublime? Does the theory of aesthetic ideas clarify or further confuse Kant's discussion of free versus dependent beauties in works of art? How can anything in nature be said to "express" anything?

These questions give a taste of the many enquiries into aesthetic experience that Kant's *Critique of the Power of Judgment* has provoked.

When Kant infamously argues that artistic genius is of such another order of originality that the scientific "genius" of an Isaac Newton is not really genius but only good learning and the application of rules (5:308–10), one can wonder where in this range Kant would place the philosopher. For his great work in aesthetics has confounded understanding ever since, and inspired many others to grasp for the meaning of beauty while deliciously never quite getting it.

Notes

1. See also the First Introduction to the *Critique of the Power of Judgment*, 20: 211–13.
2. I shall favour the more traditional rendering "purposiveness without purpose".

TEN

Organism: objective purposiveness
John Zammito

Strictly speaking, the organization of nature is not analogous with
any causality we know.   (*CJ* 5:375)

What good is it? What is it for? What is it supposed to be? Does it work?
These are the commonplace, ordinary-language queries of human
agents. They are cognitive queries with practical intent, having to do
with how we might use the entities we encounter in the world. Moreover, they betoken capacities *in ourselves* that we take, in an equally
commonplace manner, to be actual and effectual. This is the sphere of
"objective purposiveness". Kant wrote: "the human's reason knows
how to bring things into correspondence with his own arbitrary inspi-
rations" (5:368). Once we posit human beings as possessing (and comprehending) this capacity for agency, whereby things of the world are
assigned utility, such "relative" purposiveness appears to be thoroughly
unproblematic, and Kant generally proceeds exactly in that manner.[1]
Yet we must not pass too swiftly over the point that it is only because
we have posited the presence of an *actual* agent – the human being
as an entity capable of finding, for its own sake, some utility in other
entities in the world – that this very idea of a "relative purposiveness"
in the world can go through (5:368).[2] In commonplace considerations,
that need hardly give us pause. But when we are trying to understand
the transcendental strictures of Kant's critical philosophy regarding
knowledge claims, we have reason to go a bit more slowly.

Is there a transcendental warrant for these practices? What makes
"purposiveness" *really* "objective" and in what *sense* of that polymor-
phous term in Kantian philosophy? In the Introduction to the *Critique*

of the Power of Judgment, Kant distinguished the domain of such considerations as "technical" rather than "moral" – hence belonging to cognitive rather than practical philosophy (5:172). But a question then arises about the *warrant* of cognitive claims in this vein. They are not ordinary "judgments of experience" or "empirical determinant judgments"; they are "reflective" or "regulative", he informs us. It may be necessary for the judging subject to *take* entities in the world to have such "relative purposiveness", but it is not something *inherent in* the entities but only a *relation to* the subject's own interest. That is, relative purposiveness "can never be made out by mere contemplation of nature" (5:368). It "exists" only in and for the relation with the judging subject. The judging subject, all the same, has an *interest* in some entities: their *actuality* (or availability) is an indispensable element in the relation (5:296). Not only the existence of the entity but its *form* is at issue – "*what sort of thing it is supposed to be*" (5:227) – for it is in this that its *utility* ("objective *material* purposiveness") is grounded. That establishes what it is *good* for. Even purely *formal* entities – geometrical constructs – can have utility – "serviceability for all sorts of (infinitely manifold) purposes" (5:366). In pure intuition, these constructs (e.g. a circle) become available to the judging subject, aiding the subject in attaining its ends, the "solution of many problems in accordance with a single principle" (5:362). But "objective formal purposiveness" is more of an aside than a centrepiece of Kant's philosophical reconstruction of the warrant of purposiveness in the critical philosophy.

"Purpose" signifies that a representation in the mind serves as the "determining ground" or original cause of the existence of an entity or a state of affairs.[3] Human beings make sense of their own purposive activity as efficient causality in terms of the temporal and logical precedence of an idea and willed act to the actuality produced (5:220). Purposiveness, in Kant's view, is never something we perceive directly in an experience of the external world. He put it well in a marginal note to his own copy of the "First Introduction" to the *Critique of the Power of Judgment*: "we read final causes into things and do not, so to speak, abstract them from perceptions" (*CJ*, First Introduction, 24n). It is an inference, an imputation, that we make.[4] Just as when we encounter a regular hexagon in the sand of a deserted beach, we do – indeed, we are compelled to – make such imputations to entities in the external world.[5] Yet some such entities are far more mysterious, because we cannot reasonably presume an intelligent agent creating them.

The question that asserts itself, then, setting off from "objective formal purposiveness" (of mathematical forms) and "relative purposiveness" (of entities in the world that occasion interest in the judging subject for purposes of its own), is whether, *apart from a rational agent and its overt interventions*, there can be "an objective purposiveness of the things [in the world] *in themselves*" (5:368; emphasis added). This *intrinsic* purposiveness of actual entities in the world is the salient theoretical challenge in the whole notion. It is the problem of *organisms*, or what Kant terms "natural purposes" or "organized beings". That problem, taken empirically, is constitutive for biology as a natural science. Taken transcendentally, I would go further: it is the problem of the ontological character of all agency, including the human, and of our warrant to knowledge claims about this ontological character. Marcel Quarfood recognizes the importance for Kant, in the Appendix to the *Critique of Pure Reason*, of the "biological analogy ... between the systematicity of reason and the functional integration of the parts in an organism" (2004: 79). Robert Butts notes that there is a peculiar uniformity among many of the "recalcitrant particulars" in Kant's scheme of things, namely these anomalies "all presuppose an understanding of purposiveness modeled on human purposive action" (1990: 3). That is, "basic to Kant's treatment of teleology is the unquestioned assumption that we have an already perfect understanding of human purposive action because we ourselves act purposively" (*ibid.*: 15n). How it is possible *for us* to have purpose is no more *theoretically* transparent than it is for organisms to *appear* purposive for us. While in Kant's system it is possible to "think" this, and to think ourselves under that concept, it is by no means clear that it can play *any* theoretical role whatsoever. Yet the whole structure of purposiveness rests upon the presumption of the ontological coherence – the *real* possibility – of "intrinsic purposiveness" acting efficaciously in the phenomenal world.

In his *Critique of the Power of Judgment*, Kant conceived two levels of natural teleology – a general level (the "order of nature" as a system of purposes) and the individual level of organisms or species. In the two Introductions to the *Critique of the Power of Judgment*, Kant recognized that *empirical* knowledge remained (in our terms) underdetermined by the "Transcendental Analytic" of the first *Critique*. He affirmed that we must "regard nature a priori as characterized by a *logical system* of its diversity under empirical laws" (*CJ*, First Introduction, 20:214). Yet empirical laws were contingent; it was necessary to *find* them and they could be recalcitrant, perhaps even inaccessible. To undertake empirical science was a risky endeavour, needing subjective reassurance, in this case a (subjective but *a priori*) "transcendental principle" of *teleological judgement* (5:183–6). Rachel Zuckert explains: "for empirical knowledge to be possible ... we require a principle that establishes a unity of the diverse as such, a form of lawfulness that holds for the contingent aspects of nature as such" (2007: 24; see also 61).[6] This contingency of empirical knowledge is the essential concern of "reflective judging". That is, reflective judging has, as its purpose, enabling empirical concept formation and therewith the formulation and systematization of "empirical laws" (5:179–81).

But with regard to individual entities something else is at stake. "Kant's claims in the ["Critique of Teleological Judgment"] are ... narrower than those in the Appendix [to the first *Critique*], but they are also stronger" (Zuckert 2007: 95). The particular conception of natural purpose is in fact more demanding in formulation than the general one. Kant takes up what he explicitly terms a "special class" of natural entities (*CJ* 5:383). The key feature of this particular form of natural purpose is the mutual constitution of parts and whole (5:373–4). In teleological judgement of a particular organism, as Zuckert aptly notes, Kant articulated "a form of means–ends relations holding among parts *as* diverse and contingent, which are made possible by a temporal structure of future-relatedness", and he affirmed this of a "special class" of determinate empirical objects (Zuckert 2007: 20).

Kant opened his "Critique of Teleological Judgment" with a consideration of "the structure of a bird, the hollowness of its bones, the placement of its wings for movement and its tail for steering" (5:360). He asserted that there was no way that the "mere *nexus effectivus*" (i.e. efficient, mechanical causality) in nature could account for this production; it was irretrievably "contingent". Famously, he claimed we must resort to *nexus finalis* – causality according to purpose – in order to organize our reception of this phenomenon. But we do this "only ... so as to bring nature under principles of observation and investigation by *analogy* ... without presuming to *explain* it" (*ibid.*). That is, it is a causality that "we merely borrow from ourselves and ascribe to other beings, yet without wanting to think of them as similar to ourselves" (5:361).

In §§64–6 of the "Critique of Teleological Judgment", Kant offered an extended conceptualization of organic form. The essential definition entailed the reciprocal interaction of parts as means and ends for one another and for the ensemble, and, consequently, the indispensability of the whole for the parts in the constitution of the entity (5:373–4). An organism was "cause and effect of itself" (5:370–71). Kant drew a crucial contrast between a watch and an organism: "an organized being is thus not a mere machine", since its "*formative* power" vastly exceeds the mere "*motive* power" of any mechanism (5:374). Thus in §65 Kant associated with organisms "a self-propagating *formative* power" (*ibid.*). Organisms were *self*-organizing beings. With the example of a tree, in §64 Kant highlighted three features that eighteenth-century life science considered empirically established about organisms. First, "with regard to its *species* the tree produces itself: with its species, it is both cause and effect, both generating itself and being generated by itself ceaselessly" (5:371). Next, he highlighted *physiological* functions of more properly individual organisms: *nutrition and growth*.

Kant stressed the particular point that "the matter that the tree assimilates is first processed by it until the matter has the quality peculiar to the species, a quality that the natural mechanism outside the plant cannot supply" (*ibid*.). That is, the tree transforms *inorganic* materials into *organic* forms (something he believed inorganic matter could never do of itself, for that would be *generatio aequivoca* – spontaneous generation – or "hylozoism"). He went on: "in terms of the ingredients that the tree receives from nature outside it we have to consider it to be only an educt" (*ibid*.). An "educt" merely redeploys what is already given. By contrast, a "product" emerges as something new. When the tree assimilates inorganic into organic matter it *transforms* it into a *part* of itself, and hence the tree becomes a product, not merely an educt.[7] In accordance with a distinction proposed prominently by John Locke, all organic *parts* are compounded of *particles* that are drawn from the general physical–chemical order, but the form of the part is a property of a higher level than the mere materiality of the particles that compose it.[8] In our terms, substituting one atom of carbon for another makes no difference to the nature of the part, but the form of a protein plays an essential role in a cell or higher unit of organic functioning. Kant's concept of "product" articulates this point: something determinately new really does *emerge*, but it is from the vantage, and for the sake, of the organism.

Kant recognized that metabolism is a matter of *systemic* (re)integration. He distinguished emphatically between growth by internal integration and mere aggregation. Mechanism can get no further than aggregation; but *systems* do more: "The whole is thus an organized unity (*articulatio*), and not an aggregate (*coacervatio*). It may grow from within (*per intussusceptionem*), but not by external additions (*per appositionem*)" (*CpR* A 832–3/B 860–61; see Kant 1929). For this reason, Kant rejected the notion that crystal growth was proto-organic; it was in his view strictly mechanical. Concluding his discussion of this second trait in the tree as model organism, Kant noted: "the separation and recombination of this raw material show that these natural beings have a separating and forming ability [*Scheidungs- und Bildungsvermögens*] of very great originality; all our art finds itself infinitely outdistanced" (*CJ* 5:371). This emphasis on the creative spontaneity of nature as incomparably superior to human artifice is repeated in a decisive passage later in the third *Critique*, substantially curtailing the utility of the "analogy of design" for conceptualization of organisms (5:374–5).

The last of the distinguishing traits of organisms Kant formulated via the instance of a tree was the power of *regeneration*, that is, healing and even organ restoration – a matter of the most exciting experimental discoveries of mid-eighteenth-century empirical life science: the experiments of Trembley, Bonnet and ultimately Blumenbach. The regenerative powers of the polyp confirmed arguments that Caspar Friedrich Wolff would advance based on his embryological observations, namely that organic forms had the power of developmental self-organization, a capacity for internal regulation and modulation that involved a continuous and mutually responsive relation between parts and whole for the sustenance of the organism. This was the essential argument of eighteenth-century epigenesis (Vartanian 1950).

Many historians and philosophers of biology credit Kant with an elucidation of "organized being" that proved decisively enabling for the crystallization of biology as a special science (Bommersheim 1919; Ungerer 1922; Baumanns 1965; Löw 1980). Kant – drawing on his eighteenth-century predecessors – *did* provide a discerning and powerful characterization of what biologists had to explain in organic form. His difference from the rest is that he opined that it was *impossible* to explain it. All one could do was draw *analogies* to it. Its "inscrutability" was intrinsic.[9] As Marcel Quarfood explains, "organisms like all objects of experience are subject to the causal principle", but "there are features of organisms that appear to be intractable for the kind of explanations in terms of causal laws appropriate for ordinary physical objects" and thus "there is no explanation (or 'law') for how matter comes together in the ways characteristic for organisms" (2004: 146).

From the vantage of critical philosophy, the problem with organisms was that their behaviour was inconsistent with the human mode of causal explanation (5:220, 255–6). That an entity can be cause and effect of itself, Kant argued, is beyond discursive rationality. Simultaneously "ascending" and "descending" chains of determination, as Kant put it (5:372), constitute a violation of the irreversibly directional "objective time order" that is essential for application of the categories, and particularly of causality. Such judgements must, for Kant, be only subjective, however necessary. Driven to admit that it was impossible for us to see organisms other than as natural purposes, Kant held that this necessity lay in *our* projection, not in *their* nature (5:247, 221–2). In Kantian terms, there is a subjective necessity – a "need of reason" – for this move, but no objective necessity, no natural law evident in the matter at hand (the "order of nature").[10]

> The concept of a thing as in itself a natural purpose is … no con-
> stitutive concept of understanding or of reason, but it can serve
> as a regulative concept for the reflective judgment, to guide our
> investigation about objects of this kind by a distant analogy with
> our own causality. (5:222)

To take teleology as explanatory would "introduce a new causality into natural science" (5:361). This would be a quite "special kind of causality, or at least a quite distinct lawfulness [*Gesetzmäßigkeit*] of nature" and "even experience cannot prove that there actually are such purposes [*die Wirklichkeit derselben … beweisen*]" (5:359). Technically, Kant had to deny that teleology can explain anything in phenomenal nature (cf. Ginsborg 1987, 2004; Fricke 1990; Warnke 1992; Flasch 1997). What teleology is alone permitted to do is offer an *analogy* of some *heuristic* utility. It is even less than an empirical *conjecture*.

Kant directs us to read organisms as artefacts though he knows it is an inept analogy. He realizes that the analogy has a gaping flaw. "One says too little about nature and its capacity in organized products if one calls this an *analogue of art*, for in that case one conceives of the artist (a rational being) outside of it" (5:374). The last thing he wants is for us literally to take organisms as artefacts, because this would imply either that a God made them or that nature could. The first is bald theology and the second is "hylozoism", a flat contradiction in terms if (but *only if*) we accept Kant's stipulation about matter.[11] Kant fully shares the horror over "backwards causation" in teleology that haunts "function-talk" to this day (Zuckert 2007: 136, 121n, 166n).[12] Indeed, the whole language of purposiveness with reference to biology, Zuckert correctly observes, is an act of "domestication" by Kant: domestication *to* the critical system *at the expense* of any objectivity in the discernment of organisms in nature (*ibid.*: 239). "Intentional activity provides Kant with a reductive account of purposive causality that is assimilable to the efficient causal time order of necessary, irreversible succession" (*ibid.*: 141). "This reductive regulative idea allows us to 'bracket' the organisms' self-organizing character" (*ibid.*: 165).

Kant could only view the assertion of an empirically actual formative force as *hylozoism*, and there was nothing towards which he felt a stronger metaphysical animus, even though his own struggle with organic form unearthed that possibility. He wrote:

> We perhaps approach nearer to this inscrutable property if we
> describe it as an *analogon of life*, but then we must either endow

matter, as mere matter, with a property which contradicts its very being (hylozoism) or associate therewith an alien principle *standing in communion* with it (a soul). But in the latter case we must, if such a product is to be a natural product, either presuppose organized matter as the instrument of that soul, which does not make the soul a whit more comprehensible, or regard the soul as artificer of this structure, and so remove the product from (corporeal) nature. (5:374–5)

Neither seemed acceptable. The philosophical problem, Kant insisted, allowed only one solution: a transcendent creator. In Kant's words, "Nature is no longer estimated as it appears like art, but rather in so far as it actually *is* art, though superhuman art" (5:311). This conjecture gets "domesticated" to the critical philosophy via the analogy of purposiveness. Such a "Technic of Nature" was inevitable for man's discursive understanding, Kant claimed. "Nature [i.e. the "order of nature" as a system] can only be understood as meaningful if we take it at large to be designed" (Butts 1990: 5). This "supersensible" but "reflective" recourse was true not only of Kant's general notion of teleology in nature, but also of his particular view of organisms. In his Metaphysics Lectures, Kant was more explicit:

[A]ll matter that is animate has an inner principle which is separated from the object of outer sense, and is an object of inner sense ... Thus, all matter which lives is alive not as matter but rather has a principle of life and is animated. But to the extent matter is animated, to that extent it is *ensouled*. (ML 28:275)

Late in his life, in *Perpetual Peace*, Kant acknowledged the popularity of the new term *Lebenskraft* [life force], which he recognized as a substitute for the traditional concept of the soul. He welcomed this term-shift, for he held that while we can recognize an effect, we should be wary of hypostatizing a substance as its ground (PP 8:413).

The "marvelous properties of organized creatures", which Kant adumbrates with confidence in the "Analytic" of his "Critique of Teleological Judgment", are part of the empirical–experiential data available to human investigators trying to comprehend the order of nature (CJ 5:371). Even Kant appears to consider their *phenomenal description* unproblematic. But how these "marvelous properties" can be explained – and how they can be *integrated* into a unified system of empirical laws as the "order of nature" – remains, for Kant, a philosophical conundrum. I think it is essential to dwell for a moment on Kant's suggestion that there is a *radical incongruity* between his notion of organic form as "intrinsic purposiveness" and the conventions of natural science: "its form is not possible according to mere natural laws, that is, those laws which can be cognized by us through the understanding alone when applied to objects of sense" (5:370).

Still, an organism is not effectively grasped as an artefact. According to Zuckert's interpretation of Kant: "as *internally* purposive, the organism must be understood … as characterized by internal purposive temporal relations among its parts/functions, which are not only influenced by one another, but also 'anticipate' the future states of the organism". In short, "the purposive functioning of an organism is not an externally related series of events, but an internally future-directed, interdependent system of dynamic relations".

> That future state, as purpose, defines the present activities of the parts, but it also, reciprocally, is understood as determined by the present state and functioning of the parts, for it constitutes survival, that is, the continuation precisely of the present, interdependent functioning of those parts.   (Zuckert 2007: 124–5)

For herself, Zuckert writes: "life may be understood as the purposive functioning of an organism to maintain the dynamic state that it is in; … a state of dynamic self-preservation". That is, "though Kant does not so claim, this temporal structure of internal, anticipatory, reciprocal means–ends relations is also … a good characterization of life". In short, "the purposive functioning of an organism is not an externally related series of events, but an internally future-directed, interdependent system of dynamic relations" (*ibid.*: 235).

A better analogy – and, indeed, central for Zuckert – is "with our own *causality* in the technical use of reason" (*ibid.*: 122, citing *CJ* 5:383). While purposiveness is an analogy we "project" onto organisms, it is *actual* in subjective judging. In elaborating what aesthetic judgement implies about this structure of subjectivity, Zuckert characterizes Kant's "feeling of life" [*Lebensgefühl*] as "a state of dynamic self-propagation … a state of intense, heightened awareness and self-awareness" (*ibid.*: 266). It "characterizes the subject as temporally located, and as active within time, as part of the empirical world and the efficient causal nexus of appearances" (*ibid.*: 271). That entails a projective temporality, one that is, more specifically, not governed in its engagement by a prior concept, but must *anticipate* unity, "aiming *towards* an indeterminate future" in order to "render comprehensible that which is not immediately comprehensible to us" (*ibid.*: 10).

As Hannah Ginsborg puts it, "the question remains of how we can even coherently *regard* something both as a purpose and as natural" (2001: 236). The "appeal to analogy does not overcome the difficulty", she continues (*ibid.*: 238). Kant himself admitted it:

> [I]ntrinsic natural perfection, as possessed by those things that are possible only as *natural purposes* and that are hence called organized beings, is not conceivable or explicable on any analogy to any known physical ability, that is, ability of nature, not even – since we belong to nature in the broadest sense – on a precisely fitting analogy to human art. (*CJ* 5:375)

Kant concluded: "Strictly speaking, the organization of nature is not analogous with any causality we know" (*ibid.*).

Ginsborg highlights Kant's language in §68 of the third *Critique*: natural purposes are "singly and alone *explicable* according to natural laws which we can think to ourselves only under the idea of purpose as a principle, and indeed merely in this way are they so much as internally *cognizable* as regards their inner form" (Ginsborg 2001: 233, citing *CJ* 5:383). "It is indeed quite certain that we cannot even become sufficiently knowledgeable of, much less provide an explanation of organized beings and their internal possibility according to mere mechanical principles of nature" (5:400). What does "internal possibility" signify here? How does it relate to the "real possibility" that Buchdahl and others (Buchdahl 1965, 1974, 1981, 1986; Kitcher 1983) insist it is Kant's main object as philosopher of science to establish? The force of Ginsborg's argument suggests that we must take the normativity to be *immanent* in the object, a product of nature, not simply a rule of design [*Bauplan*] "analogically" referred to a nonexistent "designer", as in Kant's metaphor of a "technic of nature". Like contemporary systems theory or theory of self-organization, Ginsborg proposes to ascribe normativity to the actual and the empirical order, notwithstanding Kant's notorious insistence that this can only be "as if". That appears to signify that *purpose* characterizes something intrinsic to the *object* itself.

Ultimately, according to Kant, "we need to be able to comprehend all of nature, not as a living being, but as a rational analog of a living being" (Butts 1990: 7; McLaughlin 1990). By formulating all this as a *heuristic for enquiry*, not an *ontology of nature*, Kant preserved the "purity" of his critical philosophy from "dogmatism". Thus he transposed his metaphysical problem into a methodological one, his ontological need into an epistemological constraint. Quarfood affirms: "The distinctive feature of Kant's view is ... an *epistemic presupposition* constitutive for the study of life, rather than a definite *ontological* commitment" (2004: 145). Joan Steigerwald (2006b) agrees that Kant was concerned with the epistemic conditions of our estimation of living beings, not with the nature of living beings. That might be a possible posture for a *philosopher* of science, but it is *not* a stance that can have any appeal to practising life-scientists, for their enquiry *must* be into the "nature of living beings" and to be denied cognitive access to it is to be stipulatively stripped of a scientific domain. "Biologists not only do, but must employ the concept of a natural purpose in their investigation of organisms", Rachel Zuckert (2007: 2) affirms on Kant's behalf. But that is not quite right. First, empirical biologists simply employ the theoretical term *organism* to characterize their objects of enquiry, entities manifesting processes of intrinsic dynamism.[13] It is *Kant* who glosses this as "the concept of a natural purpose". Second, if biologists "not only do, but must" use this concept of *organism*, then it seems an *essential feature* of their science.[14] To suggest that *organism* is only a "subjective necessity" entailing no real scientific knowledge claims, as Kant does, is to render biology as an empirical science of life impossible *by definition*.

That raises a central question about the warrant and scope of *philosophy* of science. Is its task to *prescribe* or to *elucidate* scientific practice?[15] How should philosophy conceive of the practices of natural science? Today natural science is considered a *language* or *model*, an architectonic "conceptual scheme" that we *impute* to actual nature (Giere 2006; Golinski 1998). It may fit only loosely, but it must be possible for nature to *reject* the fit, at least in some places.[16] For science to be empirical, anomaly must be able to challenge theory. Organism is a capital anomaly for Kant. The paradox of organism was, in my view, far more severe and disruptive in Kant's critical philosophy than he or the conventional reception of his philosophy for the most part seem to have acknowledged. It will not fit in Kant's system of science, and yet without a good account of it, the system itself must in the end appear inadequate (Zammito 2003). While Kant continues to attract attention in current philosophy of biology, I see him more as an impediment than as a facilitator for that important pursuit.[17]

Why should we privilege Kant's terminological stipulations rather than the distinctive empirical features of nature they are meant to "analogize"? I fail to see that Kant has established that intrinsic purposiveness is so opaque to empirical enquiry. Somehow biologists and ordinary human beings discern in organisms "stronger identity and unity conditions than those that govern material objects as such", and they do so routinely. That is, "organic objects seem, by contrast to material objects as such, to be identifiable non-arbitrarily as single, unified objects (or a unified, dynamic set of activities), or closed systems" (Zuckert 2007: 108–9). Empirically, the earth throngs with them and we discern this readily. Zuckert several times refers to Charles Taylor's *The Explanation of Behaviour* as a perspicuous characterization of such discernment (*ibid.*: 108, 118). And yet she follows Kant's programme that these are all ultimately mere *projections*. They do not *really* have to do with something in the order of nature, but only with our way of judging, a "subjective necessity" of our cognitive process: "we do not have a concept that determines the single identifiable end (purpose) of the organism independently of the functioning of the parts in concert with one another" (*ibid.*: 166). When it comes to intrinsic purposiveness, we are left with "a 'bootstrapping' consideration of [one] part in reciprocal purposive relations to other parts and functions" (*ibid.*: 167).[18] Accordingly, "it is only our inability to understand this internal purposiveness that leads us to consider them in the terms of design, God, and final, external purpose" (*ibid.*: 165n).

That *is* what Kant claimed; the point is, from the vantage of contemporary biology and its philosophy, that it is not clear he was *right* to. Kant set a hard-and-fast boundary marker between attainable science and speculative metaphysics. But did he mark the boundary properly? Need we halt there? Have we halted there? McLaughlin makes the claim that sciences ought to define their own appropriate projects and practices, and that it is the role of philosophy simply to assess the "metaphysical cost" (McLaughlin 2001: 190). No less than Kant, a naturalist is concerned with the "limits of human understanding", but those limits apply across the board in empirical science; biology is not uniquely disqualified. That is, *all* natural science may ultimately need to be taken to be empirical in the radical sense of "reflective" or "regulative" judgements; biology does not warrant special targeting (Giere 1985). If organisms do not fit within Kant's categorial scheme, it is not clear that their actuality in nature must yield to revision, to "reduction" or "domestication". It is not organisms that need to be "domesticated" to Kant's system of science, but Kant's system of science that needs to be "domesticated" to the actuality of nature: the very constraint that the world *must*, even for Kant, exercise upon our logical construals (Zuckert 2007: 55). From a naturalist perspective, the status of "organism", as an object of empirical scientific enquiry, is not ontologically inferior to, say, that of gravitation or "strings". Rejection of Kant's "regulative" view of intrinsic or objective purposiveness seems essential if we are to articulate a meaningful naturalist philosophy of biology as a special but legitimate science of nature. But this also affects Kant's notion of the ontology of rational agency. What if, against Kant and from a naturalist stance, *organism* simply betokens – that is, can be intersubjectively, empirically discerned to have as its properties – those propensities of systemic, open-ended dynamism we characterize as intrinsic purposiveness? Then Kant's characterization of reason is *not* just a metaphor: it parallels organismic form because it *is* an expression of organismic function (Ingensiep 1996, 2004; Kleingeld 1998; Dörflinger 2000).

I take very seriously Paul Guyer's suggestion that starting with the *Critique of the Power of Judgment* Kant found himself driven to loosen his stipulation that mechanical explanation (in his precise sense) was *obligatory* for natural science (see Guyer 2001, 2003, 2005). I find it important that Michael Friedman (1992: 305) concluded that already with *Metaphysical Foundations of Natural Science* in 1785, the security of Kant's distinction between constitutive and regulative was imperiled. Indeed, I find this one of the most salient *historical* turns in Kant's philosophy, and one pregnant with the future in both philosophy and biology. Intrinsic purposiveness – what Kant discerned but then "domesticated" into the language of intentional action – is the starting point of actual biological science and ultimately of a naturalist philosophy of mind. And that is what, much to Kant's chagrin, his successors read out of the *Critique of the Power of Judgment*: the prospect of "a daring adventure of reason" (5:419n) (see Tuschling 1991; Zammito 2003; Huneman 2006a,b; Sloan 2006).

Notes

1. The notion "end in itself" is the most important formulation in Kant of this capacity for agency. He was quite comfortable with the *thought* ("idea" in his technical sense) of an end in itself in considering the issue of human moral agency. "*But let us suppose that there were something* whose existence has in itself an absolute worth, something which as an end in itself could be a ground of determinate laws. In it, and in it alone, would there be the ground of a possible categorical imperative" (*G* 4:428; emphasis added). There are complexities, here, as between an end in itself, a "final end" and an "ultimate end", but all these notions refer to *internal* purposiveness, and Kant's point is that "external purposiveness is an entirely different concept from the concept of internal purposiveness" (*CJ* 5:425).
2. We even take the liberty of imputing "relative purposiveness" to relations between or among entities in the natural world, like sandy soil for pine forests, although such relations are problematic as causal accounts. Kant was deeply suspicious from at least the 1760s onward of the sorts of teleological arguments along such lines rampant in eighteenth-century physical theology. See 5:368 and 5:425–28; see also Zammito (2006a).
3. The discrimination between an originating cause and its determining ground, with reference to Kant's notion of purpose, is offered by Beihart (2009).

4. "For since we do not, properly speaking, *observe* the purposes in nature as designed, but only in our reflection upon its products *think* this concept as a guiding thread for our judgment, they are not given to us through the object" (5:247).

5. Kant introduces the instance of the regular hexagon at 5:370.

6. On Zuckert's interpretation, which will be central to this analysis, see Zammito (2009).

7. The contrast between *educt* and *product* is crucial, as Kant elaborated later in the third *Critique*, 5:423. See also his *Metaphysics Lectures*, 28:684, 29:760–61, and the discussion in Zammito (2003).

8. See the discussion of Locke in McLaughlin (2001: 175–6).

9. Kant writes of an "inscrutable principle of original organization" of life forms at 5:424. See Zammito (2003).

10. "[T]he claim that there are free causes in living systems has no ontological force. It is rather a transcendental claim, that is, one concerning the possibility of our judgments" (Zumbach 1984: 107).

11. "The possibility of living matter (the concept of which contains a contradiction, because lifelessness, *inertia*, constitutes its essential characteristic), cannot even be conceived" (5:394). "The possibility of natural science proper rests entirely upon the law of inertia … The opposite of this, and therefore the death of all natural philosophy, would be hylozoism" (*MF* 4:544).

12. On "backwards causation" in "function talk" see Wright (1973), Cummins (1975) and Nagel (1977). More recently: Allen *et al.* (1998), Buller (1999), Godfrey-Smith (1993), Lewens (2001, 2004), McLaughlin (2001), Walsh (1996, 2006), Zammito (2003).

13. The concept of organism received its original elaboration by Aristotle, but it came to decisive reformulations in the eighteenth century by figures like Locke, Leibniz, Stahl, Buffon and Haller, before being taken up by Kant. For the historical background, see Huneman (2002). For contemporary discussions, see Gutmann *et al.* (2000) and Lewontin (1985).

14. See Quarfood (2004), who recognizes that for the science of biology the idea of organism must be constitutive, not regulative, yet suggests that Kant may still be warranted at a meta-level, *qua* transcendental philosopher, to regard it as merely regulative.

15. I take this to be a central element in the challenge of post-positivism to the "Received View" in philosophy of science. See Zammito (2004).

16. See the discussion in Zammito (2004: 228–31).

17. On Kant and current philosophy of biology, see Steigerwald (2006a) and Huneman (2007). For a rejoinder to my view, see Breitenbach (2009).

18. Thomas Nickles offers the appropriate rejoinder: "a defensible historicism does not rule out a bootstrap account of the development of knowledge; on the contrary, it requires it!" (1992: 116). On "bootstrapping" and naturalist epistemology, see Briskman (1977) and Axtell (1992).

ELEVEN

Nature and history: ultimate and final purpose

Stephen Houlgate

I

Kant is sometimes thought to be a thoroughly ahistorical philosopher.[1] Allen Wood points out, however, that those who think of Kant in this way "have a profoundly false image of the critical philosophy" (Wood 1999: 208). Although Kant considers reason to be a faculty with unchanging principles, he holds that our *awareness* of the rational principles of right and morality is historically conditioned and also that "our *use* of reason develops through history" (*ibid.*: 230, 248).

The key text for understanding Kant's *philosophy* of history is his essay *Idea for a Universal History with a Cosmopolitan Aim* (1784). In that essay Kant claims that history proceeds "in accordance with a determinate plan of nature" (*UH* 109). This claim itself presupposes that there is "*purposiveness*" [*Zweckmäßigkeit*] in the arrangement of nature as a whole (*UH* 115 [8:25]). Kant's philosophy of history thus forms part of his "teleological doctrine of nature" (*UH* 109).

In the *Critique of the Power of Judgment* (1790) Kant maintains that the concept of "the purposiveness of nature ... has its origin strictly in the reflecting power of judgment" (*CJ* 68). In particular, such judgement presupposes that nature's universal empirical laws are purposefully suited to *our* understanding of them (*CJ* 72). Kant also claims, however, that the concept of an *objective* purposiveness of nature – the idea that nature does not just accommodate our aim of understanding it but has purposes or "ends" of its own – is "a critical principle of *reason* [*Vernunft*] for the reflecting power of judgment", rather than a principle of reflecting judgement itself (*CJ* 268 [5:397]; see also *CJ* 274). In the essay on history, too, it is reason that requires that we regard nature and history as purposive.[2] Before examining that essay, therefore, we need to look briefly at Kant's discussion of reason's idea of purposiveness in the *Critique of Pure Reason* (1781, 1787).

In that text Kant explains that the principal interest of reason – that is, speculative, *theoretical* reason – is to bring about the "systematic completeness of all cognitions" (*CpR* B 683). A "systematic" connection, in Kant's view, is one that is "based on one principle" (673). Reason thus seeks completeness of cognition by directing the understanding [*Verstand*] to search for something in nature that can serve as that one principle, for example the "*fundamental power*" or "highest genus" (677, 686). The highest formal unity in nature that reason can conceive, Kant tells us, is the "*purposive* unity of things" (714). Like other principles of reason (such as those of homogeneity and specification), this principle of purposiveness is a purely *regulative* one (719).[3] Reason does not know *a priori* that purposive unity *must* be found in nature. It directs the understanding to search for evidence of such unity, and presumes that it will indeed be found, but it lets the understanding discern that evidence in nature as far as it can and in that sense leaves undetermined what will actually be found there.[4]

Kant insists that theoretical reason seeks purposiveness nowhere other than in *nature* itself. Nonetheless, he argues that such purposiveness has to be thought as grounded in the "intentions" of a "divine will" that lies beyond nature (*CpR* B 726–7; see Allison 2009: 35). Yet theoretical reason, in Kant's view, is not justified in asserting that a divine being *actually exists* and *causes* there to be purposiveness in the world. The most such reason can do is look upon nature "*as if* this being, as the highest intelligence, were the cause of everything according to the wisest aim" (*CpR* B 716).

For Kant, a purpose or "end" [*Zweck*] is "an object of the choice (of a rational being)", that is, something set by beings, such as ourselves, with intelligence (*MMV* 513 [6:381]). The purposiveness that reason seeks in nature thus also has to be grounded in a being with intelligence, namely a divine being with divine intelligence and intentions. Kant insists that we have no choice in the matter: "we *must* presuppose such a being" (*CpR* B 725). It lies in the nature of reason to seek purposive unity in things, and so "the *speculative* interest of reason makes it necessary to regard every ordinance in the world as if it had sprouted from the intention of a highest reason" (714). The point of doing so, however, is not to provide a "hyperphysical", divine explanation for the purposiveness in nature (727–8); rather, it is only in this way that reason can form a properly determinate conception of *natural purposiveness* itself.

Reason's speculative interest is in, and its focus is on, nature: that is the "proper field" for the speculative use of reason (729). We can think of nature as properly *purposive*, however, only if we think of it – by analogy with the purposes of finite, rational beings (726) – *as if* it were grounded in God's wisdom.

The idea of a divine being thus provides what Kant calls a "schema" for thinking of nature itself as a systematic, purposive unity (702). The purposiveness in which speculative reason is interested, therefore, is one that is fulfilled in nature by means of nature's own laws, not one that is "foreign and contingent in relation to the nature of things" (721). This is central to Kant's idea of purposiveness: whenever he talks of the "wisdom" of nature what he is interested in is the way in which the mechanisms of nature fulfil the purposes of nature *by themselves*.

II

Kant begins his essay on history by reminding us of one of the conclusions of the first *Critique*: actions, which are the manifestations or "appearances" of *free will* in the sensuous world, are nonetheless determined "in accordance with universal laws of nature" (*UH* 108; see also *CpR* B 826; *PracR* 232). This does not mean that there is no observable difference in experience for Kant between mere physical events and free actions. The latter are events that are determined by principles of reason, rather than mere sensuous impulses or physical causes. In that sense, Kant maintains in the first *Critique*, "practical freedom can be proved through experience" (*CpR* B 830), even if the transcendental freedom that such practical freedom presupposes is not manifest in experience. As objects of experience, however, actions determined by principles of reason still have causes and effects within the spatiotemporal world and so are subject to laws of nature. This is evident, Kant contends, in the case of marriages and births, which are greatly influenced by the free will of human beings, but are proven by the "annual tables of them in large countries" to happen in accordance with constant laws of nature (*UH* 108). This fact that *free* human actions are subject to *laws of nature* gives us hope, Kant thinks, that we might be able to discern a certain lawfulness or "regular course" not just in particular cases but in the play of human freedom as a whole, that is, in the whole course of *history*.

Kant concedes that human actions taken *as a whole* can appear to constitute a "planless *aggregate*", "woven together out of folly [and] childish vanity" (*UH* 118, 109). To understand history in this way, however, would be at odds with the interest of speculative, theoretical reason, which seeks lawfulness and "systematic unity" throughout nature (which, for Kant, includes history). As we saw above, the highest formal unity that reason can conceive is "the *purposive* unity of things" (*CpR* B 714). The speculative interest of reason requires it, therefore, to look for purposive unity – and to assume that it can be found – in the history of free human actions. If we were not to do this, we would find purposiveness in certain parts of nature (such as organisms), but not in nature as a whole. We would thus not encounter a thoroughly "lawful nature", but in nature viewed as a whole "desolate chance" would take the place of the "guideline of reason" (*UH* 109).[5]

Note that Kant does not himself provide a fully worked-out teleological account of human history. He does no more in his essay than provide the *idea* or "guiding thread" for a history of freedom "in accordance with a determinate plan of nature" (*UH* 109, 119); that is, he suggests how the course of history would have to be understood *if* it were understood as fulfilling nature's purpose. Kant's idea for a universal history is thus a merely *regulative* idea that is meant to guide the understanding in its study of history. Experience and the examination of historical records will show whether or not there is actually any purposeful development in history itself; Kant's idea of history just directs the understanding to look for purposiveness in history in the first place and sets out briefly what purposive *historical* (as opposed to biological) development would involve.

III

Kant understands history to be the fulfilment of the aims of *nature*. We need, therefore, briefly to clarify what he understands by the term "nature". In his essay *On the Use of Teleological Principles in Philosophy* (1788) Kant suggests that nature is "the sum total of all that exists as determined by laws". This includes, he writes, both "the world" and "its supreme cause". He adds, however, that only the world, as the object of physics, is "nature properly so called" (*TP* 195). Nature, for Kant, is thus the realm of objects in space and time that are governed by efficient causality: the realm of "appearance".

In the first *Critique* Kant argues that the understanding, whose object of cognition is this realm of appearance, must also think of an "object in itself" beyond appearance as a "transcendental object, which is the cause of appearance" (*CpR* B 344). He also contends that theoretical reason must produce ideas of the soul and God as purely intelligible (as opposed to empirical) objects (*CpR* B 710–14). Kant insists, however, that neither the understanding nor theoretical reason may assume that objects in themselves or the objects of ideas actually exist. For theoretical reason, therefore, nature does not include the noumenal, intelligible world beyond the realm of appearance (assuming that there is such a world).

Another way of putting the point is to say that nature is not equivalent to *creation* [*Schöpfung*]: for, as Kant claims in the *Critique of Practical Reason* (1788), "the concept of a creation ... can only be referred to noumena" and signifies the "creation of things in themselves" (*PracR* 222 [5:102]). Nature "properly so called" cannot be understood by theoretical reason to be created by, or explained through, an actually existing creator God, because, as we have seen, such reason is entitled to look upon nature only *as if* it were grounded in God's wisdom (*CpR* B 716).

From the perspective of theoretical reason, therefore, it is nature (rather than a creator God) that gave us reason and the (practical) freedom that is grounded on it (*UH* 110; see also *CB* 170). Moreover, nature gave us reason and freedom for a purpose. The purpose that nature, as it were, had (and has) "in mind" for us is that we actually come to use our reason and so come to think and act freely and rationally. Alongside reason itself, therefore, nature also gave the human being certain "predispositions" (*Anlagen*) *to use* his reason in various ways. The purpose or aim of nature can thus be restated as follows: it is that the *"predispositions [within the human being] whose goal is the use of his reason"* should be fully developed. Indeed, Kant argues that in the "teleological doctrine of nature" *"all natural predispositions of a creature are determined sometime to develop themselves completely and purposively"* (*UH* 109 [8: 18]).

Two things should be noted about Kant's claim that the "highest intention [*Absicht*] of nature" is "the development of all the predispositions in humanity" (*UH* 112 [8: 22]).[6] On the one hand, for Kant (from the theoretical point of view), it is *nature* that "intends" us to use our reason and exercise our freedom. In other words, we are *born* to be free. In this respect Kant's position differs from that of Hegel, for whom our freedom is rooted in our *spirit* – that is, in our own consciousness and self-consciousness – rather than in what nature determines us to be.[7]

On the other hand, nature intends us to be *free and rational* and so to liberate ourselves from being determined by nature alone. Reason is defined by Kant in his essay on history as "a faculty of extending the rules and aims of the use of all its powers far beyond natural instinct" (*UH* 109). Our goal in life, therefore, is to use our reason to set ends and formulate principles through which we *freely* determine ourselves to act in various ways. Indeed, in Kant's view, nature intends us to use our reason and act freely in every aspect of our lives:

> Since [nature] gave the human being reason, and the freedom of the will grounded on it, that was already a clear indication of its intention [*Absicht*] in regard to that endowment. For he should now not be guided by instinct or cared for and instructed by innate knowledge; rather he should produce everything out of himself.[8]

We should feed ourselves, clothe ourselves, provide for our own safety and defence, and "all gratification that can make life agreeable, all [the human being's] insight and prudence and even the generosity of his will, should be entirely his own work" (*UH* 110). We are to become, through the use of our own reason, fully self-productive beings. In this respect, despite other differences between them, the perspectives of Kant and Hegel (and, indeed, Marx) are similar.

The condition in which "all talents come bit by bit to be developed" and we attain "the greatest skillfulness" [*Geschicklichkeit*] is named by Kant "culture" [*Kultur*] (*UH* 110–11 [8: 20–21]). The highest intention or aim of nature can thus be said to be the achievement of culture. In the *Critique of the Power of Judgment* Kant makes the same point by calling culture "the ultimate end" or purpose of nature. Reason, he writes, is the "capacity to set voluntary ends" for oneself – to determine freely for oneself what one is to do and how one is to do it – and culture is the "production of the *aptitude* [*Tauglichkeit*] of a rational being for any ends in general" (*CJ* 298–9 [5:431]). Culture, therefore, is not just the predisposition, but the actual aptitude, to use our reason freely in different ways.[9]

In the third *Critique*, however, Kant distinguishes sharply between the "ultimate end of nature" [*letzter Zweck der Natur*] and the "final end of creation" [*Endzweck der Schöpfung*] (*CJ* 298–303 [5:431–6]). As Henry Allison points out, Kant actually introduces two conceptions of the final end (Allison 2009: 42). On the one hand, the final end or purpose of creation "to which the whole of nature is subordinated" is simply "*the human being* (each rational being in the world) *under moral laws*" (*CJ* 303, 314). On the other hand, "the final end in the world" [*Endzweck in der Welt*] is the end that human beings are themselves under an unconditional duty to pursue, namely, the "happiness of rational beings harmoniously coinciding with conformity to the moral law" (*CJ* 316 [5:451]), or what Kant also calls "the *highest good in the world* possible through freedom" (*CJ* 315; see also *PracR* 244–5). In neither sense, however, is the final end something that *nature* is able to bring about: "morality and a causality subordinated to it according to ends is absolutely impossible by means of nature; for the principle of its determination for action is supersensible" (*CJ* 303). It cannot, therefore, be the *aim* or *end* of nature to bring about that final end either now or in the future (302). As Allison puts it, "nature's ultimate end cannot be to make us moral" (2009: 40).

Certain statements made by Kant in the third *Critique* make it look, however, as though nature does aim to make us moral, and so to bring about the final end or purpose, after all. He says, for example, that "we must seek out that which nature is capable of doing *in order to prepare* [the human being] for what he must himself do in order to be a final end" (*CJ* 298), and he talks of what "nature can accomplish *with a view to* [*in Absicht auf*] the final end that lies *outside* of it" (299 [5:431]) (my emphasis in each case). Kant also insists, however, that the very idea of a "final end" is "a concept of our practical reason", not our theoretical reason (319–20). The idea that nature aims in some way at bringing about the final end is thus the result of Kant's combining the theoretical *and* the practical points of view. This is perfectly appropriate in a discussion of how we should *judge* nature, for one of the roles of reflecting judgement, in Kant's view, is precisely to make possible, through the concept of purposiveness, "the transition from the purely theoretical to the purely practical" (81–2). Kant insists, however, that from the perspective of purely *theoretical* cognition no use of the concept of a "final end" is justified or possible (320).[10] From the perspective of theoretical reason, therefore, the aim of nature is culture within nature and history, *not* moral freedom or holiness beyond this world.

Yet Kant reminds us in the essay on history that "the idea of morality" itself "belongs to culture" (*UH* 116; see Wood 1999: 296). Furthermore, other remarks in that essay suggest that, even from the perspective of purely theoretical reason, nature's intention is that we should become not only "cultivated" but also "*moralized*" [*moralisiert*] (*UH* 116 [8:26]), albeit *within* history rather than *beyond* it. Kant writes, for example, that "it appears to have been no aim at all to nature that [the human being] should live well; but only that he should labour and work himself up so far that he might make himself *worthy* [*würdig*] of well-being through the conduct of life" (*UH* 110 [8:20], my emphasis); and, as he states in the *Critique of Practical Reason*, "all worthiness [*Würdigkeit*] depends upon moral conduct" (*PracR* 244 [5:130]). He also states that, with the progress towards culture,

> a beginning is made toward the foundation of a mode of thought which can with time transform the rude natural predisposition

to make moral [*sittlich*] distinctions into determinate practical principles and hence transform a *pathologically* compelled agreement to form a society finally into a *moral* [*moralisch*] whole.

(*UH* 111 [8:21])

It appears, therefore, that, for Kant, *nature* intends us to become, through the use of our own free reason, virtuous *moral* beings within history.

It remains the case, however, that the aim of nature "properly so called" is not to make us moral in the sense of giving rise to the noumenal foundation of morality, that is, to our supersensible freedom. That foundation of morality, like everything that belongs to the intelligible world, can only be the result of divine *creation* and cannot be generated, or given to us originally, by mere nature.[11] Yet this does not mean that human beings are incapable of moral progress in history. Kant thinks, for example, that our awareness and understanding of the moral law can and does develop (in the individual and the species) and that "morality must have more power over the human heart the more purely it is presented" (*PracR* 265).[12] He believes that certain "subjective conditions" can "hinder people or help them in *fulfilling* the laws of a metaphysics of morals", conditions that include education and "popular instruction" (*MMR* 372). And he states explicitly in one essay that "in our age, as compared with all previous ages, the human race as a whole has actually made considerable moral [*moralisch*] progress" (*CS* 307 [8:310]). Nature's aim is thus not to give rise to the foundation of morality in humanity, or to bring about the highest good that is the end of creation beyond nature and history, but to promote the progress in understanding and fulfilling the moral law of which we are capable *in history*.[13]

Note that, strictly speaking, nature aims *indirectly* at our becoming morally virtuous. The "ultimate end of nature" is *culture*: the full development of all our natural predispositions into actual aptitudes. One of our predispositions, however, is to use our reason in a moral, rather than purely pragmatic or prudential, way: as Kant puts it, we have a "moral [*sittlich*] vocation" (*CB* 169 [8:116–17]). Nature's aim must, therefore, include our becoming virtuous moral beings (see Kleingeld 2009: 185).[14]

Even when "morality" is understood to be something towards which we can make progress in history, however, nature itself cannot *make* us moral. Moral conduct, for Kant, always requires "supersensible" freedom, as well as education and discipline in this world: we cannot, therefore, be forced into it by nature or anything else.[15] All nature can do is *facilitate* our becoming morally virtuous by forcing us through natural means to become cultivated (see Deligiorgi 2005: 107; Allison 2009: 40). The distinction between free, rational activity that we can be forced by nature to undertake and moral conduct that we cannot be forced to undertake is, I think, what Kant has in mind when he talks of thought transforming "a *pathologically* compelled agreement to form a society finally into a *moral* [*moralisch*] whole" (*UH* 111 [8:21]).

The goal of nature, for Kant, can thus be summarized in the following way. We are to develop all manner of skills and eventually become "*cultivated* in a high degree by art and science". At the same time, we are to become "*civilized* ... by all sorts of social decorum and propriety". Finally, through our own efforts, we are to become "*moralized*" (*UH* 116).[16] Kant maintains that the development of our use of reason, which is to lead to culture, civilization and morality, requires "attempts, practice and instruction in order gradually to progress from one stage of insight to another" (*UH* 109). In his view, however, this means "every human being would have to live exceedingly long in order to learn how he is to make a complete use of all his natural predispositions". Yet human beings have been allotted only a short period of life by nature. Kant concludes, therefore, that "nature perhaps needs an immense series of generations, each of which transmits its enlightenment to the next, in order finally to propel its germs in our species to that stage of development which is completely suited to its aim". Accordingly, nature's aim is not that every individual human being should fully develop his or her predispositions, but that these predispositions be fully developed over a long period "*in the species*". Nature's aim is that the human species should eventually *end up* being cultivated, civilized and moralized (*UH* 109–10).

In the *Critique of Practical Reason*, Kant states that "complete conformity of the will with the moral law" is "*holiness*, a perfection of which no rational being of the sensible world is capable at any moment of his existence". Practical reason requires us, therefore, to assume an "*endless progress* toward that complete conformity" that extends beyond this world, that is, to postulate the immortality of the soul (*PracR* 238). As we have seen, however, there is no good reason from the perspective of *theoretical* reason to accept the existence of anything beyond nature and history, although its possibility cannot be excluded. Theoretical reason thus has to locate the goal of nature – the human species becoming a "*moral* whole" – *within* history itself, and so does not understand nature to act "with a view to the final end" that lies outside of nature and history (*CJ* 299).

IV

It was noted above that the purposiveness that theoretical reason seeks in nature is one that is fulfilled in accordance with nature's own laws (see *CpR* B 719). In the essay on history, therefore, Kant examines the *natural mechanism* through which nature achieves its purpose. (What follows below is, of course, an account of what nature does according to the *idea* of history that Kant sets out. Whether nature actually does any of this must be discovered by experience and historical research that are guided by this idea.) The natural mechanism at work in history is identified by Kant as the *"unsociable sociability"* [*ungesellige Geselligkeit*] of human beings or their propensity for *"antagonism"* in their social relations with one another (*UH* 111 [8:20]). Kant claims that human beings have an "inclination to become *socialized*" – to join together with others in pursuit of their aims – but that the human being also has "a great propensity to *individualize* (isolate) himself" and to try to "direct everything so as to get his own way". We come together with others, therefore, expecting and encountering *resistance* from them as they seek to get their own way just as we do. It is this resistance, Kant writes, that "awakens all the powers of the human being, brings him to overcome his propensity to indolence, and, driven by ambition, tyranny, and greed, to obtain for himself a rank among his fellows, whom he cannot *stand*, but also cannot *leave alone*". By awakening our powers in this way – that is, by making us use our reason – the resistance we expect and encounter forces us to take the first steps "from crudity toward culture" and to develop all our talents (*ibid.*).

Kant concedes that the qualities of unsociability from which resistance arises are "not at all amiable in themselves", but he insists that without them "all talents would ... remain eternally hidden in their germs" (*UH* 111–12). These "natural incentives" to the use of our reason are thus the means through which nature, as it were, *cunningly* achieves its own purpose.[17]

Two things need to be noted at this point. First, Kant writes that *nature* brings about the development of all our predispositions (*UH* 111). It should be borne in mind, however, that all nature actually does, on Kant's account, is give us our initial predispositions and the two inclinations towards sociability and unsociability. Those two inclinations then awaken *our* powers and cause us to use *our own* reason in our effort to "get our own way" in society with others. We are then the ones who, *through our own activity*, further develop our predispositions to use reason in various ways. It is thus "humanity by itself" that fulfils the purpose of nature (*UH* 112): nature's work in history is actually (as

Kant puts it elsewhere) *"the work of the human being"* (CB 169). It is true that nature *forces* us to be free by giving us the relevant inclinations; but it is equally true that nature forces us – pretty well immediately – to be *free*. Kant puts the point nicely later in the essay on history: "nature here follows a regular course, leading our species from the lowest step of animality gradually up to the highest step of humanity, and indeed *through the human being's own art*, albeit one extorted from him" (*UH* 115). For Kant, as for Hegel and Marx, therefore, history is the sphere of *human* activity. Kant and Hegel would both agree with Marx's famous statement that "human beings make their own history, but they do not make it just as they please" (Marx 1852: 329).

Second, although transcendental freedom cannot be explained by the laws of nature, *practical* freedom within the world (and the use of reason that grounds it) can – at least in part – be so explained. Indeed, this is precisely what a teleological approach to history reveals: nature, through natural means, leads us directly to use our reason and *freely* formulate rational principles that guide our conduct. Note, however, that the use of reason does not immediately turn us into cultivated or civilized (let alone moralized) beings. On the contrary, our use of reason, for Kant, is initially in the service of our unsociability and fuels our ambition, greed and desire "to dominate" (*UH* 112; see Wood 1999: 267). (Like Hegel and Nietzsche, therefore, Kant sees the desire for dominance as a necessary stage on our journey towards becoming moral beings.)

V

In Kant's view, our natural inclinations do not lead us into problems that *extort* moral conduct from us as their solution. Moral conduct is motivated by pure respect for the moral law and so is not something we can be compelled by nature to engage in. Our natural inclinations do, however, lead us into problems that compel us to find solutions to them. The supreme "task" [*Aufgabe*] that nature sets us is how to establish "a perfectly *just civil constitution*", that is, a *"civil society universally administering right"* (*UH* 112 [8:22]).[18] Human beings are compelled to enter into such a society because their antagonistic inclinations make it impossible for them to subsist long next to one another in "wild freedom". They can thrive and develop their predispositions only in "that society which has the greatest freedom, hence one in which there is a thoroughgoing antagonism of its members, and yet the most precise determination and security of the boundaries of this freedom so that the latter can coexist with the freedom of others" (*ibid.*). Nature does not, however, construct such a society for us; we have to do it ourselves.[19] This task presents a particular problem, in Kant's view, because human beings will always abuse their freedom unless there is someone to exercise authority over them in accordance with law, but the highest supreme authority, which has to be "just [*gerecht*] *in itself*", will itself be a human being with no one in authority over him. A perfect solution to this problem, Kant writes, is impossible, so the task that nature sets us is to *approximate* to the idea of perfect justice as well as we can (*UH* 113 [8:23]; see also *CJ* 299–300).

As Kant points out elsewhere, there will have to have been "some arrangement for a civil constitution and public justice" early in human history (*CB* 172). The task or problem that Kant has in mind in the essay on history is that of establishing a *perfectly just* civil constitution. This problem, we are told, is "*the latest to be solved by the human species*" and, in Kant's view, had not yet been solved in his own time, even approximately (*UH* 113). Furthermore, it cannot be solved without simultaneously solving another problem: that of establishing a "lawful *external relation between states*" or "federation of nations". Such a federation would constitute a "cosmopolitan condition of public state security", which would be "not wholly without *dangers*" but which would nonetheless exhibit a "united might" and protect the security and rights of every state "in accordance with laws of its united will" (*UH* 114, 116).[20]

States are required to form such a federation because, like individual human beings, they too are *antagonistic* towards one another. "Through wars", Kant writes, and "through the overstrained and never ceasing process of armament for them", states suffer "many devastations, reversals and even thoroughgoing exhaustion of their powers", and this "condition of need" drives them to enter into a federation of states. "Nature has therefore once again used the incompatibility of human beings, even of great societies and state bodies of this kind of creature, as a means to seek out in their unavoidable *antagonism* a condition of tranquility and safety" (*UH* 114).

For Kant, then, the problem of securing justice within the state is inseparable from the problem of securing justice between states. Nature, in Kant's view, compels us through our "unsociable sociability" to seek the solution to both problems together. When these two problems of justice have been solved, or at least when we have reached approximate solutions, the human species, Kant states, will be "almost halfway through its formation" (*UH* 116). What remains to be completed is the task of *moralizing* the human species, of developing virtue and spreading it across the globe. There is, however, no more that *nature* can do by herself to facilitate the development of virtue. In that sense, the highest intention of nature – the one that it can fulfil by means of the natural inclinations implanted in human beings – is the achievement of a "universal *cosmopolitan condition*", a law-governed federation of just law-governed states (*UH* 118).[21]

Nature does not, however, pursue the aim of political justice for its own sake: the "ultimate end of nature" is *culture* within the sphere of civil and international justice (see *CJ* 299–300). Furthermore, a law-governed federation of just states, in which we live cultivated, civilized lives, is itself the necessary precondition of human society's becoming a "*moral* whole" (*UH* 111). The highest aim of nature is thus to bring about "a universal *cosmopolitan condition*, as the womb in which all original predispositions of the human species will be developed" (*UH* 118), including the predisposition to use practical reason to fulfil our moral vocation.

VI

In his essay on history Kant presents no more than an "idea of how the course of the world would have to go *if* it were to conform to certain rational ends" (*UH* 118, emphasis added). He thinks, however, that the speculative interest of reason requires us to conceive of nature as a purposive unity and to understand history as the fulfilment of nature's "aims" for humanity. Furthermore, he believes that experience (which includes the testimony of historians) provides some evidence that history is actually taking the course set out in his "idea" (*UH* 116). If, for example, we trace the influence of the Greeks on the Romans and of the latter on the "barbarians", and so on "down to the present time", Kant maintains that "one will discover a regular course of improvement of state constitutions in our part of the world" (*UH* 119).[22] He also believes that "civil freedom" within states is gradually advancing in his own time and that, although a federation of just states still lies a long way off in the future, a "feeling" is now beginning to stir among European states that we should move in that direction (*UH* 117–18).[23] All of this opens up for us a "consoling prospect into the future" in which we can foresee the human species "in the remote distance" finally working itself upward "toward the condition in which all germs nature has placed in it can be fully developed and its vocation here on earth can be fulfilled" (*UH* 119). Moreover, Kant thinks that the philosophical activity of identifying the aim of nature itself furthers the fulfilment of that aim, for it means that we can now work more self-consciously than hitherto to bring about that fulfilment (and in the process enable heads of state who promote that aim to secure their "glorious remembrance" in the eyes of "the latest age") (*UH* 116, 118, 120).

Kant thus sets out his "idea for a universal history" in part to enable us to work for a better *future*, and in that respect his approach to history finds a later echo in the thought of Marx. Kant's principal concern, however, is to provide a "guideline" that will enable speculative reason to understand history as a *rational*, systematic unity (*UH* 109). In that respect, Kant's approach to history appears to be closer to Hegel's. Kant differs from Hegel, however, in seeing human activity in history as fulfilling *nature's* plan, rather than as the (free, human) "*spirit's* efforts to attain knowledge of what it is in itself" (Hegel 1830: 54, emphasis added).

VII

In his essay on teleological principles in philosophy, Kant writes that "I do not find it advisable to use a *theological* language in matters that concern the mere cognitions of nature and their reach (where it is quite appropriate to express oneself in *teleological* terms)" (*TP* 213; see also *CJ* 253–4). The most we can do, from the standpoint of theoretical reason, is approach nature *as if* it were grounded in God. Practical reason, by contrast, requires that we postulate the *existence* of God as the ground of nature. Kant's reasoning, very briefly, is as follows: the moral law commands that we strive to promote the "highest good", which is the unity of morality and happiness. Since we *ought* to promote the highest good, the latter must be possible. As finite beings, however, we are incapable by ourselves of making nature "harmonize" with the principles of morality, such that it leads us to happiness at the same time as we make ourselves worthy of that happiness by achieving moral virtue. We must, therefore, postulate the existence of a "supreme cause of nature" – God – who can ensure that the course of nature is in harmony with the principles of morality and that we are able to achieve happiness and moral virtue together. It is "morally necessary", therefore, "to assume the existence of God" (*PracR* 240–41).

The postulate or "rational belief" that God exists is a *theoretical* proposition, but one that is made necessary by pure *practical* reason (*PracR* 238). This practical extension of our theoretical cognition does not alter the way in which we understand nature and history themselves, but it situates both of them in a broader moral–theological context. First, we are now justified in assuming the purposiveness in nature and history to be grounded in the wisdom of an existing God (with moral intentions). Nature must still be understood as achieving its purpose "in accordance with universal and necessary laws of nature", but these laws themselves must be understood to "have their origin in the absolute necessity of a single original being" (*CpR* B 844; see also *PracR* 252). Second, the meaning of the term "nature" is expanded to include both sensible and *supersensible* nature (which, for the sake of practical reason, must now be assumed to exist) (*PracR* 174). Nature "properly so called" – that is, sensible, this-worldly nature – is thus now to be understood explicitly as part of *creation* as a whole. Third, creation is to be understood as having its own goal, which transcends what sensible nature aims to achieve. "*God's final end* in creating the world" is the "*highest good*" – the unity of morality and happiness – which can be achieved only *beyond* sensible nature in the intelligible world (*PracR* 245, 247). The final end of creation, however, incorporates the highest aim of sensible nature; this is because the development of humanity into a fully *moral* species presupposes the establishment of a law-governed federation of law-governed states, in which all the original predispositions of humanity will be developed.[24] With the addition of the perspective of practical reason, therefore, it becomes legitimate to think of nature "properly so called" not just as aiming at culture, justice and morality *within* history, but as aiming at them (as Kant puts it in the third *Critique*) "with a view to the final end" that lies *beyond* nature and history (*CJ* 299; see also *CJ* 63).[25]

Notes

1. See, for example, Walsh: "as has often been remarked by critics of his general philosophy, his [Kant's] outlook was singularly unhistorical" (1967: 120).
2. See *Universal History* 109: "guideline of reason". Katerina Deligiorgi points out that Kant "conspicuously avoids all references to reflective teleological judgment in his writings on history" (2005: 106).
3. On the regulative principles of homogeneity and specification, see *CpR* B 676–89.
4. Like the principles of homogeneity and specification, the principle of purposiveness can thus be said to have "objective but indeterminate validity" (*CpR* B 691). See also *CpR* B 719–20: "we have a regulative principle of the systematic unity of a teleological connection, which, however, *we do not determine beforehand*, but may only expect while pursuing the physical–mechanical connection according to universal laws" (emphasis added).
5. Allen Wood and Henry Allison have both stressed – rightly in my view – that what motivates Kant to try to understand history teleologically is a *theoretical* interest in comprehending what there *is*, rather than a moral interest in determining what we should do. See Allison (2009: 24) and Wood (1999: 214–15).

Walsh, by contrast, sees in Kant's philosophy of history "a pendant to moral philosophy". See Walsh (1967: 121).

6. Wood translates "*Absicht*" as "aim" rather than "intention".

7. See Hegel: "Just as gravity is the substance of matter, so also can it be said that freedom is the substance of spirit" (1830: 47).

8. Wood again translates "*Absicht*" as "aim" rather than "intention".

9. On the difference between the culture of skill and the culture of discipline (*Zucht*) in Kant's account, see Deligiorgi (2005: 116–17) and Allison (2009: 40–41).

10. See Makkreel: "Whereas a final purpose is a rational moral ideal that transcends nature, within a natural context we can only speak of ultimate purposes" (1995: 125).

11. See *Faculties* 307 [7:92]: "without the moral foundation [*Grundlage*] in humanity having to be enlarged in the least; for that, a kind of new creation [*Schöpfung*] (supernatural influence) would be necessary".

12. See also *CpR* B 845: "a greater refinement of moral ideas". Fackenheim even talks of the "*discovery* of moral law" in history as Kant understands it. See Fackenheim (1956–7: 387, emphasis added).

13. On the idea of moral progress in Kant, see especially Kleingeld (1999).

14. Deligiorgi points out that "culture opens the way for morality because it thematizes our identity as end-*setting* beings, which is a prerequisite for considering ourselves as morally beholden". See Deligiorgi (2005: 118) and Roulier (2004: 93–6).

15. See *CJ* 61: "morally practical precepts, which are grounded entirely on the concept of freedom"; "their principle ... rests on the supersensible, which the concept of freedom alone makes knowable through formal laws".

16. On the specific differences between cultivation, civilization and moralization, see *Lectures on Pedagogy*, 444.

17. On the idea of the "cunning of nature" in Kant, see Yovel (1980: 8, 140), and Allison (2009: 27). For Hegel's related idea of the "cunning of reason", see Hegel (1830: 89).

18. Wood translates "*Aufgabe*" as "problem".

19. See Fackenheim: "nature cannot compel man to *be* what he ought to be. She can at best compel him to *make himself* what he ought to be" (1956–7: 395).

20. Later in the essay on history Kant describes this federation of nations as a "future large state body" (*UH* 118). On the relation between Kant's views on such a federation in *Idea for a Universal History* and *Toward Perpetual Peace*, see Kleingeld (2009).

21. Paul Guyer points out, however, that, for Kant, "the solution of the problem of establishing a just state" (and, by implication, a federation of just states) actually "require[s] purely *moral* motivation, not just prudence, at some point" (2009: 131, emphasis added).

22. Hegel, of course, also understands historical progress to entail progress in the constitution of the state; see Hegel (1830: 93–104, esp. 97): "the state is the more specific object of world history in general".

23. Kant also claims, famously, that although "we" – at the end of the eighteenth century – do not live in an *enlightened* age, "we do live in an *age of enlightenment*" (*E* 21).

24. See *Perpetual Peace* 343: "thereby a great step is taken *toward* morality". Also see Surprenant (2007: 99–100).

25. "We could thus say that morality opens a perspective on history that leads us *beyond* history" (Deligiorgi 2005: 126).

TWELVE

Rational faith:
God, immortality, grace

Patrick Frierson

In 1786, as Kant's philosophy became prominent in Germany, it remained marginal to the hottest philosophical issue of the day: the relationship between faith and reason. The preceding year had seen two posthumous biographies of Gotthold Lessing, the dominant intellectual presence in Germany for a generation. In one, F. H. Jacobi claimed that in Lessing's dying days, he confessed to being a "pantheist", which was essentially synonymous with atheism. In another, Moses Mendelssohn defended Lessing against such charges. The apparently biographical disagreement became a hotly contested philosophical dispute about the Enlightenment: could one be an "enlightened", rational philosopher without giving up religion and morality? Into this debate came a series of "Letters on the Kantian Philosophy" by an early disciple of Kant's philosophy. Karl Reinhold argued that the apparently arcane and incomprehensible *Critique of Pure Reason* actually "secures ... a better future for our descendents" by providing "universally satisfying" answers to "the most pressing philosophical needs of our time" (Reinhold 2006: 16).

Today's philosophical scene is quite different. It is no longer assumed that atheism is immoral or dangerous. If anything, most professional philosophers hold the opposite view, that "God is not great" and religion is a dangerous "God delusion" (see Dawkins 2006; Hitchens 2007). But we continue to deal with problems Reinhold hoped Kant had solved forever. Despite atheism's popularity *among philosophers*, many people still find mere reason insufficient for making sense of human life. At the same time, the recent rise of religiously motivated violence brings an increasingly acute awareness of the dangers of religion severed from rational moral ideals. If, as Reinhold suggests, Kant provides a path whereby "supernatural religion and natural religion dissolve into ethical religion", where "superstition and non-belief give [way] to rational faith" (Reinhold 2006: 64), this path is still urgently needed today.

Kant's approach to religion involves three stages. First, the *Critique of Pure Reason* "denies *knowledge* in order to make room for *faith*" (B xxx). Kant argues that questions about immortality or God's existence are unanswerable with the rational capacities used to understand the empirical world. This limitation of reason, however, is not a rejection of *belief* in God or immortality, but simply of *knowledge*. Second, the *Critique of Practical Reason* fills in this "faith" with *practical proofs* of immortality and God.[1] Finally, *Religion within the Boundaries of Mere Reason* expands this faith with grace as a response to human beings' "radical evil".

Kant versus theistic proofs

Kant's *Critique of Pure Reason* "denies knowledge in order to make room for faith" (B xxx). The refutation of religious knowledge occurs both at a general level and through specific arguments against classic theological arguments. At the general level, Kant's *Critique* is based on a "Copernican" turn whereby we have *a priori* knowledge of the world only by rejecting the assumption that "cognition must conform to objects" and instead "assuming that objects must conform to our cognition" (B xvi). Kant's general idea is that metaphysics, as an *a priori* science of objects, is possible only in so far as the structure of human cognition contributes to the make-up of the world. Since a non-spatial or non-temporal world could never be experienced by us, we can know – *a priori* – that the world must be spatial and temporal. This shift in perspective provides the basis for a positive *a priori* metaphysics of experience. But this shift also implies that metaphysics is *limited* to the world *of possible human experience*: "Our exposition establishes the ... objective validity of space [and other *a priori* categories] in ... whatever can be presented to us ... but also ... the ideality of space [for] things ... considered in themselves ... without regard to [our] constitution" (A 28/B 44). Things *in the world* (of experience) must be spatial, but we can make no claims at all about things "in themselves" independent of our structures of cognition. Because classic metaphysical questions of freedom, God and immortality go beyond possible human experience, Kant's Copernican turn is "very disadvantageous to ... metaphysics" and "sever[s] the very root of materialism, fatalism, atheism ... and superstition" (B xxxiv).

Beyond this general philosophical approach, within which arguments about God and immortality are irresolvable, Kant also offers detailed arguments against traditional proofs for (or against) the existence of God or immortality, proofs highlighting the dangers of trying to extend knowledge beyond its proper limits. For example, Kant takes on three central arguments for God's existence: the "ontological", "cosmological" and "physico-teleological" proofs.[2] The ontological argument uses the definition of God as "that than which nothing greater can be conceived" or "the most perfect being" to prove that God, so defined, must exist (see Anselm 2001: ch. 2; Descartes 2006). Since it is better to exist than not, and since God must be the best (by definition), God must exist. Kant's key objection is that existence "is ... not a real predicate, that is, a concept of something that could add to the concept of a thing" (A 598/B 626).

A hundred actual dollars does not contain the least bit more than a hundred possible ones. For since the latter signifies the concept and the former its object ... [if] the former contained more than the latter, my concept would not express the entire object and would not be the suitable concept of it.   (A 599/B 627)

If an *actual* hundred dollars is an instantiation of the concept of "hundred dollars", the content of the actual hundred dollars better match the concept exactly, nothing more or less. But this means that "existence" cannot be included *within* the concept, since in that case, no instantiation could ever match its concept. To exist is for one's entire concept to be "posited" or "actualized". "When I think a thing ... not the least bit gets added to the thing when I posit in addition that this thing is" (A 600/B 618). Since existence cannot be part of the definition of *any* concept, it cannot be part of the concept of God. If God actually exists, then God must have all of the properties of a most perfect being (omnipotence etc.), but if one denies the existence of these properties, one must – and can without contradiction – also deny God's existence.

The "cosmological" argument states, "If something exists, then an absolutely necessary being also has to exist. Now I myself, at least, exist; therefore, an absolutely necessary being exists" (A 604/B 633). The minor premise, which Kant describes as "I exist", can be any empirical claim that *something* exists, whether oneself, the world or any particular object. The main work of the proof is done in the major premise, and the argument for this premise is typically set up in terms of a dilemma. Either the existing thing in the minor premise is self-caused, in which case it is already absolutely necessary, or it is caused by something else.

In the latter case, either the cause is absolutely necessary, or it is in turn caused by something else. But since "it is not possible to go on to infinity" (Aquinas 1981: q.2, a.3), one must eventually stop at a "first cause" that is absolutely necessary. This first cause is God.

Kant offers two main objections to this proof. First, to prove the existence of *God*, the proof must show that its "absolutely necessary being" is also that most perfect being that we call "God". But "[i]f [this] proposition is correct ... then it must be convertible" (A 608/B 637), that is, if it is an *a priori* truth that "absolutely necessary being = most perfect being", then it is also true that "most perfect being = absolutely necessary being". But the latter claim is the essence of the ontological argument, so unless the ontological argument is valid, the cosmological argument fails to show that its "necessary being" is a "most perfect being". Since the ontological argument is not valid, neither is the cosmological. Even if there is a necessary first cause, this being need not be God. Kant's second objection involves claiming both that the conditions of possibility of experience *preclude* an absolutely necessary cause in the world of possible experience and that reason's need to look for causes of contingent things does not actually require that there *be* a first cause. Kant argues that the cause of anything contingent must begin to act at some moment (otherwise its effects would be just as necessary as itself). But human beings cannot conceive of an uncaused beginning of action, so any cognizable cause must be caused and hence not absolutely necessary (see A 188–211/B 232–56). Kant then scrutinizes the claim that "it is not possible to go on to infinity" and finds in this reason's demand for an unconditioned, absolutely sufficient explanation of events in the world. If one considers this demand as a basis for proving claims about a world independent of human cognition, one must think of there actually *being* such a first cause. But once one sees that thinking of the first cause in this way contradicts the conditions of possibility of experience, one will recognize that reason's demand for an unconditioned is a demand on human cognition not to be satisfied with partial explanations but to constantly seek out more and more complete ones (see A 508/B 536ff.; Grier 2001). As a *task* for speculative enquiry, this demand provokes greater understanding of the world of experience, rather than assertions about things beyond possible experience.

The final proof for God's existence is physico-teleological, which, like the cosmological, is based on empirical premises. Here, however, the premises refer not merely to existence but to the world's "immeasurable ... manifoldness, order, purposiveness, and beauty" (A 622/B 650). As William Paley famously put it (2008: 7–20; see also Hume

1998), if one finds a watch, one assumes that an intelligent designer built it; when one finds an even more complex network of causes and effects in the world, one should assume that an even more intelligent designer built it. Just as Kant objected to the cosmological argument by showing its dependence upon the ontological, here he reduces the physico-teleological argument to the cosmological. Based merely on the world one observes, the physico-teleological argument cannot establish any determinate concept of God, but only that the world's cause is something like an intelligence and in some sense greater than ordinary human intelligence. We cannot know whether this "architect of the world" is a *single* architect, nor *how* powerful this architect is, nor how wise and so on (A 627/B 655).

> After one has gotten as far as admiring the magnitude of the wisdom, power, etc. of the world's author and cannot get any farther ... one suddenly ... goes back to the contingency ... inferred right at the beginning ... The physico-theological proof, stymied in its undertaking, suddenly jumps over to the cosmological proof.
>
> (A 629/B 657)

Since the cosmological in turn depends upon the ontological and the latter upon the erroneous attempt to use pure reason to go beyond the limits of possible experience, all three proofs ultimately fail to prove God's existence.

Kant's moral religion

Kant's philosophy of religion is not, however, entirely negative. His *Critique of Pure Reason* opposes not only dogmatism but also "scepticism", not only religious "fanaticism" but also "atheism" (B xxxiv). And Kant insists that he denies *knowledge* of God (and immortality) only "*in order to make room for faith*" (B xxx). Moreover, Kant is no fideist recommending a "leap of faith" here. The "faith" that he has in mind is wholly grounded in reason, but in *practical* rather than theoretical reason. The positive part of Kant's philosophy of religion thus comes in his *Critique of Practical Reason*. Whereas the *Critique of Pure Reason* finds conditions of possibility of *experience* in *a priori* forms of intuition and categories of understanding, the *Critique of Practical Reason* looks for conditions of possibility of obligation. The consciousness that we are morally obligated is a "fact of reason" from which Kant deduces claims that outstrip theoretical knowledge, the most important of which is that we are transcendentally free causes of our actions: one "judges ... that he *can* do something because he is aware that he *ought* to do it" (*PracR* 5:30). Freedom is the first object of practical "faith", but the moral law provides rational grounds for two further "postulates of pure practical reason": immortality and God.

Neither immortality nor God's existence are conditions of the possibility of morality *per se*. Whereas unfree beings would not be bound by categorical imperatives (see G 4:445ff., 5:28–9), free human beings are bound even if we are mortal and God does not exist: "on its own behalf, morality in no way needs religion" (*RBR* 6:3). But humans are not *merely* free morally bound agents. We are also *finite* agents with a volitional structure whereby we act not only on principles but also for the sake of ends (see 4:427, 5:109, 6:211). Thus the moral law is not only a necessary principle; it also gives us necessary *ends* (see 5:109, 6:4–5). The "whole *object* of pure practical reason" (5:109) is the "highest good", which refers either to a "supreme good ... not subordinate to any other" or the "complete good", that "whole which is not part of a still greater whole" (5:110). But making either highest good an object of will requires cognitive commitments to immortality and God, so by giving human beings certain objects of volition, the moral law makes the associated beliefs "morally necessary" (5:125).

Kant's key claim is that one can aim only for what one takes to be possible at least in part through one's effort. I cannot aim to win a race if my defeat is literally certain, nor to build a house out of materials that I know will not stand. I can, of course, run along a track or put nails in materials without the relevant beliefs, but I cannot aim for goals that I take to be impossible or unrelated to my efforts. Kant's arguments for God and immortality proceed by clarifying the necessary objects of pure practical reason and arguing that pursuing those objects is unreasonable without the relevant beliefs.

The argument for God's existence begins with the central thesis of Kant's moral philosophy, that "virtue (as worthiness to be happy)" is the "supreme good" (see 4:393). Kant adds that for the "*complete* good ... *happiness* is also required" (5:110). To one familiar with Kant's moral theory, this claim might be surprising, since Kant repeatedly opposes duty and inclination and insists that "the direct opposite of the principle of morality is the principle of one's own happiness" (5:25). Still, Kant never claims that happiness is not good, and *Groundwork* even implies what Kant here confirms, that for one "worthy" of it, happiness is good (4:393, 396). To avoid confusion, however, Kant emphasizes that this complete good can never "be taken as [the] *determining ground*" of the good will (5:109); that is, we do not obey the moral law for the sake of attaining the complete good. Rather, we seek the complete good only because doing so is required in order to obey the moral law. Moreover, we do not include happiness in our conception of the complete good simply because we want happiness; it is required not "merely in the partial eyes of a person who makes himself an end" (5:110) but rather for specifically *moral* reasons: "For to need happiness [and] also be worthy of it and yet not to participate in it cannot be consistent with the perfect volition of a rational being that would at the same time have all power" (*ibid.*). In an unfortunate rhetorical blunder, Kant might seem here to assume the existence of God – a "perfect ... rational being" with "all power" – in order to establish a premise he later uses to prove God's existence. But Kant is merely drawing attention to the morally required content of the complete good by asking, not what we would *want* to have included in that goal, but what our "impartial reason" *demands*. Given that humans are finite creatures with worldly needs, having virtuous people who are worthy to be happy yet nonetheless unhappy is a condition towards which a morally good agent cannot deliberately aim. We must, if we are really morally good, aim for a state wherein virtue is rewarded with happiness.

Once Kant argues that happiness proportionate to virtue is a morally necessary aim, he asks after the conditions of possibility of this aim. The complete good requires that virtue and happiness be "necessarily" combined such that one is to be happy *because* one is virtuous, but these elements can be combined "either as analytic (logical connection) or as synthetic (real connection)" (5:111). An "analytic" connection, advocated by "the ancient Greek schools", denies a real difference between virtue and happiness. For Stoics, "happiness" is nothing more than virtue itself, while for Epicureans, "virtue" is nothing more than the effective pursuit of happiness. Against both schools, Kant reminds us, on the basis not only of common sense but also of his argument earlier in the *Critique of Practical Reason* (see 5:21ff.), that these concepts are in fact "extremely heterogeneous" (5:111). "Happiness is the state of a rational being in the world in the whole of whose existence everything goes according to his wish and will" (5:124), and however virtuous he may be, the Stoic sage being tortured on the rack is not "happy". And because virtue requires doing one's duty *for the sake of duty*, an Epicurean who acts virtuously for the sake of pleasure has no true virtue.

Having dismissed "analytic" connections between virtue and happiness, Kant offers an "antinomy of practical reason", considering a causal relationship between happiness and virtue such that either "happiness [is] the motive of maxims to virtue" or "virtue [is] the efficient cause of happiness" (5:113). The former is *"absolutely* impossible because ... maxims that put the determining ground of the will in the desire for happiness are not moral" (*ibid.*). Even if acting in accordance with duty leads to happiness, doing duty *for the sake of* happiness undermines moral worth. But the latter idea – that virtue ends up causing happiness – is "*also impossible* because any practical connection of causes and effects in the world ... does not depend upon the moral dispositions of the will but upon knowledge of the laws of nature and the physical ability to use them for one's purposes" (*ibid.*). While attempting to get virtue from seeking happiness is evil, hoping for happiness as a fringe benefit of virtue is stupid. The way to satisfy desires is through knowing how the world works and putting that knowledge to use. Cleverness and strength, not one's moral disposition, effect changes in the world that bring happiness.

If his discussion of the highest good ended there, Kant would offer little more than despair. One ought to pursue the highest good and thus believe it possible, but no way of making sense of it seems consistent with one's knowledge of the nature of duty and the way of the world. But Kant offers a "resolution of the antinomy" that shows how one *can* combine virtue and happiness in a necessary way by discarding an assumption underlying the previous analysis. For Kant, "antinomies" are apparently intractable conflicts of reason that are resolved "by showing that there is no true conflict if the ... world ... [is] regarded merely as" a world of experience rather than the world "in itself" (5:114). In particular, the claim that virtue can lead to happiness is false only *if* one's moral disposition is taken as a "form of causality in the sensible world" (*ibid.*). One need not, however, think of the moral disposition in this way. Instead, one can and should see oneself (with one's moral disposition) as a "noumenon", existing in an intelligible world that is the ground of but not reducible to the empirical world (5:115; cf. A 546/B 574ff.). This perspective opens the possibility that one's noumenal moral disposition can be a *non-empirical* cause with happiness as its (empirical) effect. And this opens room for claiming that virtue leads to happiness, albeit not on grounds of any empirically observed correlation between the two.

Merely admitting the possibility that one's moral disposition *could* somehow provide a noumenal ground for happiness is insufficient. Happiness "rests ... on the harmony of nature with [one's] whole end" (5:124). But "the acting rational being in the world is ... not also the cause of the world ... itself" (*ibid.*), so human beings lack the capacity to ensure that good moral dispositions will noumenally ground happiness.

> Nevertheless, in the ... necessary pursuit of the highest good, such a connection [between virtue and happiness] is postulated as necessary ... Accordingly, the existence of a cause of all nature, distinct from nature, which contains the ground of this connection, namely of the exact correspondence of happiness with morality, is *postulated*. (5:125)

To pursue a morally required end (the complete good), human beings must assume that their pursuit of virtue brings about a world in which happiness is proportionate to virtue. For that world to come about, something must ground necessary connections between virtue and happiness. Since this something cannot be human beings (we are not powerful enough) nor nature itself (as merely empirical, it makes no reference to noumenal dispositions), we must assume a separate noumenal ground that Kant calls "God". "It is morally necessary to assume the existence of God" (5:125).

Like traditional rational theologians, Kant moves from a proof that God exists to a discussion of the nature of God. Unlike proofs Kant rejected earlier, the moral proof establishes "an author of the world possessed of the highest perfection ... *omniscient* in order to cognize my conduct even to my inmost disposition ... *omnipotent* in order to bestow results appropriate to it, and so too *omnipresent, eternal,* and so forth" (5:140). Moreover, because God secures the morally required highest good, God must be omnibenevolent, just and so on. And because belief in God follows *from* dutiful effort to attain the highest good, it is not a basis *for* that effort. If speculative theology proved the existence of a just and all-powerful God, "transgression of ... law would ... be avoided ... but because ... the spur to activity ... would be external ... most actions conforming to law would be done from fear, only a few from hope, and none at all from duty" (5:147). *Knowledge* of a just God undermines true virtue, while morally motivated *faith* in such a God completes the virtuous disposition with a basis for moral hope.

By connecting virtue and happiness, God provides *part* of what makes the highest good possible, but the difficulty attaining the highest good is not limited to connecting happiness and virtue. Virtue itself seems out of reach, at least without *immortality*.

1. Virtue requires "*complete conformity* of dispositions with the moral law" (5:122).
2. "This conformity must therefore be ... possible" (given that we are obliged to pursue it).

3. But this conformity is not possible in any finite period of time.
4. Thus we must have literally *"endless progress* toward that complete conformity" (*ibid.*).
5. Thus we must "presuppos[e] ... the *existence* ... of the same rational being continuing *endlessly* ([that is,] immortality of the soul)" (*ibid.*).

Kant's explanation of the third and key step in this proof is sparse: "Complete conformity of the will with the moral law is ... *holiness,* a perfection of which no rational being of the sensible world is capable at any moment of its existence" (*ibid.*). Kant says nothing more (here) about *why* complete conformity of will is impossible for temporally limited, sensible, rational beings. And there are at least three ways of reading Kant's argument, none of which precisely fit Kant's claims.

First, one might examine other passages in which Kant discusses "holiness". There "holiness" distinguishes God's will from human wills. A *"holy* will" is one that "by its subjective constitution ... can be determined *only* through the representation of the good" (4:414, cf. 5:82–3). Such a will necessarily follows the moral law, so this law is not an "imperative" for it. If Kant means this by "holiness" in the proof above, human beings are clearly incapable of it. As sensible beings, we are beholden to an interest in happiness that, even if wholly subordinated to the moral law, nonetheless provides an alternative possible motivation for the will. But this version of the argument makes it unclear why Kant would think that human beings, even *with* endless time, would be able to attain holiness. Kant denies that "we could *ever* bring it about that ... we ... like the Deity raised beyond all dependence, could come into possession of holiness of will" (5:82–3, emphasis added). Moreover, why should human virtue *require* holiness of will? Kant emphasizes that the moral law does not *"strike down"* but "merely *infringes upon* self-love, inasmuch as it only restricts it, as natural and active in us even prior to the moral law, to the condition of agreement with this law" (5:73). For virtuous agents, the moral law *trumps* other motivating grounds, but need not eliminate them altogether.

Alternatively, Kant might be making a general point about how to express complete conformity with morality in a temporally extended series. For God, who does not have a temporal existence, conformity with the moral law might be a single eternal act. But for a rational, *sensible* being, the only expression of a will in *complete* conformity with the moral law might be a will that conforms to that law over endless duration. At the "end" of our immortal lives, we will have brought about an accord with morality that can "never be disturbed" (see 5:83), not because all possibility of temptation has vanished, but because we have withstood every temptation.

Finally, Kant's claims here might anticipate his later argument in *Religion within the Boundaries of Mere Reason* that human beings "started from evil" (6:72) not merely in the sense that we have inclinations that *can* conflict with the moral law but that we "corrupt ... the subjective supreme ground of all [our] maxims" (6:37). In this case, the best we can do is to make "progress ... from the worse to the morally better" (5:123, cf. 5:127–8) by gradually strengthening respect for the moral law and increasingly subordinating self-love to that law. This reading has the advantage of drawing on Kant's extensive discussion of evil and moral progress in *Religion*, but does not fit well with the specific argument in the *Critique of Practical Reason*. It does not explain the *Critique*'s emphasis on *holiness*, nor why "no rational being of the sensible world" is capable of perfect virtue. Kant's argument for radical evil in *Religion* is specifically about *human beings,* and while Kant admits the possibility of other finite, rational agents in the universe, he nowhere claims such agents *in general* are evil.[3] Any radical-evil-based argument is inadequate to show why immortality is necessary for all "rational but finite being[s]" (5:123). In the end, however, even if the *Critique of Practical Reason* does not make clear why sensible rational beings are incapable of complete conformity with the moral law, one can remedy this gap in Kant's proof by taking *Religion* as the requisite supplement to the *Critique*, or by appealing to the complete good and arguing for immortality as necessary to provide time for apportioning happiness to virtue.

Kant's proofs for immortality and God have not escaped criticism. Some criticisms focus on the arguments' details, while others attack Kant's overall proof-structure. Discussing even a substantial fraction of these criticisms is impossible in this short chapter, but one objection is worth noting. Bertrand Russell and others have argued that Kant's argument represents the worst sort of irrational justification of wishful thinking. After summarizing Kant's moral arguments for God and immortality, Russell objects:

> That is a very curious argument. If you looked at the matter from a scientific point of view, you would say, "After all, I only know this world. I do not know about the rest of the universe, but so far as one can argue at all on probabilities one would say that probably this world is a fair sample, and if there is injustice here the odds are that there is injustice elsewhere also". Supposing you got a crate of oranges that you opened, and you found all the top layer ...

bad, you would not argue, "The underneath ones must be good, so as to redress the balance". You would say, "Probably the whole lot is a bad consignment"; and that is ... what a scientific person would argue about the universe. He would say, "Here we find in this world a great deal of injustice, and ... that is a reason for supposing that justice does not rule in the world; and therefore ... it affords a moral argument against deity and not in favour of one. (Russell 1957: 13)[4]

While Kant's response to such objections ultimately involves virtually the entirety of his *Critique of Pure Reason*, its basic structure can be summarized easily. Kant entirely agrees that if you look scientifically, you find no reason to think injustice will be remedied, since one sees injustice prevailing here and now. But this "scientific" perspective is only half of a practical antinomy that *seems* to make moral hope irrational. Russell's objection, like the antinomy itself, assumes that science is the only legitimate point of view on questions about reality. Once Kant's *Critique of Pure Reason* limits science to claims about appearances, he *can* postulate God's existence. And once the *Critique of Practical Reason* shows that it is morally necessary, this postulate becomes *necessary*.

Postulates' status as postulates *of practical reason* is extremely important here. While these postulates' *content* is theoretical (there is a God; humans are immortal), their *epistemic grounds* are moral. Precisely how to interpret their practical status is an issue of contention among Kant scholars, with some claiming that one must merely "act as if" the postulates are true and others insisting that one must actually believe *that* they are true but without claiming scientific or metaphysical warrant for this belief. On either interpretation, however, claims about God and immortality are defended and applied solely in terms of their practical import, without the traditional rational–metaphysical theorizing of the tradition against which Kant argues in the *Critique of Pure Reason*.

Religion within the Boundaries of Mere Reason

Kant's most comprehensive religious work – *Religion within the Boundaries of Mere Reason* – was an attempt to reinterpret and defend traditional Christian doctrines such as sin, grace, atonement and the kingdom of God. The attempt successfully got Kant in enough trouble with Prussian censors for "misus[ing his] philosophy to distort and disparage ... basic teachings of ... Christianity" (*CF* 7:6) that he had to promise, "as Your Majesty's most loyal subject, [to] refrain altogether from discoursing publicly ... on religion" (7:10).[5] Among the wide range of theological issues Kant's *Religion* enters into, the most important are his philosophical defences of *radical evil* and God's *grace*, and the related development of his argument for immortality.

Kant's argument that human beings are evil depends on both "anthropological research" (*RBR* 6:25) and an "*a priori*" inference. From "the multitude of woeful examples that the experience of human deeds parades before us" (6:32–3), one infers evil maxims by assuming that human agents are free. Given the specific nature of the moral law (requiring universal and thus unwavering adherence), one can infer from a single evil deed the presence of a fundamental ("radical") willingness to subordinate moral incentives to non-moral ones if the "price" is right (6:39). Given human freedom and the rigour of the moral law, the implication of universal human misdeeds is that "what the Apostle says ... hold[s] true of human beings universally, 'There is no distinction here, they are all under sin – there is none righteous ... no, not one'" (6:39).

For Kant, the fact that human beings are radically evil generates a problem akin to those that motivated the *Critique of Practical Reason*'s postulates:

> [Human] evil is radical, since it corrupts the grounds of all maxims ... it is also not to be extirpated through human forces, for this could happen only through good maxims – something that cannot take place if the subjective supreme ground of all maxims is presupposed to be corrupted. (6:37, cf. 6:45)

The willingness to make an exception to the moral law when the price is right shows that evil lies at the root of human choice, which implies that one cannot extirpate it through that same (evil) power of choice. The problem is even worse because, for Kant, human evil involves tendency to cultivate a *propensity* to further evil. And even if one somehow reformed oneself and overcame self-wrought evil propensities, one can never be someone who always chooses in accordance with the moral law since one has chosen wickedly in the past: "however steadfastly a human being may have persevered in such a [good] disposition in a life conduct conformable to it, he nevertheless started from evil, and this is a debt which is impossible for him to wipe out" (6:72).

Despite these challenges to virtue, "the command that we ought to become better human beings still resounds unabated in our souls" (6:45). Consistent with the key move in his arguments for the postulates,

Kant argues that "consequently, we must ... be capable of it" (*ibid.*). As with the postulates, whatever must be believed to rationally make moral reform an object of will can and should become an article of rational faith. Because evil cannot be extirpated "through human forces" alone (6:37) and thus "some supernatural cooperation is also needed to [a person] becoming good or better" (6:44, cf. 7:43–4, 328), belief in divine assistance, or "grace", is needed. For us to pursue virtue as an attainable end of our endeavours, we "can admit an effect of grace" (6:53) and "must accept this help" (6:44). As with the postulates, this belief is justified only in order to rationally pursue virtue as an attainable end, so one must see grace as something one "makes oneself antecedently worthy of receiving" (*ibid.*) and never make use of grace to promote moral complacency (6:53).

The rest of *Religion* gives further detail as to how grace functions in human beings' moral lives, including a long discussion of how his conception of grace relates to the traditional Christian doctrine of substitutionary atonement (see esp. 6:66–78). For this essay, grace's most important implication is its supplement to Kant's earlier arguments for God and immortality. Kant's argument for grace to solve the problem of human evil implies the existence of a God that at least arguably needs to have the traditional properties Kant ascribes to God (omniscience, omnipotence etc.), but *Religion* adds an emphasis on the need for a God of grace and mercy as well as justice and goodness. With respect to immortality, because "the distance between the goodness which we ought to effect in ourselves and the evil from which we start is ... infinite" (6:66), humans reach goodness only through "infinite progression" of a life that "steadily improves" (6:67–8). This provides either a further argument for immortality or a better explanation of the second *Critique*'s argument.

Conclusion

Kant's arguments for God, immortality and grace remain forces to be reckoned with. This chapter laid out only the beginnings of debates about the legitimacy of Kant's theological arguments. Some continue to defend traditional theistic proofs against Kant's objections and others attack Kant's own arguments for God, immortality and grace. More important than these particular arguments, however, Kant's philosophy of religion reflects an important philosophical *approach* to religion. The *Critique of Pure Reason* is an important step towards freeing religion from domination by scientific and metaphysical arguments. Kant provides both detailed arguments and a general strategy for showing why neither science nor metaphysics in any traditional sense is capable of grappling with religion. Moreover, Kant helpfully points out that even if science and metaphysics provide no reason for believing in God, there are aspects of life that are at least as important as science and metaphysics, aspects that may require beliefs that go beyond what science can prove. Kant provides a way of making non-scientific arguments that are rigorous and rational without being *metaphysical*, and even if his arguments have problems in details, the strategy of developing such arguments continues to be worth pursuing.

Kant's focus on religion's practical importance is also relevant today. Absent convincing scientific evidence for it, many today see no point in religion. But Kant shows how religious beliefs can be rationally and psychologically necessary to ward off either moral lenience or moral despair. In his *Critique of Practical Reason*, religious beliefs are a way of maintaining moral demands in the face of a human life that seems too limited and a world that seems unjust. In *Religion*, religious beliefs prevent moral despair in the face of a rigorous moral law and the recognition of one's own corrupt tendencies. Human finitude and moral imperfection continue to tempt us either to soften the demands of morality or to give up hope of meeting them. Kant shows that this apparent choice is illusory, that religion provides a way to combine rational moral hope with an uncompromised conception of virtue. But Kant also models how faith could solve other apparently intractable dilemmas within practical reason. By recasting dilemmas as "antinomies", Kantian philosophies of religion can highlight the extent to which conflicts between strict duty and corporate welfare, or between duty and authenticity, or between fairness and moral progress, can be alleviated by faith.

Religion's practical import implies not only (nor even primarily) that those who are non-religious should become more religious. When many continue to use religion to defend immoral violations of rights, Kant's moral arguments justify religion *within moral limits*. If one believes in God and immortality *for moral reasons*, then one should *not* hold beliefs that require or even allow moral violations or compromise. Without theoretical grounds for religion, the *only* basis for believing religious claims is that such belief is required to adhere to moral demands, so religious belief can never require *transgressing* these demands. Kant's lesson to those who want to be morally good is that they should be open to religious faith; his lesson to those who want to be religious is that they can – and must – restrain that faith within limits, not only of reason, but also of respect for the dignity of all human beings. Today, both lessons remain worth heeding.

Notes

1. Kant's argument here is not the so-called "moral argument" that God has to exist in order to legislate moral laws. For Kant, one legislates moral laws to oneself, and so would have moral obligations whether God exists or not. But because of the sorts of beings that we are – imperfect and needy of happiness – we must believe in God and personal immortality in order to make sense of our morally required pursuit of the "highest good".
2. For the purpose of this chapter, I pass over Kant's discussion of human immortality in his "Paralogisms of Pure Reason". See Ameriks (2000b).
3. For a detailed defence of this reading, see Wood (2009).
4. For a strikingly similar criticism phrased in much different terms, see Hegel (1977: §622ff.).
5. Kant emphasizes the phrase "as Your Majesty's most loyal subject" when, after the King's death, he publishes his *Conflict of the Faculties* (1798), his final published work on religion.

Chronology

1724 Born 22 April in Königsberg (now Kaliningrad), a fairly cosmopolitan commercial and university town with numerous international trading companies, as son of the saddler Johann Georg Kant (1683–1746) and his wife Anna Regina (1697–1737), a pietist family.

1726 Death of Isaac Newton. Newtonian physics has an enormous impact on Kant's thought.

1732–40 Attends the Collegium Fridericianum.

1737 Death of his mother.

1740 Enrolment on 24 September at the Albertina, the University of Königsberg; studies philosophy. Unlike most philosophers of his time, he does not study theology and does not aspire to the presbyterate. His most important teacher is Martin Knutzen, a rationalist thinker who tries to reconcile rationalism with Newtonian physics and holds, contrary to Leibniz, the so-called *"influxus physicus"* theory that substances have a physical impact on one another. Death of Friedrich Wilhelm I of Prussia; Friedrich the Great is crowned king of Prussia. Friedrich the Great wants to be an enlightened monarch who is the first servant of his state. He introduces freedom of religion.

1746 Death of Kant's father.

1748–54 Private tutor in manor houses around Königsberg. Kant becomes acquainted with Johann Georg Hamann, who is regarded as a precursor of *Sturm and Drang*.

1749 First publication: *Thoughts on the True Estimation of Living Forces*. This work was a dissertation, written in Latin in 1746, but not fully printed until 1749.

1751 Death of Kant's teacher Martin Knutzen (1713–51).

1754 Death of Christian Wolff, leading figure of German scholasticism or German rationalism in the tradition of Gottfried Wilhelm Leibniz. Works: *Investigation of the Question, Whether the Axial Rotation of the*

217

Earth, through which Day and Night are brought about, has Changed since its Beginning, and How One Can be Certain of this, which the Royal Academy of Sciences in Berlin has offered a Prize for the current year and *The Question Whether the Earth is Aging, Considered Physically.*

1755   A German translation of Hume's *Enquiry Concerning Human Understanding* is published. There is evidence that Kant took notice of it and that it had some influence on his work as early as 1756. Kant begins teaching at the Albertina. He teaches numerous classes, about twenty hours a week, since he has to make his living from direct payments from students. It is common to teach in one's own private rooms. He reads mathematics, geology, metaphysics, logics, ethics and physics. Later he also reads pedagogy, natural theology, mineralogy, natural right and even military fortification.
        Works: *Universal Natural History and Theory of the Heavens, or Essay on the Constitution and Mechanical Origin of the Entire Universe, Treated in Accordance with Newtonian Principles; Short Exposition of Some Thoughts about Fire* (MA thesis, published only posthumously); *New Illumination of the First Principles of Metaphysical Knowledge* (thesis that gives Kant the licence to teach at the University).

1756   Kant applies unsuccessfully for the chair of his late teacher Knutzen.
        Works: *On the Causes of the Terrestrial Convulsions, on the Occasion of the Disaster Afflicting the Western Countries of Europe towards the End of Last Year.*

1758   22 January: Occupation of Königsberg by Russian troops until 1762. December: Unsuccessful application for the chair of Kypke.
        Works: *New Theory of Motion and Rest, and the connected Consequences in the First Principles of the Natural Sciences, whereby he also announces his lectures for this semester, the 1st of April, 1758.*

1759   Works: *An Attempt at Some Reflections on Optimism by Immanuel Kant, also containing an announcement of his lectures for the coming semester. 7th October 1759.*

1760   Works: *Thoughts on the Premature Death of Mr. Johann Friedrich von Funk.*

1762   Herder studies with Kant until 1764.
        Works by others: Jean-Jacques Rousseau, *Émile, Social Contract* and *The False Subtlety of the Four Syllogistic Figures Demonstrated by M. Immanuel Kant.*

1763   Works: *The Only Possible Ground in Support of a Demonstration of the Existence of God; Attempt to Introduce the Concept of Negative Magnitudes into Philosophy.*

1764   Works: *Observations on the Feeling of the Beautiful and the Sublime; Essay on the Maladies of the Mind;* Review of Silberschlag's essay "Theory of the Fireball that Appeared on July 23, 1762"; *Inquiry Concerning the Distinctness of the Principles of Natural Theology and Morality.*
        Works by others: Johann Heinrich Lambert, *Novum Organum.*

1765   Initiation of correspondence with Johann Heinrich Lambert, a mathematician and philosopher, which was an important source of inspiration

218

for Kant. Supposedly in 1765, no later than 1766, Kant meets his lifelong close friend Joseph Green (1727–86), an English merchant. It is assumed that Green had a great influence on Kant's way of life. After meeting Green, Kant develops his legendary discipline, quits card-playing, billiard-playing and going to the theatre. Kant himself called it "not an aesthetic but a moral friendship". A little later both made friends with Green's colleague, Robert Motherby (1736–1801).
Works: *Announcement of the Programme of his Lectures for the Winter Semester 1765–1762.*

1766   Position as sub-librarian at the palace library of Königsberg until 1772.
Works: *Dreams of a Spirit-Seer Elucidated by Dreams of Metaphysics.*
Works by others: Moses Mendelssohn, *Phaedon or about the Immortality of the Soul.*

1768   Works: *Concerning the Ultimate Ground of the Differentiation of Directions in Space.*

1769   Offered a Chair at the University of Erlangen in October, and turned it down in December.

1770   Offered a Chair at the University of Jena in January. Appointed Professor of Logic and Metaphysics at the University of Königsberg, 31 March.
Works: *De mundi sensibilis atque intelligibilis forma et principiis.*

1771   Beginning of Kant's so-called "silent decade" (1770–81) during which he publishes only a few minor essays but works intensely on a project to revise all former philosophy, the *Critique of Pure Reason.*
Works: "Review of Moscati's Book: *On the Essential Bodily Difference in the Structure of Animals and Human Beings*".

1775   Works: *On the Different Races of Humankind, and to announce the lectures on physical geography for the summer semester 1775.*

1776–77   Works: *Essays Concerning the Philanthropin.*
Works by others: Johannes Nikolaus Tetens, *Philosophical Essays*, a work trying to reconcile empiricism with German scholasticism, was to have a huge impact on Kant.

1778   Turns down an offer from the University of Halle.

1781   *Critique of Pure Reason*, first edition.

1782   Dean of the University of Königsberg.
Works: "A Notice of Johann Bernoulli's Edition of Lambert's Correspondence"; *Report to Physicians.*

1783   Kant buys his first and only house, where every day his friends gather for dinner.
Works: *Prolegomena to any Future Metaphysics that will be able to present itself as a Science*; "Review of Johann Heinrich Schulz's *Essay on the Moral Instruction of all Humans, regardless of their Religion*".

1784   Works: *Idea for a Universal History with a Cosmopolitan Purpose; An Answer to the Question: What is Enlightenment?*

1785   Dean of the University.
Works: "Review of Herder, *Ideas on the Philosophy of Human History*"; *On the Volcanoes on the Moon; Groundwork of the Metaphysics of*

Morals; *On the Wrongfulness of Unauthorized Publication of Books*; *Determination of the Concept of a Human Race.*

1786 President of the University, and external member of the Berlin Academy of Sciences. Death of Friedrich the Great of Prussia and enthronement of Friedrich Wilhelm II. Kant organizes the festivities of the University for this event. Numerous articles, reviews and books concerning Kant's philosophy were published in the following decades. Some explained Kant's transcendental idealism to the public, others tried to mend its alleged imperfections, and yet others criticized Kant for either destroying traditional metaphysics or not destroying it thoroughly enough. A journal was dedicated to fight Kant's philosophy, the *Philosophical Magazine* (*Philosophisches Magazin*), edited by Johann August Eberhard. Further inveterate enemies of Kant were Christian Garve and Johann Georg Heinrich Feder. Kant reacted to their attacks with a number of polemic articles.
Works: *Conjectural Beginning of Human History*; *Metaphysical Foundations of Natural Science*; "Review of Gottlieb Hufeland's *Essay on the Principle of Natural Right*"; "Some Remarks on L. H. Jakob's *Examination of Mendelssohn's Morgenstunden*"; *What Does it Mean to Orient Oneself in Thinking?*
Works by others: Karl Leonhard Reinhold, *Letters on the Kantian Philosophy.*

1787 Friedrich Heinrich Jacobi publishes *David Hume or About Faith, or Idealism and Realism*, and formulates an influential and rather harsh critique of Kant's transcendental idealism that motivates the young Schelling, Fichte and Hegel to turn away from Kantian philosophy.
Works: *Critique of Pure Reason*, second edition, which is a substantial revision of the first edition.

1788 9 July: Religious edict demanding orthodox views of all clergymen in Prussia; it is one device of the counter-reconnaissance-movement under the reign of Friedrich Wilhelm II.
19 December: Edict introducing stricter censorship.
Works: *Critique of Practical Reason*; *On the Use of Teleological Principles in Philosophy.*

1789 Start of the French Revolution. Kant notices first signs of an impairment of his mental capacities that will progressively deteriorate over the years. By about 1800 his mental capacities were severely damaged. There are varying views about the extent to which this had an impact on his late philosophical work.

1790 Works: *First Introduction to the Critique of the Power of Judgment* (published posthumously); *Critique of the Power of Judgment*; *On a Discovery, according to which any new Critique of Pure Reason is made Dispensable through an Older*; *On the Propensity to Fanaticism and the Means to Oppose it.*

1791 Dean of the University.
Works: *On the Miscarriage of all Philosophical Trials in Theodicy.*

1792 Louis XVI of France is executed. Issue of a stricter religious edict in Prussia. An essay by Kant is banned by the censor.
Works: *On Radical Evil in Human Nature.*

Works by others: Johann Gottlieb Fichte publishes his first work, *Critique of all revelation*, anonymously. The public supposes it to be the work of Kant. Kant publishes a clarification that he is not the author.

1793   Works: *Religion within the Boundaries of Mere Reason*; *What Real Progress Has Metaphysics Made in Germany since the Time of Leibniz and Wolff?*; *On the Common Saying: "That may be Correct in Theory, but it is of no Use in Practice".*

1794   Member of the St Petersburg Academy of Science. The Prussian Civil Code is introduced.
1 October: Kant receives an admonition from the King, accusing Kant of the vilification of Christianity in his work "Religion within the Boundaries of Mere Reason". Kant was threatened with the loss of his chair and even being banned from Prussia.
12 October: Kant answers the King.
Works: *On the Influence of the Moon on the Weather*; *The End of All Things*.

1795   Works: *Toward Perpetual Peace: A Philosophical Project*.
Works by others: Friedrich Wilhelm Joseph Schelling, *About the I as a Principle in Philosophy*.

1796   23 April: Death of his long-time friend Hippel.
23 July: Kant's last lecture.
Works: *Remarks on Sömmering's "On the Organ of the Soul"*; *On a New Superior Tone in Philosophy*; *Settlement of a Mathematical Controversy which is Resting on a Misunderstanding*; *Announcement of the Near Conclusion of a Treaty for Eternal Peace in Philosophy*.
Works by others: Fichte, *Foundations of Natural Law*.

1797   Death of Friedrich Wilhelm II and enthronement of Friedrich Wilhelm III.
Works: *The Metaphysics of Morals: Doctrine of Right*; *The Metaphysics of Morals: Doctrine of Virtue*; *On a Supposed Right to Lie from Philanthropy*.
Works by others: Friedrich Wilhelm Joseph Schelling, *Ideas for a Philosophy of Nature*. Supposedly, Kant did not take notice of the new philosophies of Schelling and Hegel.

1798   Works: *The Conflict of the Faculties*; *Anthropology from a Pragmatic Point of View*; *On Turning Out Books: Two Letters to Mr. Friedrich Nicolai from Immanuel Kant*.

1799   Works: *Declaration Regarding Fichte's "Wissenschaftslehre"*.

1800   Works: "Preface to Reinhold Bernhard Jachmann's *Examination of the Kantian Philosophy of Religion*"; "Afterword to Christian Gottlieb Mielcke's *Lithuanian–German and German–Lithuanian Dictionary*"; *Logic: A Handbook for Lectures*, edited by Gottlieb Benjamin Jäsche.
Works by others: Friedrich Wilhelm Joseph Schelling, *System of Transcendental Idealism*.

1802   Works: *Immanuel Kant's Physical Geography,* edited by Friedrich Theodor Rink.
Works by others: G. W. F. Hegel, *Faith and Knowledge*.

1803   April: Writes his last letter.

October: Kant falls sick.

Works: *On Education*, edited by Friedrich Theodor Rink.

1804   Napoleon enthrones himself emperor.

12 February: Death.

28 February: Funeral. In Kant's estate were found several manuscripts of great philosophical interest.

Works: *Handwritten Notes* (Reflections written between 1765 and 1800) and the much discussed fragmentary manuscript, *Opus Postumum* (which Kant started writing around 1796).

Details from Cassirer (1921); Gulyga (2004); Kuehn (2001).

Bibliography

Works by Kant

Kant, I. 1900ff. *Kants Gesammelte Schriften*, Königlich Preußische (spaeter Deutsche) Akademie der Wissenschaften (ed.). Berlin: Georg Reimer, later Walter de Gruyter & Co. Referred to as Akademie-Ausgabe (Ak).

Kant, I. Various dates. *The Cambridge Edition of the Works of Immanuel Kant*, 20 vols, Paul Guyer & Allen W. Wood (eds). Cambridge: Cambridge University Press.

Kant, I. 1929. *The Critique of Pure Reason*, Norman Kemp Smith (trans.). London: Macmillan. Reprinted 1992.

Kant, I. 1973. *Kants Gesammelte Schriften*. Translated in the Kant–Eberhard Controversy, H. Allison (ed.). Baltimore, MD: Johns Hopkins University Press.

Kant, I. 1983. *Grounding for the Metaphysics of Morals*, James Ellington (trans.). Indianapolis, IN: Hackett.

Kant, I. 1985. *Philosophy of Material Nature*, James Ellington (trans.). Indianapolis, IN: Hackett.

Kant, I. 1997. *Lectures on Ethics*, Peter Heath and J. B. Schneewind (eds). Cambridge: Cambridge University Press.

Kant, I. 2004a. *Prolegomena to any future Metaphysics that Will Be Able to Present Itself as Science*, G. Zöller (ed.). Oxford: Oxford University Press.

Kant, I. 2004b. *Vorlesung zur Moralphilosophie*, W. Stark (ed.). Berlin: Walter de Gruyter.

Other works

Al-Azm, S. 1972. *The Origins of Kant's Arguments in the Antinomies*. Oxford: Oxford University Press.

Allen, C., M. Bekoff & G. Lauder (eds) 1998. *Nature's Purposes: Analyses of Function and Design in Biology*. Cambridge, MA: MIT Press.

Allison, H. 2004. *Kant's Transcendental Idealism: An Interpretation and Defense*, 2nd edn. New Haven, CT: Yale University Press.

Allison, H. 2009. "Teleology and History in Kant: the Critical Foundations of Kant's Philosophy of History". In *Kant's Idea for a Universal History with a Cosmopolitan Aim: A Critical Guide*, A. O. Rorty & J. Schmidt (eds), 24–45. Cambridge: Cambridge University Press.

Ameriks, K. 1981. "Kant's Deduction of Freedom and Morality". *Journal of the History of Philosophy* 19: 53–79.

Ameriks, K. 1992. "The Critique of Metaphysics". In *The Cambridge Companion to Kant*, P. Guyer (ed.), 249–79.

Ameriks, K. 2000a. *Kant and the Fate of Autonomy*. Cambridge: Cambridge University Press.

Ameriks, K. 2000b. *Kant's Theory of Mind: An Analysis of the Paralogisms of Pure Reason*, 2nd edn. Oxford: Oxford University Press.

Anselm 2001. *Proslogion*, T. Williams (trans.). Indianapolis, IN: Hackett.

Aquinas, T. 1981. *Summa Theologica*. Fathers of the English Dominican Province (trans.). Notre Dame, IN: Christian Classics.

Axtell, G. 1992. "Normative Epistemology and the Bootstrap Theory". *Philosophical Forum* 23: 329–43.

Baumanns, P. 1965. *Das Problem der organischen Zweckmäßigkeit*. Bonn: Bouvier.

Beck, L. W. 1960. *A Commentary to Kant's Critique of Practical Reason*. Chicago, IL: University of Chicago Press.

Beihart, C. 2009. "Kant's Characterization of Natural Ends". *Kant Yearbook* 1: 1–30.

Bennett, J. 1966. *Kant's Analytic*. Cambridge: Cambridge University Press.

Betzler, M. (ed.) 2008. *Kant's Ethics of Virtue*. Berlin & New York: Walter de Gruyter.

Bird, G. 2006. *The Revolutionary Kant: A Commentary on the Critique of Pure Reason*. Peru, IL: Open Court.

Bohman, J. & M. Lutz-Bachmann (eds) 1997. *Perpetual Peace: Essays on Kant's Cosmopolitan Ideal*. Cambridge, MA: The MIT Press.

Bommersheim, P. 1919. "Der Begriff der organischen Selbstregulation in Kants Kritik der Urteilskraft". *Kant-Studien* 23: 209–20.

Brandt, R. 1988. "Der Zirkel im dritten Abschnitt von Kants Grundlegung zur Metaphysik der Sitten", in *Kant: Analysen – Probleme – Kritik*, H. Oberer & G. Seel (eds), 169–91. Würzburg: Königshausen & Neumann.

Breitenbach, A. 2009. "Teleology and Biology: A Kantian Perspective". *Kant Yearbook* 1: 31–56.

Briskman, L. 1977. "Historicist Relativism and Bootstrap Rationality". *Monist* 60: 509–39.

Buchdahl, G. 1965. "Causality, Causal Laws and Scientific Theory in the Philosophy of Kant". *British Journal for Philosophy of Science* 16: 187–208.

Buchdahl, G. 1974. "Transcendental Reduction: A Concept for the Interpretation of Kant's Critical Method". In *Akten des 4. Internationalen Kant-Kongresses*, vol. 1, G. Funke (ed.), 28–44. Berlin: Walter de Gruyter.

Buchdahl, G. 1981. "Zum Verhältnis von allgemeiner Metaphysic der Natur und besonderer metaphysischer Naturwissenschaft bei Kant". In *Probleme der "Kritik der reinen Vernunft"*, B. Tuschling (ed.), 97–142. Berlin: Walter de Gruyter.

Buchdahl, G. 1986. "Kant's 'Special Metaphysics' and the *Metaphysical Foundations of Natural Science*". In *Kant's Philosophy of Physical Science*, R. E. Butts (ed.), 121–61. Dordrecht: Reidel.

Buller, D. J. (ed.) 1999. *Function, Selection and Design*. Albany, NY: SUNY Press.

Burke, E. 1990. *A Philosophical Enquiry Into the Origin of Our Ideas of the Sublime and the Beautiful*, A. Phillips (ed.). Oxford: Oxford University Press.

Butts, R. E. 1990. "Teleology and Scientific Method in Kant's *Critique of Judgment*". *Nous* 24: 1–16.

Byrd, B. Sharon 1989. "Kant's Theory of Punishment: Deterrence in its Threat, Retribution in its Execution". *Law and Philosophy* 8: 151–200.

Byrd, B. Sharon & J. Hruschka 2010. *Kant's Doctrine of Right: A Commentary*. Cambridge: Cambridge University Press.

Carson, E. 1999. "Kant on the Method of Mathematics". *The Journal of the History of Philosophy* 37(4): 79–102.

Cassirer, E. 1921. *Kants Leben und Lehre*. Berlin: E. Cassirer.

Cummins, R. 1975. "Functional Analysis", *Journal of Philosophy* 72: 741–64.

Dawkins, R. 2006. *The God Delusion*. Boston, MA: Houghton Mifflin Harcourt.

Dean, R. 2006. *The Value of Humanity in Kant's Moral Theory*. Oxford: Oxford University Press.

Deligiorgi, K. 2005. *Kant and the Culture of Enlightenment*. Albany, NY: SUNY Press.

Descartes 2006. *Meditations, Objections and Replies*. R. Ariew & D. Cress (trans.). Indianapolis, IN: Hackett.

Dicker, G. 2004. *Kant's Theory of Knowledge: An Analytical Introduction*. Oxford: Oxford University Press.

Dörflinger, B. 2000. *Das Leben theoretischer Vernunft*. Berlin: Walter de Gruyter.

England, F. E. 1968. *Kant's Conception of God*. New York: Humanities Press.

Engstrom, S. 2002. "The Inner Freedom of Virtue". In *Kant's Metaphysics of Morals: Interpretative Essays*, M. Timmons (ed.), 289–315. Oxford: Oxford University Press.

Fackenheim, E. 1956–7. "Kant's Concept of History". *Kant-Studien* 48: 381–98.

Falkenstein, L. 1995. *Kant's Intuitionism: A Commentary on the Transcendental Aesthetic*. Toronto: University of Toronto Press.

Finnis, J. 1980. *Natural Law and Natural Rights*. Oxford: Clarendon Press.

Flasch, W. 1997. "Kants Empiriologie: Naturteleologie als Wissenschaftstheorie". In *Grenzen der kritischen Vernunft*, P. Schmid & S. Zurbuchen (eds), 273–89. Berlin: Schwabe.

Flikschuh, K. 2000. *Kant and Modern Political Philosophy*. Cambridge: Cambridge University Press.

Flikschuh, K. 2008. "Reason, Right, and Revolution: Kant and Locke". *Philosophy and Public Affairs* 36(4): 375–404.

Flikschuh, K. 2010a. "Justice without Virtue". In *Kant's Metaphysics of Morals: A Critical Guide*, L. Denis (ed.), ch.3. Cambridge: Cambridge University Press.

Flikschuh, K. 2010b. "Kant's Sovereignty Dilemma: A Contemporary Analysis". *Journal of Political Philosophy* 18(4): 469–93.

Fricke, C. 1990. "Explaining the Inexplicable: The Hypotheses of the Faculty of Reflective Judgment in Kant's Third Critique". *Nous* 24: 45–62.

Friedman, M. 1992. *Kant and the Exact Sciences*. Cambridge, MA: Harvard University Press.

Gardner, S. 1999. *Kant and the Critique of Pure Reason*. London: Routledge.

Giere, R. 1985. "Philosophy of Science Naturalized". *Philosophy of Science* 52: 331–56.

Giere, R. 2006. *Scientific Perspectivism*. Chicago, IL: University of Chicago Press.

Ginsborg, H. 1987. "Kant on Aesthetic and Biological Purposiveness". In *Reclaiming the History of Ethics*, A. Reath, B. Herman & C. Korsgaard (eds), 329–60. Cambridge: Cambridge University Press.

Ginsborg, H. 2001. "Kant on Understanding Organisms". In *Kant and the Sciences*, E. Watkins (ed.), 231–58. Oxford: Oxford University Press.

Ginsborg, H. 2004. "Two Kinds of Mechanical Inexplicability in Kant and Aristotle". *Journal of the History of Philosophy* **42**: 33–65.

Godfrey-Smith, P. 1993. "Functions: A Consensus without Unity". *Pacific Philosophical Quarterly* **74**: 196–208.

Golinski, J. 1998. *Making Natural Knowledge: Constructivism in the History of Science*. Cambridge: Cambridge University Press.

Gregor, M. 1963. *Laws of Freedom: A Study of Kant's Method of Applying the Categorical Imperative in the* Metaphysik der Sitten. Oxford: Basil Blackwell.

Gregor, M. 1988. "Kant's Theory of Property". *Review of Metaphysics* **41**: 757–87.

Gregor, M. (trans.) 1991. *Kant: The Metaphysics of Morals*. Cambridge: Cambridge University Press.

Gregor, M. 1993a. "Kant on 'Natural Rights'". In *Kant and Political Philosophy: The Contemporary Legacy*, R. Beiner & W. J. Booth (eds), 50–75. New Haven, CT: Yale University Press.

Gregor, M. 1993b. "Kant on Obligation, Rights and Virtue". In *Jahrbuch für Recht und Ethik/Annual Review of Law and Ethics* **1**: 69–102.

Gregor, M. (trans.) 1996. *Kant: The Metaphysics of Morals*, 2nd edn. Cambridge: Cambridge University Press.

Grier, M. 2001. *Kant's Doctrine of Transcendental Illusion*. Cambridge: Cambridge University Press.

Gulyga, A. 2004. *Immanuel Kant*. Frankfurt: Suhrkamp.

Gutmann, M., E. Neuman-Held & C. Rehmann-Sutter (eds) 2000. *"Organism" – Historical and Philosophical Issues. Theory in Biosciences* **119** (special issue).

Guyer, P. 1979. *Kant and the Claims of Taste*. Cambridge, MA: Harvard University Press.

Guyer, P. 1987. *Kant and the Claims of Knowledge*. Cambridge: Cambridge University Press.

Guyer, P. 1990. "Reason and Reflective Judgment: Kant on the Significance of Systematicity". *Nous* **24**: 17–43.

Guyer, P. (ed.) 1998. *Kant's Groundwork of the Metaphysics of Morals: Critical Essays*. Lanham, MD: Rowman & Littlefield.

Guyer, P. 2001. "Organism and the Unity of Science". In *Kant and the Sciences*, E. Watkins (ed.), 259–81. Oxford: Oxford University Press.

Guyer, P. 2002. "Kant's Deductions of the Principles of Right". In *Kant's Metaphysics of Morals: Interpretative Essays*, M. Timmons (ed.), 23–64. Oxford: Oxford University Press; reprinted in P. Guyer, *Kant's System of Nature and Freedom*, 198–242. Oxford: Oxford University Press, 2005.

Guyer, P. 2003. "Kant and the Systematicity of Nature: Two Puzzles". *History of Philosophy Quarterly* **20**: 277–95.

Guyer, P. 2005. *Kant's System of Nature and Freedom*. Oxford: Oxford University Press.

Guyer, P. 2006. *Kant*. London: Routledge.

Guyer, P. 2007. "Naturalistic and Transcendental Moments in Kant's Moral Philosophy". *Enquiry* **50**: 444–64, 497–510.

Guyer, P. 2008. "Proving Ourselves Free". In *Recht und Frieden in der Philosophie Kants: Akten des X. Internationalen Kant-Kongresses*, V. Rhoden *et al.* (eds), 115–38. Berlin: Walter de Gruyter.

Guyer, P. 2009. "The Crooked Timber of Mankind". In *Kant's Idea for a Universal History with a Cosmopolitan Aim: A Critical Guide*, A. O. Rorty & J. Schmidt (eds), 129–49. Cambridge: Cambridge University Press.

Habermas, J. 1997. "Kant's Idea of Perpetual Peace, with the Benefit of Two Hundred

Years' Hindsight". In *Perpetual Peace: Essays on Kant's Cosmopolitan Ideal*, J. Bohman & M. Lutz-Bachmann (eds), 113–154. Cambridge, MA: MIT Press.

Hanna, R. 2009. "Kant's Theory of Judgment". In *Stanford Encyclopedia of Philosophy*, plato.stanford.edu/entries/kant-judgment/ (accessed November 2010).

Hare, J. 2006. "Kant on the Rational Instability of Atheism". In *Kant and the New Philosophy of Religion*, C. Firestone & S. Palmquist (eds), 60–78. Bloomington, IN: Indiana University Press.

Hegel, G. W. F. 1830. "Second Draft (1830): The Philosophical History of the World". In G. W. F. Hegel, *Lectures on the Philosophy of World History. Introduction: Reason in History*, H. B. Nisbet (trans.). Cambridge: Cambridge University Press.

Hegel, G. W. F. 1977 (1807). *Phenomenology of Spirit*, A. W. Miller (trans.). Oxford: Clarendon.

Hegel, G. W. F. 1991 (1820). *Elements of the Philosophy of Right*, A. W. Wood (ed.), H. B. Nisbet (trans). Cambridge: Cambridge University Press.

Heidemann, D. 2010. "Appearance, Thing-in-Itself and the Skeptical Hypothesis". In *Kant's Idealism: New Interpretations of a Controversial Doctrine*, D. Schulting & J. Verburgt (eds). Dordrecht: Springer Verlag.

Henrich, D. 1969. "The Proof-Structure of Kant's Transcendental Deduction". *Review of Metaphysics* 22: 640–59.

Henrich, D. 1975. "Kant's Deduktion des Sittengesetzes". In *Denken im Schatten des Nihilismus*, A. Schwan (ed.), 55–110. Darmstadt: Wissenschaftliche Buchgesellschaft. Partially translated in Guyer (ed.) 1998, 303–41.

Herman, B. 1993. *The Practice of Moral Judgment*. Cambridge, MA: Harvard University Press.

Herman, B. 2007. *Moral Literacy*. Cambridge, MA: Harvard University Press.

Hill, Th. E. Jr 1997. "Kant on Punishment: A Coherent Mix of Deterrence and Retribution?" *Jahrbuch für Recht und Ethik/Annual Review of Law and Ethics* 5: 291–314; reprinted in Th. E. Hill, Jr, *Respect, Pluralism, and Justice. Kantian Perspectives*, 173–99. Oxford: Oxford University Press, 2003.

Hitchens, C. 2007. *God is Not Great: How Religion Poisons Everything*. New York: Twelve Books.

Höffe, O. 1989. "Kant's Principle of Justice as a Categorical Imperative of Law". In *Kant's Practical Philosophy Reconsidered*, Y. Yovel (ed.), 149–67. Dordrecht: Springer.

Höffe, O. (ed.) 1995. *Zum Ewigen Frieden*. Berlin: Akademie.

Hruschka, J. 1987. "Die Konkurrenz von Goldener Regel und Prinzip der Verallgemeinerung in der juristischen Diskussion des 17./18. Jahrhunderts als geschichtlich Wurzel von Kants kategorischem Imperativ". *Juristen Zeitung* 42(20): 941–52.

Hruschka, J. 2004. "The Permissive Law of Practical Reason in Kant's Metaphysics of Morals". *Law and Philosophy* 23: 45–72.

Hume, D. 1973. *Enquiries Concerning Human Understanding and Concerning the Principles of Morals*, 3rd edn, L. A. Selby-Brigge (ed.). Oxford: Oxford University Press.

Hume, D. 1998. *Dialogues Concerning Natural Religion: The Posthumous Essays of the Immortality of the Soul and of Suicide*, 2nd edn, R. Popkin (ed.). Indianapolis, IN: Hackett.

Hume, D. 2000. *A Treatise of Human Nature*, D. F. Norton & M. J. Norton (eds). Oxford: Oxford University Press.

Huneman, P. 2002. *Métaphysique et biologie: Kant et la constitution du concept d'organisme*. Villeneuve: Presses Universitaires du Septentrion.

Huneman, P. 2006a. "From the *Critique of Judgment* to the Hermeneutics of Nature". *Continental Philosophy Review* 39: 1–34.

Huneman, P. 2006b. "Naturalising Purpose: From Comparative Anatomy to the 'Adventure of Reason'". *Studies in History and Philosophy of the Biological and Biomedical Sciences* 37: 649–74.

Huneman, P. (ed.) 2007. *Understanding Purpose: Collected Essays on Kant and Philosophy of Biology*. Rochester, NY: University of Rochester Press.

Ingensiep, H.-W. 1996. "'Die Welt ist ein Thier: aber die Seele desselben ist nicht Gott': Kant, das Organische und die Weltseele". In *NaturStücke: Zur Kulturgeschichte der Natur*, H.-W. Ingensiep & R. Hoppe-Sailer (eds), 101–20. Ostfildern: Edition Tertium.

Ingensiep, H.-W. 2004. "Organismus und Leben bei Kant". In *Kant-Reader: Was kann ich wissen? Was soll ich tun? Was darf ich hoffen?* H.-W. Ingensiep, H. Baranzke & A. Eusterschulte (eds), 107–36. Würzburg: Königshausen & Neumann.

Kaufmann, M. 1997. "The Relation between Right and Coercion: Analytic or Synthetic?" *Jahrbuch für Recht und Ethik/Annual Review of Law and Ethics* 5: 72–84.

Kemp Smith, N. 1962. *Commentary to the Critique of Pure Reason*, 2nd edn. New York: Humanities Press.

Kitcher, P. 1983. "Kant's Philosophy of Science". *Midwest Studies in Philosophy* 8: 387–407.

Kleingeld, P. 1998. "The Conative Character of Reason in Kant's Philosophy". *Journal of the History of Philosophy* 36: 77–97.

Kleingeld, P. 1999. "Kant, History, and the Idea of Moral Development". *History of Philosophy Quarterly* 16: 59–80.

Kleingeld, P. 2004. "Approaching Perpetual Peace: Kant's Defence of a League of States and His Ideal of a World Federation". *The European Journal of Philosophy* 12(3): 304–25.

Kleingeld, P. 2009. "Kant's Changing Cosmopolitanism". In *Kant's Idea for a Universal History with a Cosmopolitan Aim: A Critical Guide*, A. O. Rorty & J. Schmidt (eds), 171–86. Cambridge: Cambridge University Press.

Korsgaard, C. 1997. "Taking the Law into Our Own Hands: Kant on the Right to Revolution". In *Reclaiming the History of Ethics: Essays for John Rawls*, A. Reaths, B. Herman & C. Korsgaard (eds), 297–328. Cambridge: Cambridge University Press.

Korsgaard, C. 2009. *Self-Constitution: Agency, Identity, and Integrity*. Oxford: Oxford University Press.

Kuehn, M. 2001. *Kant: A Biography*. Cambridge: Cambridge University Press.

Kummiskey, D. 1996. *Kantian Consequentialism*. Oxford: Oxford University Press.

Lewens, T. 2001. "No End to Function Talk in Biology". *Studies in History and Philosophy of Biology and the Biomedical Sciences* 32: 179–90.

Lewens, T. 2004. *Organisms and Artefacts: Design in Nature and Elsewhere*. Cambridge, MA: MIT Press.

Lewontin, R. 1985. "The Organism as Subject and Object of Evolution". In R. Levins & R. Lewontin, *The Dialectical Biologist*, 85–106. Cambridge, MA: Harvard University Press.

Longuenesse, B. 1998. *Kant and the Capacity to Judge*, C. Wolfe (trans.). Princeton, NJ: Princeton University Press.

Louden, R. B. 2002. *Kant's Impure Ethics: From Rational Beings to Human Beings*. Oxford: Oxford University Press.

Löw, R. 1980. *Philosophie des Lebendigen: der Begriff des Organischen bei Kant, sein Grund und seine Aktualität*. Frankfurt: Suhrkamp.

Ludwig, B. 1988. *Kants Rechtslehre. Ein Analytischer Kommentar*. Hamburg: Felix Meiner.

Ludwig, B. 2002. "Whence Public Right? The Role of Theoretical and Practical Reasoning in Kant's Doctrine of Right". In *Kant's Metaphysics of Morals: Interpretative Essays*, M. Timmons (ed.), 159–84. Oxford: Oxford University Press.

Makkreel, R. A. 1995. "Differentiating Dogmatic, Regulative, and Reflective Approaches to History in Kant". In *Proceedings of the Eighth International Kant Congress* [2 vols], H. Robinson (ed.), vol. 1, 123–37. Milwaukee, WI: Marquette University Press.

Manson, N. & O. O'Neill 2007. *Rethinking Informed Consent in Bioethics*. Cambridge: Cambridge University Press.

Marx, K. 1852. "The Eighteenth Brumaire of Louis Bonaparte". In *Karl Marx. Selected Writings*, 2nd edn, D. McLellan (ed.), 329–55. Oxford: Oxford University Press.

McLaughlin, P. 1990. *Kant's Critique of Teleology in Biological Explanation: Antinomy and Teleology*. Lewiston, ME: Mellen.

McLaughlin, P. 2001. *What Functions Explain: Functional Explanation and Self-Reproducing Systems*. Cambridge: Cambridge University Press.

Merle, J.-C. 2000. "A Kantian Critique of Kant's Theory of Punishment". *Law and Philosophy* 19: 311–38.

Mill, J. S. 1963–91. *Utilitarianism* [1861]. In *The Collected Works of John Stuart Mill* [33 vols], D. F. Norton & M. J. Norton (eds). Toronto: University of Toronto Press.

Mulholland, L. A. 1990. *Kant's System of Rights*. New York: Columbia University Press.

Murphy, J. G. 1970. *Kant: The Philosophy of Right*. New York: Macmillan.

Nagel, E. 1977. "Goal-Directed Processes in Biology". *Journal of Philosophy* 74: 261–79.

Nickles, T. 1992. "Good Science as Bad History". In *The Social Dimensions of Science*, E. McMullin (ed.), 85–129. Notre Dame, IN: Notre Dame University Press.

Niesen, P. 2007. "The 'West Divided'? Bentham and Kant on Law and Ethics in Foreign Policy". In *Rethinking Ethical Foreign Policy: Pitfalls, Possibilities and Paradoxes*, D. Chandler & V. Heins (eds), 93–115. New York: Routledge.

O'Neill, O. 1975. *Acting on Principle*. New York: Columbia University Press.

O'Neill, O. 1989a. *Constructions of Reason*. Cambridge: Cambridge University Press.

O'Neill, O. 1989b. "Consistency in Action". In O. O'Neill, *Explorations of Kant's Practical Philosophy*, 81–104. Cambridge: Cambridge University Press.

O'Neill, O. 1992. "Vindicating Reason". In *The Cambridge Companion to Kant*, P. Guyer (ed.), 280–308. Cambridge: Cambridge University Press.

O'Neill, O. 1996. *Towards Justice and Virtue*. Cambridge: Cambridge University Press.

O'Neill, O. 2000a. *Bounds of Justice*. Cambridge: Cambridge University Press.

O'Neill, O. 2000b. "Kant and the Social Contract Tradition". In *Kant Actuel: Hommage à Pierre Laberge*, F. Duchesneau, G. Lafrance & C. Piché (eds), 185–200. Montréal: Bellarmin.

O'Neill, O. 2002. "Instituting Principles: Between Duty and Action". In *Kant's Metaphysics of Morals: Interpretive Essays*, M. Timmons (ed.), 331–47. Oxford: Oxford University Press.

O'Neill, O. 2003a. "Constructivism in Rawls and Kant". In *The Cambridge Companion to Rawls*, S. Freeman (ed.), 347–67. Cambridge: Cambridge University Press.

O'Neill, O. 2003b. "Autonomy: The Emperor's New Clothes". *Proceedings and Addresses of the Aristotelian Society* 77(1): 1–21.

O'Neill, O. 2004a. "Autonomy, Plurality and Public Reason". In *New Essays in the History of Autonomy*, N. Brender & L. Krasnoff (eds), 181–94. Cambridge: Cambridge University Press.

O'Neill, O. 2004b. "Self-Legislation, Autonomy and the Form of Law". In *Recht, Geschichte, Religion: Die Bedeutung Kants für die Gegenwart*, Sonderband der *Deutschen Zeitschrift für Philosophie*, H. Nagl-Docekal & R. Langthaler (eds), 13–26. Berlin: Akademie Verlag.

O'Neill, O. 2004c. "Kant: Rationality as Practical Reason". In *The Oxford Handbook of Rationality*, A. R. Mele & P. Rawling (eds), 93–109. Oxford: Oxford University Press.

Paley, W. 2008. *Natural Theology*, M. Eddy & D. Knight (eds). Oxford: Oxford University Press.

Parsons, C. 1992. "The Transcendental Aesthetic". In *The Cambridge Companion to Kant*, P. Guyer (ed.), 62–100. Cambridge: Cambridge University Press.

Paton, H. J. 1947. *The Categorical Imperative*. New York: Harper.

Paton, H. J. 1965. *Kant's Metaphysic of Experience: A Commentary on the First Half of the "Kritik der reinen Vernunft"*, 2nd vol., 4th edn. London: Allen & Unwin.

Pippin, R. 1982. *Kant's Theory of Form*. New Haven, CT: Yale University Press.

Pogge, T. 2002. *World Poverty and Human Right*. Cambridge: Polity.

Quarfood, M. 2004. *Transcendental Idealism and the Organism: Essays on Kant*. Stockholm: Almqvist & Wiksell.

Quarfood, M. 2006. "The Circle and the Two Standpoints". In *Groundwork for the Metaphysics of Morals*, C. Horn & D. Schönecker (eds), 285–300. Berlin: Walter de Gruyter.

Rawls, J. 2000. *Lectures on the History of Moral Philosophy*. Cambridge, MA: Harvard University Press.

Reinhold, K. 2006. *Letters on the Kantian Philosophy*, K. Ameriks & J. Hebbeler (eds and trans.). Cambridge: Cambridge University Press.

Riley, P. 1986. *The General Will Before Rousseau: The Transformation of the Divine into the Civic*. Princeton, NJ: Princeton University Press.

Ripstein, A. 2004. "Authority and Coercion". *Philosophy and Public Affairs* 32: 2–35.

Ripstein, A. 2009. *Force and Freedom: Kant's Legal and Political Philosophy*. Cambridge, MA: Harvard University Press.

Ross, W. D. 1930. *The Right and the Good*. Oxford: Oxford University Press.

Roulier, S. M. 2004. *Kantian Virtue at the Intersection of Politics and Nature: The Vale of Soul-Making*. Rochester, NY: University of Rochester Press.

Russell, B. 1957. *Why I Am Not a Christian and Other Essays on Religion and Related Subjects*. New York: Simon & Schuster.

Schneewind, J. B. 1991. "Natural Law, Skepticism, and Methods of Ethics". *Journal of the History of Ideas* 52(2): 289–308.

Schnoor, C. 1989. *Kants Kategorischer Imperativ als Kriterium der Richtigkeit des Handelns*. Tübingen: J. C. B. Mohr.

Schönecker, D. 1999. *Kant: Grundlegung III – Die Deduktion des Sittengesetzes*. Freiburg: Verlag Karl Alber.

Seel, G. 2009. "How Does Kant Justify the Universal Objective Validity of the Law of Right?" *International Journal of Philosophical Studies* 17(1): 71–94.

Sellars, W. 1968. *Science and Metaphyiscs: Variations on Kantian Themes*. London: Routledge & Kegan Paul.

Sextus Empiricus 1934. *Outlines of Pyrrhonism*. In *Works* [4 vols], Rev. R. G. Bury (trans.). Cambridge, MA: Harvard University Press.

Shabel, L. 2004. "Kant's 'Argument from Geometry'". *The Journal of the History of Philosophy* 42(2): 195–215.

Sinnott-Armstrong, W. 2006. *Moral Skepticisms*. New York: Oxford University Press.

Sloan, P. 2006. "Kant on the History of Nature: The Ambiguous Heritage of the Critical Philosophy for Natural History". *Studies in History and Philosophy of the Biological and Biomedical Sciences* 37(4): 627–48.

Steigerwald, J. (ed.) 2006a. *Kantian Teleology and the Biological Sciences. Studies in History and Philosophy of Biological and Biomedical Sciences* 37(4) (special issue).

Steigerwald, J. 2006b. "Kant's Concept of Natural Purpose and the Reflecting Power of Judgement". *Studies in History and Philosophy of Biological and Biomedical Sciences* 37(4): 712–34.

Strawson, P. F. 1966. *The Bounds of Sense: An Essay on Kant's Critique of Pure Reason*. London: Methuen.

Surprenant, C. W. 2007. "Cultivating Virtue: Moral Progress and the Kantian State". *Kantian Review* 12: 90–112.

Tuschling, B. 1991. "The System of Transcendental Idealism: Questions Raised and Left Open in the *Kritik der Urteilskraft*". *Southern Journal of Philosophy* 30 (Supplement): 109–28.

Ungerer, E. 1922. *Die Teleologie Kants und ihre Bedeutung für die Logik der Biologie.* Berlin: Borntraeger.

Vartanian, A. 1950. "Trembley's Polyp, La Mettrie and Eighteenth-Century French Materialism". *Journal of the History of Ideas* 11: 259–86.

Walford, D. (ed.) 1992. *Theoretical Philosophy, 1755–1770*. Cambridge: Cambridge University Press.

Walsh, D. M. 1996. "A Taxonomy of Functions". *Canadian Journal of Philosophy* 26: 493–514.

Walsh, D. M. 2006. "Organisms as Natural Purposes: The Contemporary Evolutionary Perspective". *Studies in History and Philosophy of the Biological and Biomedical Sciences* 37(4): 771–91.

Walsh, W. H. 1967. *An Introduction to the Philosophy of History*, 3rd edn. London: Hutchinson.

Warnke, C. 1992. "'Naturmechanismus' und 'Naturzweck': Bemerkungen zu Kants Organismus-Begriff". *Deutsche Zeitschrift fur Philosophie* 40: 42–52.

Warren, D. 1998. "Kant and the apriority of space", *The Philosophical Review* 107(2): 179–224.

Watkins, E. 2001. "Kant on Rational Cosmology". In *Kant and the Sciences*, E. Watkins (ed.), 70–89.

Westphal, K. R. 1995. "How 'Full' is Kant's Categorical Imperative?" *Jahrbuch für Recht und Ethik/Annual Review of Law and Ethics* 3: 465–509.

Westphal, K. R. 1997. "Do Kant's Principles Justify Property or Usufruct?" *Jahrbuch für Recht und Ethik/Annual Review of Law and Ethics* 5: 141–94.

Westphal, K. R. 1998. "Hegel's Solution to the Dilemma of the Criterion". In *The Phenomenology of Spirit Reader: A Collection of Critical and Interpretive Essays*, J. Stewart (ed.), 76–91. Albany, NY: SUNY Press.

Westphal, K. R. 2002. "A Kantian Justification of Possession". In *Kant's Metaphysics of Ethics: Interpretive Essays*, M. Timmons (ed.), 89–109. New York: Oxford University Press.

Westphal, K. R. 2004. *Kant's Transcendental Proof of Realism*. Cambridge: Cambridge University Press.

Westphal, K. R. 2010a. "From 'Convention' to 'Ethical Life': Hume's Theory of Justice in Post-Kantian Perspective". *The Journal of Moral Philosophy* 7(1): 105–32.

Westphal, K. R. 2010b. "Constructivism, Contractarianism and Basic Obligations: Kant and Gauthier". In *Reading Kant's Doctrine of Right*, J.-C. Merle (ed.). Cardiff: University of Wales Press.

Westphal, K. R. 2010c. "Kant's Constructivism and Rational Justification". In *Politics and Metaphysics in Kant*, S. Baiasu, S. Pihlström & H. Williams (eds). Cardiff: University of Wales Press.

Westphal, K. R. 2010d. "Urteilskraft, gegenseitige Anerkennung und rationale Rechtfertigung". In *Ethik als prima philosophia?* H.-D. Klein (ed.), 171–93. Würzburg: Königshausen & Neumann.

Willaschek, M. 1997. "Why the Doctrine of Right Does Not Belong in the Metaphysics of Morals". *Jahrbuch für Recht und Ethik/Annual Review of Kaw and Ethis* 5: 205–27.

Willaschek, M. 2009. "Right and Coercion. Can Kant's Conception of Right be Derived from his Moral Theory?" *International Journal of Philosophical Studies* 17(1): 49–70.

Williams, B. 1980. "Internal and External Reasons". Reprinted in *Moral Luck: Philosophical Papers 1973–1980*, 101–13. Cambridge: Cambridge University Press.

Wolff, M. 2009. "Warum das Faktum der Vernunft ein Faktum ist. Auflösung einiger Verständnisschwierigkeiten in Kants Grundlegung der Moral". *Deutsche Zeitschrift für Philosophie*. 57(4): 511–49.

Wood, A. 1978. *Kant's Rational Theology*. Ithaca, NY: Cornell University Press.

Wood, A. 1999. *Kant's Ethical Thought*. Cambridge: Cambridge University Press.

Wood, A. 2002. "The Final Form of Kant's Practical Philosophy". In *Kant's Metaphysics of Morals: Interpretative Essays*, M. Timmons (ed.), 1–22. Oxford: Oxford University Press.

Wood, A. 2009. *Kant's Moral Religion*. Ithaca, NY: Cornell University Press.

Wright, L. 1973. "Functions". *Philosophical Review* 82: 139–68.

Yovel, Y. 1980. *Kant and the Philosophy of History*. Princeton, NJ: Princeton University Press.

Zammito, J. 2003. "'This Inscrutable *Principle* of an Original *Organization*': Epigenesis and 'Looseness of Fit' in Kant's Philosophy of Science". *Studies in History and Philosophy of Science* 34: 73–109.

Zammito, J. 2004. *A Nice Derangement of Epistemes: Post-Positivism in the Study of Science from Quine to Latour.* Chicago, IL: University of Chicago Press.

Zammito, J. 2006a. "Kant's Early Views on Epigenesis: The Role of Maupertuis". In *The Problem of Animal Generation in Modern Philosophy*, J. E. Smith (ed.), 317–54. Cambridge: Cambridge University Press.

Zammito, J. 2006b. "Teleology Then and Now: The Question of Kant's Relevance for Contemporary Controversies over Function in Biology". *Studies in History and Philosophy of Biological and Biomedical Sciences* 37(4): 748–70.

Zammito, J. 2009. "Kant's Notion of Intrinsic Purposiveness in the *Critique of Judgment*: A Review Essay (and an Inversion) of Zuckert's *Kant on Beauty and Biology*". *Kant Yearbook* 1: 223–47.

Zuckert, R. 2007. *Kant on Beauty and Biology: An Interpretation of the Critique of Judgment*. Cambridge: Cambridge University Press.

Zumbach, C. 1984. *The Transcendent Science: Kant's Conception of Biological Methodology*. The Hague: Nijhoff.

Index